POSTCARD HISTORY SERIES

Lower Bucks County

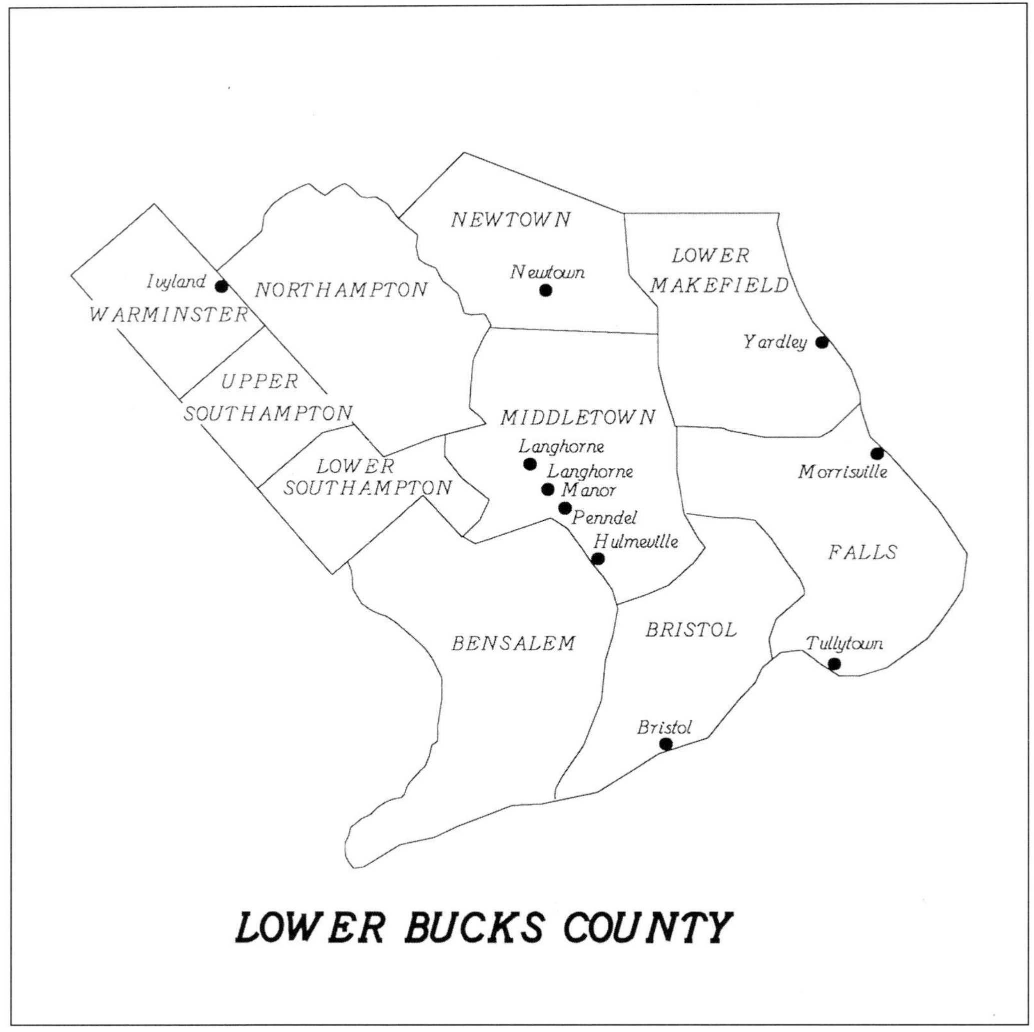

A Map of Lower Bucks County. This map shows the boundaries and places in lower Bucks County that are pictured in this book.

POSTCARD HISTORY SERIES

Lower Bucks County

Andrew Mark Herman

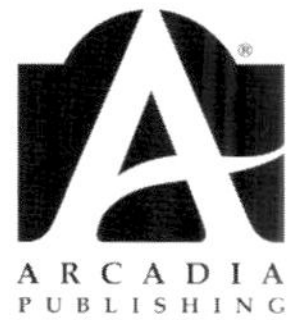

ISBN 978-0-7385-0525-1

Published by Arcadia Publishing
Charleston SC, Chicago IL, Portsmouth NH, San Francisco CA

Printed in the United States of America

Library of Congress Catalog Card Number: 00108595

For all general information contact Arcadia Publishing at:
Telephone 843-853-2070
Fax 843-853-0044
E-mail sales@arcadiapublishing.com
For customer service and orders:
Toll-Free 1-888-313-2665

Visit us on the Internet at www.arcadiapublishing.com

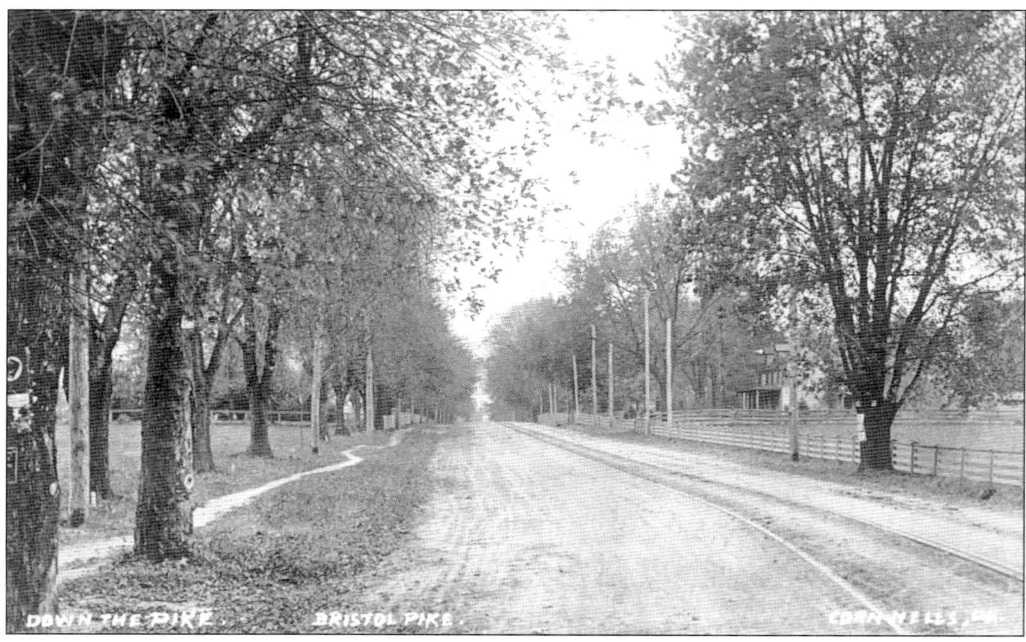

Bristol Pike, Cornwells. Picturesque farms and old trees dominated the lower Bucks County landscape until the middle of the 20th century. This glimpse of Bristol Pike in 1913 illustrates the rustic country scenery of the area quite well.

CONTENTS

ACKNOWLEDGMENTS AND BIBLIOGRAPHY

Special thanks to my wife, Claudia, whose support and assistance is greatly appreciated. Thanks also to my children, Lauren, Allison, and Madeleine, and to my immediate family, Marvin, Paula, Robin, Vivian, and my father-in-law, Marvin.

Davis, Bertha, Olive Steele, and Charlotte Cutshall. *Postcards of Bucks County, Pa*. Printed by the Arnold Brothers, Abington, Pa.: Cassidy Printing, Inc., 1980.

Green, Doran. *History of Old Homes on Radcliffe Street*. n.p., 1938.

Hennessy, Raymond. *Newtown 275 Anniversary*. Bristol, Pa.: Bucks County Printing House, 1959.

Historic Langhorne Association. *Langhorne Centennial 1876 to 1976*. Langhorne, Pa.: The Advance of Bucks County, 1975.

Historical Society of Bensalem Township. *Traveling Through Bensalem 1692–1984*. n.p., 1984.

Howard, Martin. *Hulmeville Borough Centennial 1872 to 1972*. Southampton, Pa.: Ollard Printing, 1972.

MacReynolds, George. *Place Names in Bucks County*. n.p., 1976.

Northampton Township Historical Commission. *Winds of Change*. n.p., 1985.

Snipes, Samuel M., Jeffrey L. Marshall, and Stephanie Will. *Falls Township, Bucks County: A 300th Anniversary History*. n.p., 1992.

Upper Southampton Township Historical Advisory Commission. *Southampton 1685–1985*. Jostens, Inc., 1985.

INTRODUCTION

Bucks County was one of the three original counties in Pennsylvania, dating to 1682. The name Bucks was derived after Buckinghamshire, William Penn's home in England. The original boundaries of the county covered almost all the present eastern half of Pennsylvania. The original townships of Bensalem, Falls, Makefield, Middletown, and Newtown date to 1692. Later townships were Southampton in 1703, Warminster in 1712, Bristol in 1720, and Northampton in 1722.

The beautiful landscape, fertile fields, thick forests, and abundant waterways have been luring people to the area since the 1680s, when William Penn chose a Falls Township site for his plantation, Pennsbury Manor. In the 1700s and 1800s, the Bucks County landscape changed depending on location. Bristol Borough had developed into a prominent business center, and its sophisticated Radcliffe Street was lined with handsome riverside homes. Many of these were home to foreign ambassadors and consuls when Philadelphia was the capital of the United States. Ship captains, physicians, and other wealthy people also resided along the street. Newtown was also an early colonial center, while Langhorne developed into a refined residential borough. Tullytown and Hulmeville were small commercial towns.

The surrounding countryside, blessed with fine natural resources, was home to many farms. Along old roads such as Bristol Pike, Street Road, and Lincoln Highway, villages of varying sizes were important aspects of life. General merchandise stores, churches, meetinghouses, and local tradesmen's shops were also found in these villages. Historic taverns such as the Red Lion and the Buck Hotel were host to important colonial figures. Stagecoach routes between Philadelphia and New York traversed lower Bucks County. All of these were important influences in the development of the area.

Lower Bucks County had also been a magnet for people seeking a resort in the country. In the 1700s, the Bristol area had natural springs that attracted many. In the 1800s, places like Hulmeville, Parkland, Bridgewater, and Neshaminy Falls boasted small picnic and amusement parks, with swimming and boating in the Neshaminy Creek.

In the 1900s, more people discovered lower Bucks County. Then, with the advent of Levittown, suburbia arrived. Today, most farms and extensive woodlands, along with old buildings, have been lost with the increased development. Yet to the keen observer, many old landmarks can still be found.

The postcards presented in this book show life in lower Bucks County in the early 1900s.

These postcards include views of old hotels, street scenes, places of worship, and private homes. Natural scenery, such as creeks and even a noteworthy tree, is included. Many of the things in these images still exist, although quite a few are gone forever. Postcard images captured the precious aspects of everyday life that would otherwise have been lost.

Bucks County was fortunate to have a few dedicated postcard publishers. Bristol Borough appears to be the postcard publishing center of lower Bucks County. Three publishers worked out of Bristol. The Hay Photo Studios operated on Mill Street. Harry Wharton and J.K. Streeper & Son also were from Bristol. Charles and Newton Arnold of Rushland & Ivyland were unique because they photographed the entire county. Their numbered postcard series is greatly sought after by local collectors. Linford Craven worked from a studio on West State Street in Doylestown. He photographed much of central and upper Bucks County, including Holland, Newtown, and Yardley in lower Bucks County. Philadelphia photographer William H. Sliker, from Bridesburg, made postcards of several counties in the area. He focused on the area of Cornwells Heights to Davisville in lower Bucks County. Thanks to these photographers, images of lower Bucks County can be preserved for generations to come.

Having lived in lower Bucks County for 15 years and being a 1977 graduate of Bensalem High School and a 1979 graduate of Bucks County Community College, I have always been interested in this historic region. During that time, I photographed many old buildings, spent summer days along the Neshaminy Creek, and bicycled along many roads. The highlight of that period was when I traveled to England in 1981 with a tour group, tracing the life of William Penn and visiting his ancestral home and grave site. Although much of lower Bucks County has changed over the years, its spirit can be evoked through the wonderful images in this book. It is my hope that readers will find that spirit.

One

Andalusia to Bridgewater

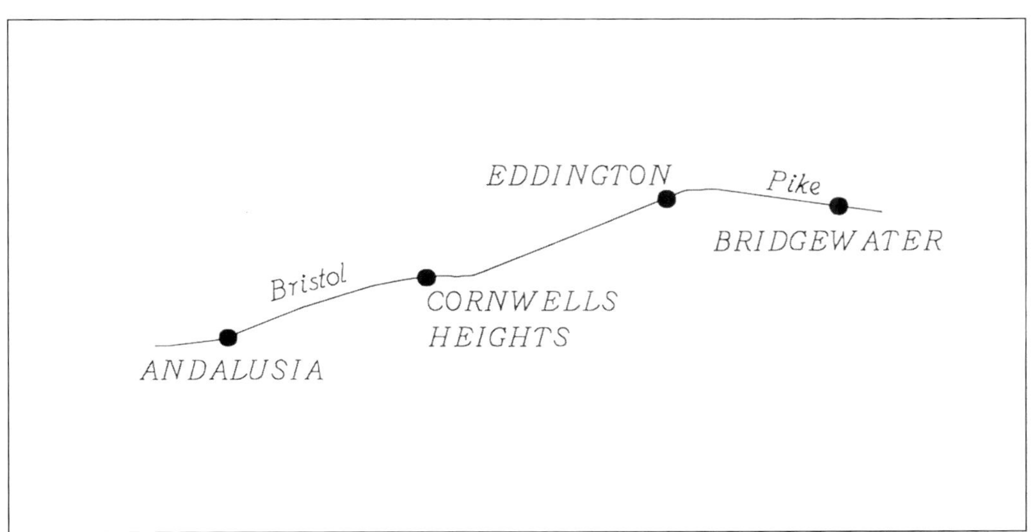

Andalusia to Bridgewater. This chapter deals with the towns of Andalusia, Cornwells Heights, Eddington, and Bridgewater. Images will follow the Bristol Pike from the Poquessing Creek at the county line to the Neshaminy Creek. These places are closely associated with the old Kings Highway, now Route 13, and represent the extreme southern section of Bucks County.

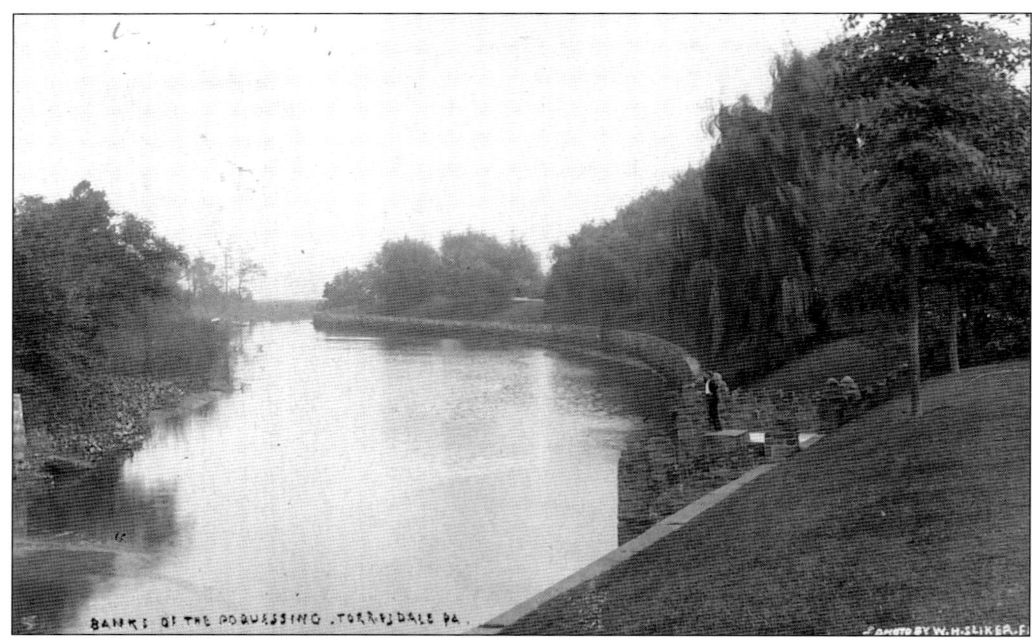

Poquessing Creek. The Poquessing Creek forms a natural boundary between the city of Philadelphia and Bucks County. This view looks east toward the Delaware River with Bucks County to the left. (Sliker postcard.)

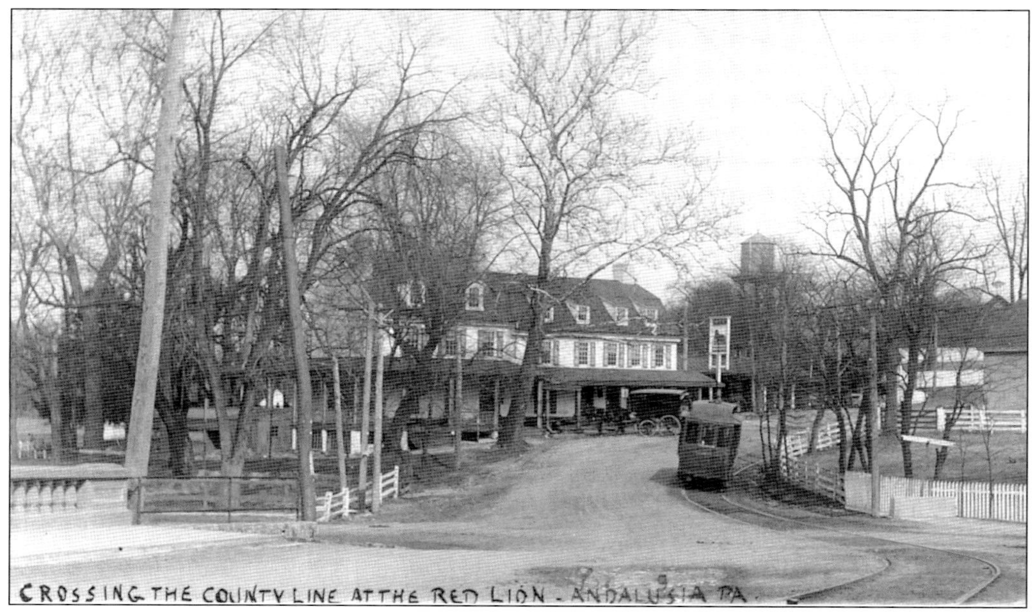

Crossing the County Line, Andalusia. This wonderful view shows the old Red Lion Hotel and a trolley along Bristol Pike in Andalusia. The bridge in the foreground is over the Poquessing Creek at the county line. The white picket fences and old trees make this 1910 image of Andalusia a picturesque view. (Sliker postcard.)

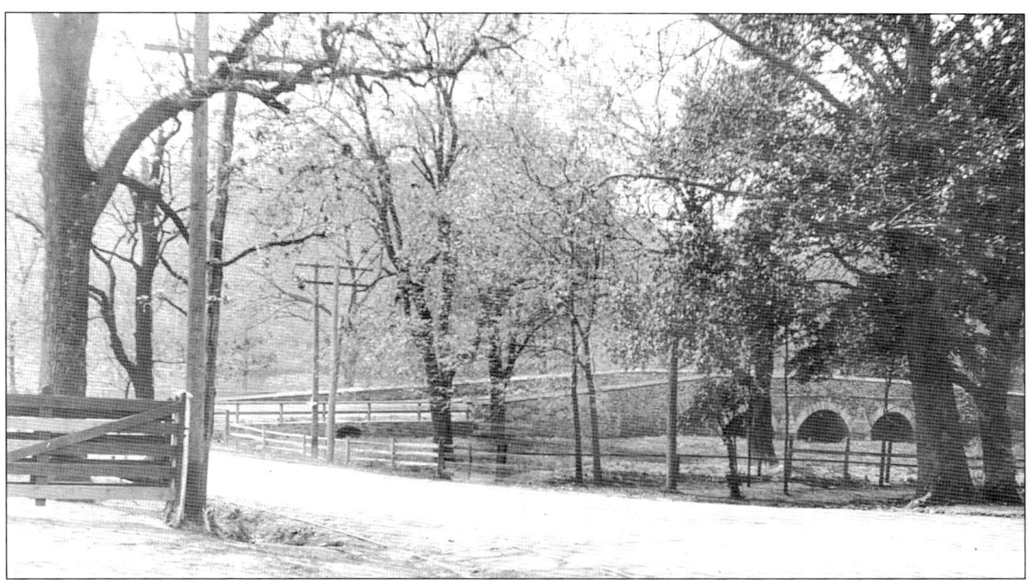

Bristol Pike at the County Line, Andalusia. This 1910 view of Bristol Pike looks south from in front of the Red Lion Hotel. The arch bridge on the right carried the Red Lion Road over the Poquessing Creek. The date stone on the bridge is from 1845. Bristol Pike takes a sharp turn toward the left in this view. (Sliker postcard.)

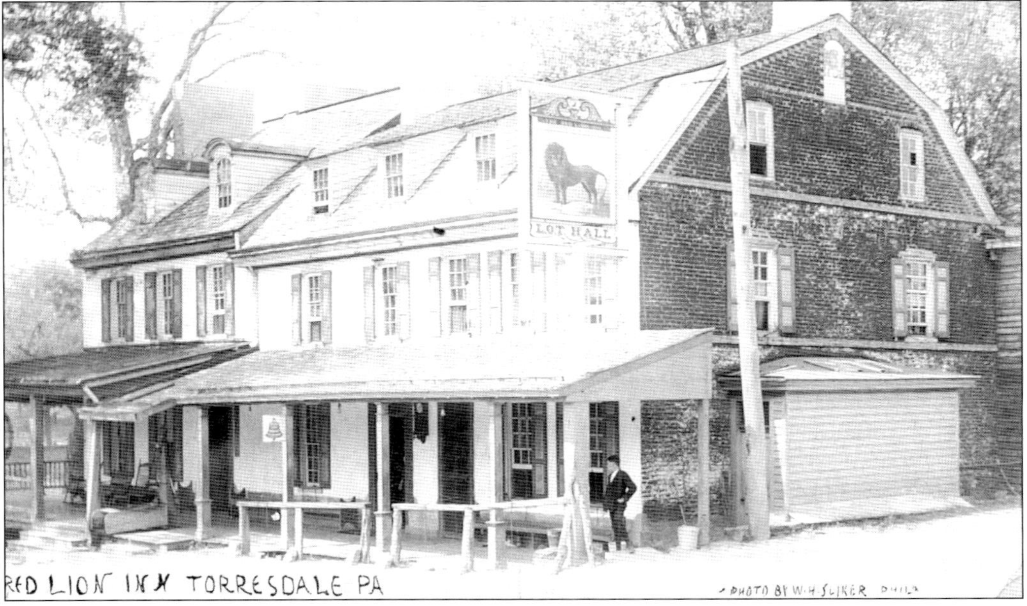

The Red Lion Hotel. The historic and majestic Red Lion Hotel once stood where the Poquessing Creek and Bristol Pike meet. Dating to 1730, it was Bucks County's most important tavern. Many famous people lodged at the inn, including George Washington, Samuel Adams, Robert Morris, and Thomas Jefferson. A sad ending to this old landmark occurred in 1991, when a fire destroyed the hotel. This was a great loss to those who value historic places and especially to those who held personal memories of the hotel. (Sliker postcard.)

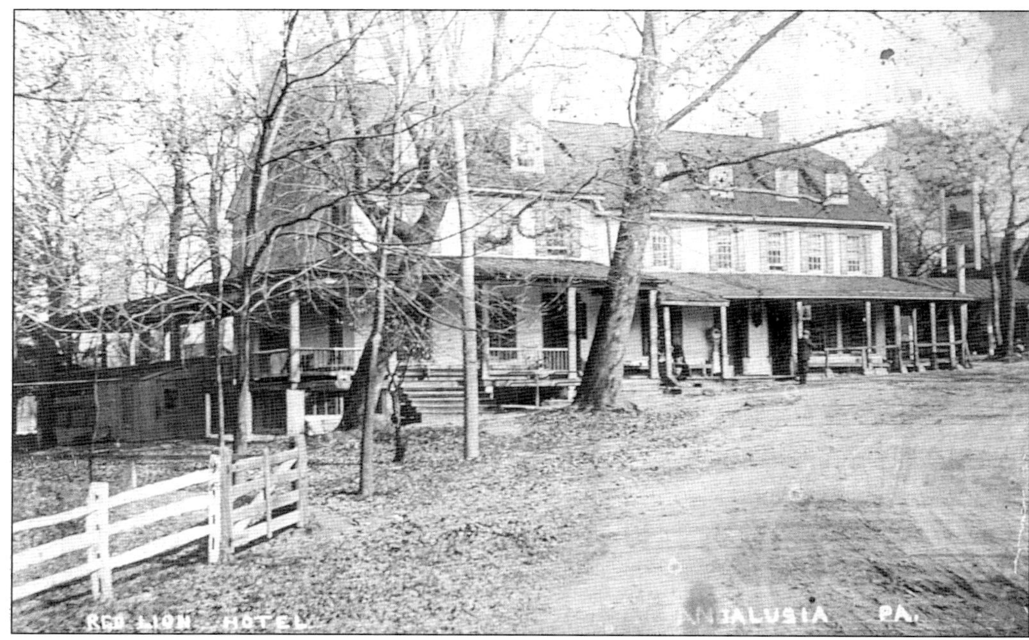

The Red Lion Hotel, 1910. This 1910 view shows the Red Lion Hotel on Bristol Pike, then a dirt lane winding past the old inn. In later years, the porches were enclosed to allow more seating at the inn, and Bristol Pike was moved to the right. The trees were eliminated, and a small parking lot was created. Despite all the changes, the upper windows, shutters, and its Colonial roof remained intact.

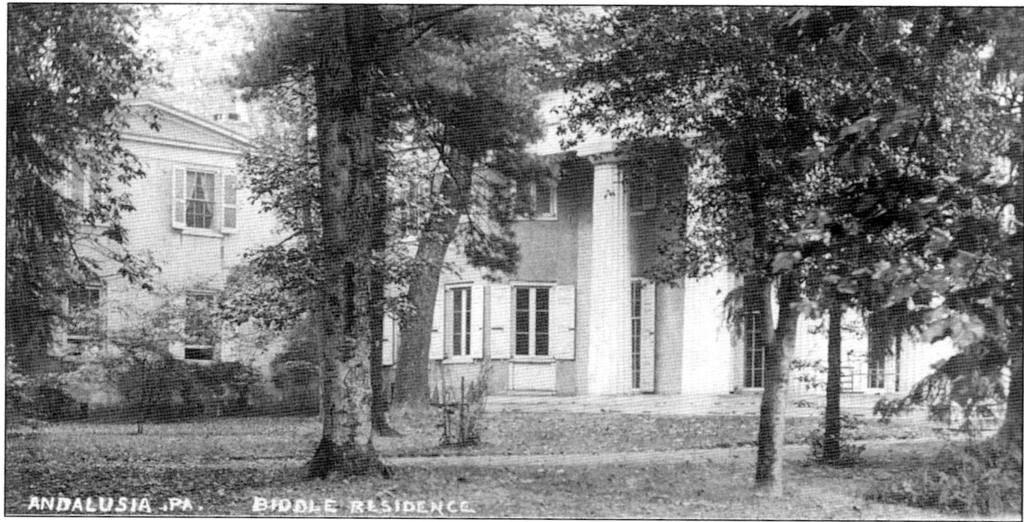

Biddle Residence, Andalusia. The town of Andalusia in Bensalem Township was named after the old Biddle estate situated on the Delaware River. An existing farmhouse from the 1700s was remodeled in the 1830s to become one of this country's greatest examples of Greek Revival architecture. With its classic pillared columns and gently sloping lawn, stretching to the Delaware River, the Biddle estate is one of lower Bucks County's most impressive historic sites. It is a rare survivor of the elegant estates that once lined the banks of the Delaware River. (Sliker postcard.)

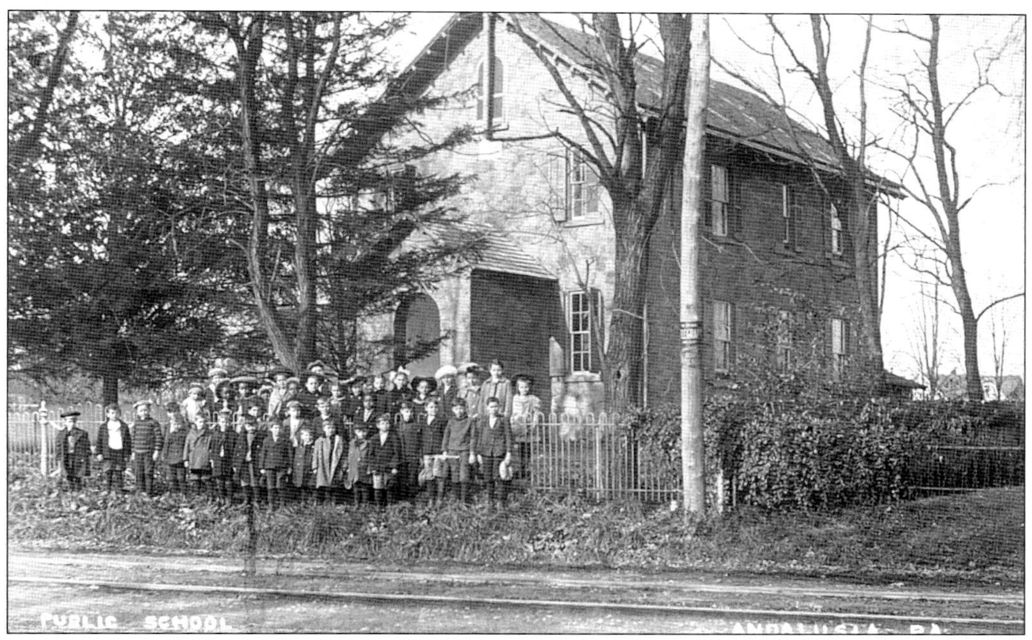

A Public School, Andalusia. The Andalusia Public School was built in 1878 on Bristol Pike at Poquessing Avenue. It is typical of a two-room schoolhouse, with one classroom on each floor. Shown *c.* 1910, the school was demolished in the mid-1960s. (Hay Photo Postcard Company.)

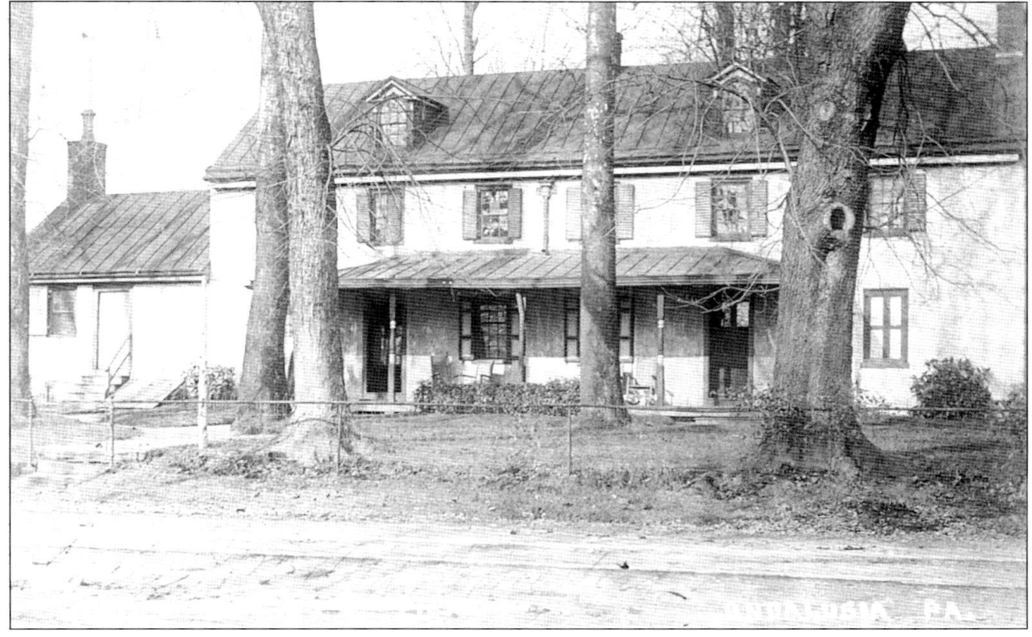

The Old Fox Chase Hotel, Andalusia. Further evidence of the importance and popularity of the Kings Highway (Bristol Pike) in the 1700s is that two taverns existed in the same vicinity. The Red Lion Hotel was a half mile below the Fox Chase Hotel. The Fox Chase Hotel was first licensed as a tavern in 1785, although it was a private home at the time of this postcard in 1909.

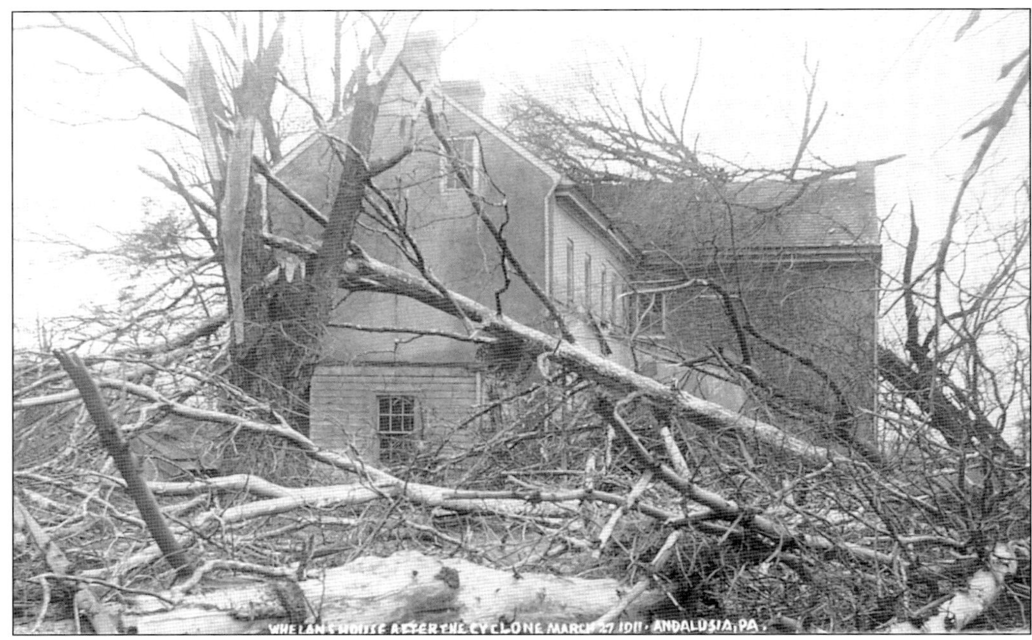

WHEELAN'S HOUSE, MARCH 27, 1911. An early spring windstorm of rare intensity traveled up the Delaware River corridor from Frankford through Tacony, Torresdale, and north to Andalusia on March 27, 1911. Bridesburg photographer William Sliker documented the destruction on at least 20 different postcards. This view shows the devastation to the landscape at the Wheelan house in Andalusia. It appears that the sturdy farmhouse survived with minimal damage.

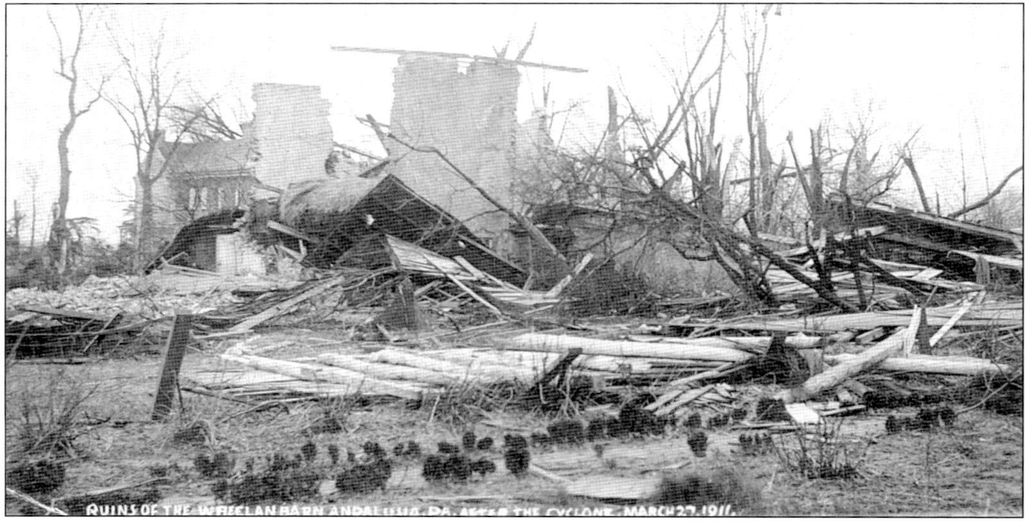

WHEELAN'S BARN, MARCH 27, 1911. The damage to the Wheelan barn was much more substantial, with only two partial walls left standing. Interestingly, Sliker labeled some of his views as "windstorm," while others were described as "cyclones." Judging from the narrow path the storm took, it is possible that a small twister traveled up the Route 13 corridor. What actually occurred may remain a mystery, but it appears that these views of the destruction were quite a curiosity in their day.

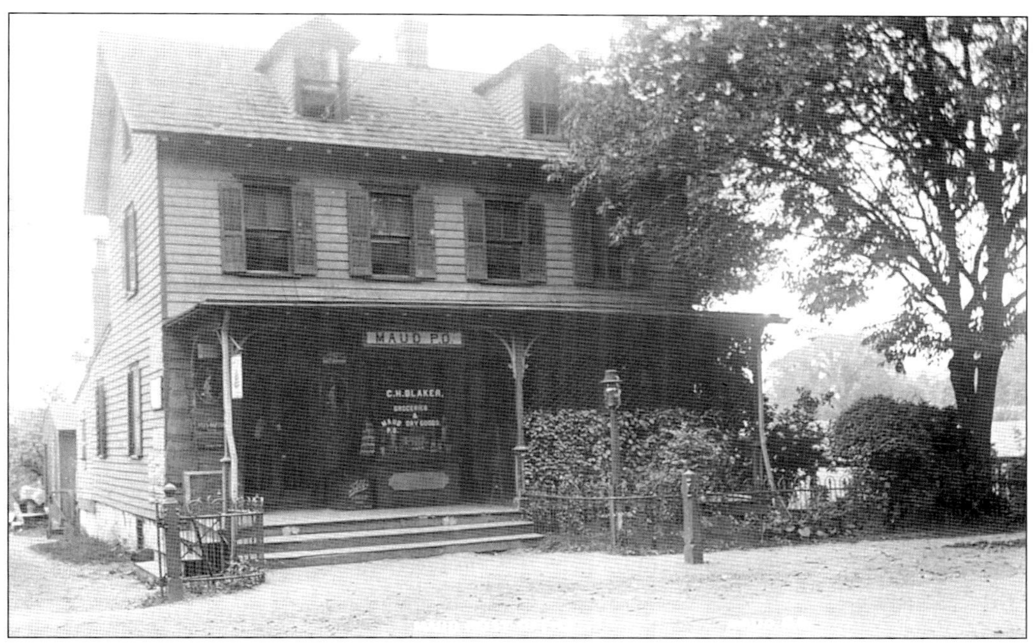

The Maud Post Office. If many people have never heard the name Maud in Bucks County, there is a reason why. Originally it was called Cornwells Post Office, then several months later in 1881 the name was changed to Maud. In 1915, the name was changed back to Cornwells Heights. This building on Bristol Pike is no longer standing. (Sliker postcard.)

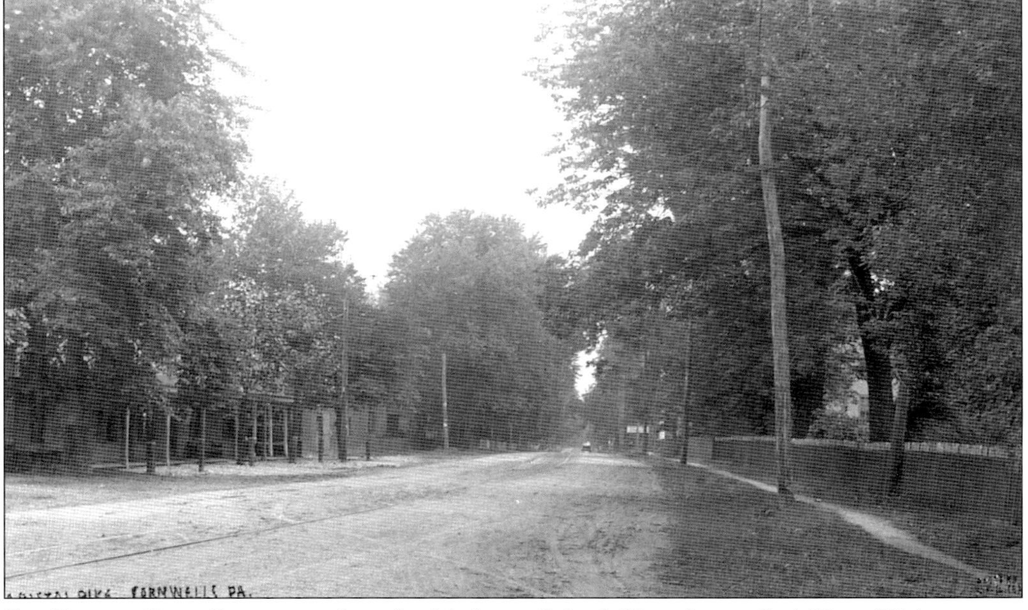

The Bristol Pike, Cornwells. In colonial times, Bristol Pike, then called Kings Highway, was the oldest and most important route in lower Bucks County. Dating to 1686, it became a major stagecoach route between Philadelphia, Bristol, and New York. This 1910 view shows a quiet Bristol Pike at Cornwells Heights. (Sliker postcard.)

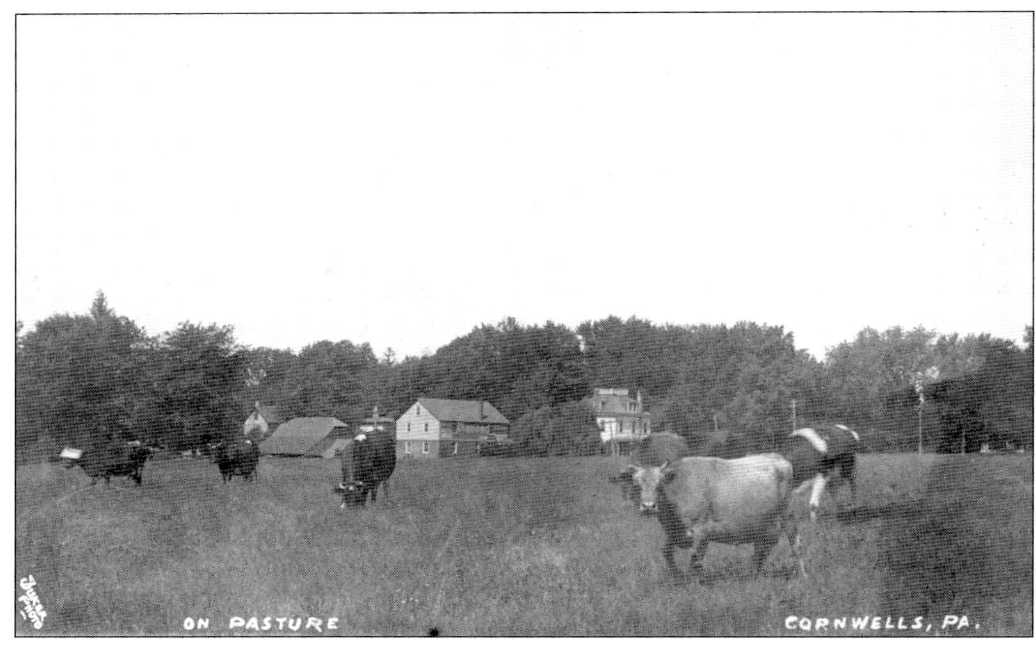

ON PASTURE, CORNWELLS. Farming and agriculture were important aspects of life in lower Bucks County from the time of the first settlement in the late 1600s to the middle of the 1900s. This Sliker view captures a bucolic setting in Cornwells Heights *c.* 1915.

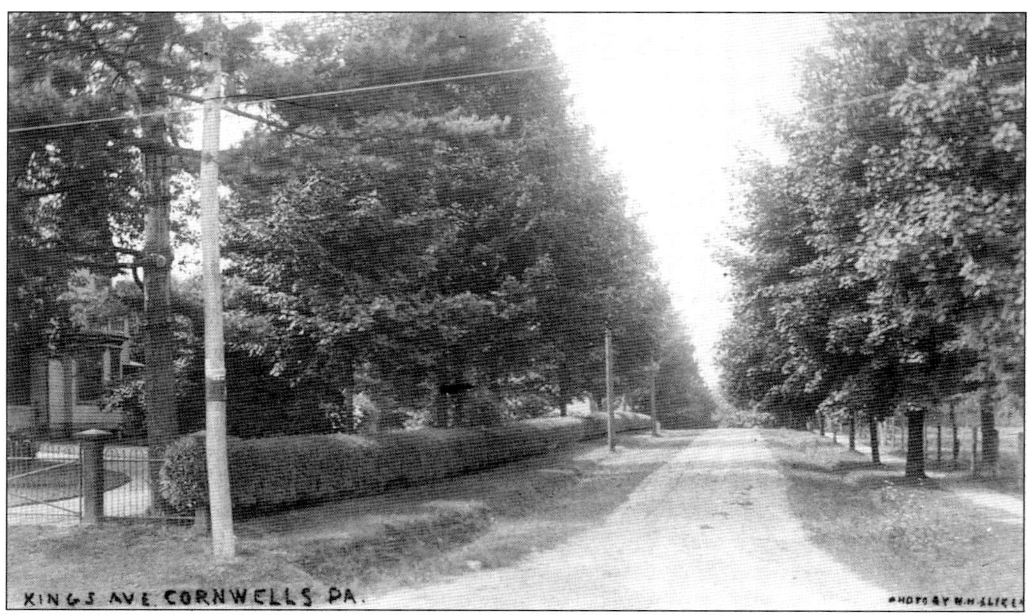

KINGS AVENUE, CORNWELLS. In 1912, Kings Avenue was an attractive residential street with beautiful tress and hedges. As seen here, the road was unpaved. (Sliker postcard.)

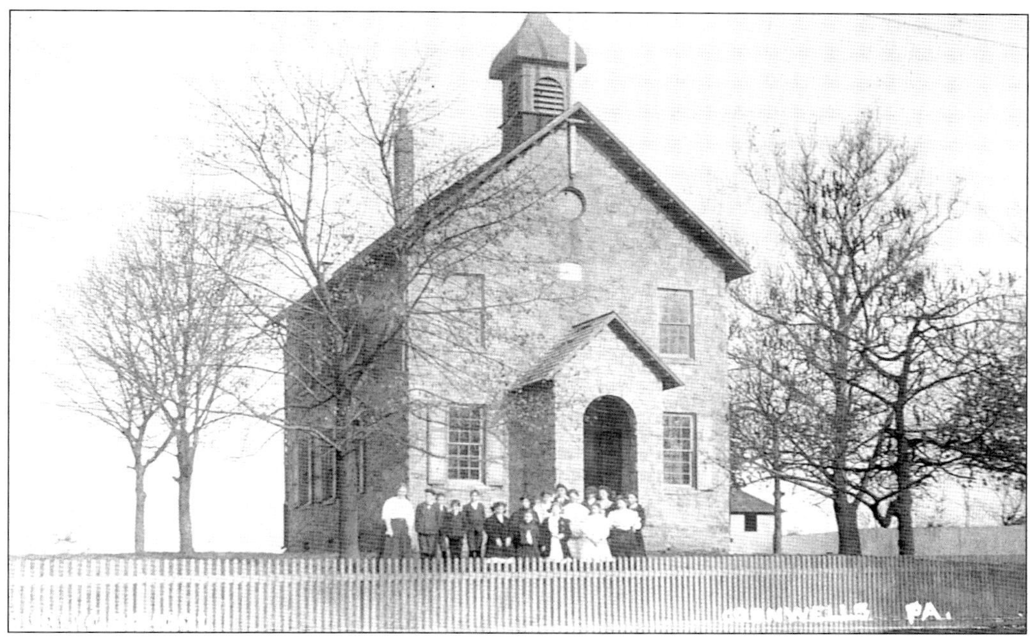

PUBLIC SCHOOL, CORNWELLS. The Cornwells Heights School was the first in Bensalem Township. In 1823, a one-room schoolhouse was built and was replaced by this two-room building in 1893. Over the years, the school has had numerous additions and has been remodeled. Supposedly, the 1893 classrooms are incorporated into the present building at Bristol Pike and School Lane. This view is from 1908.

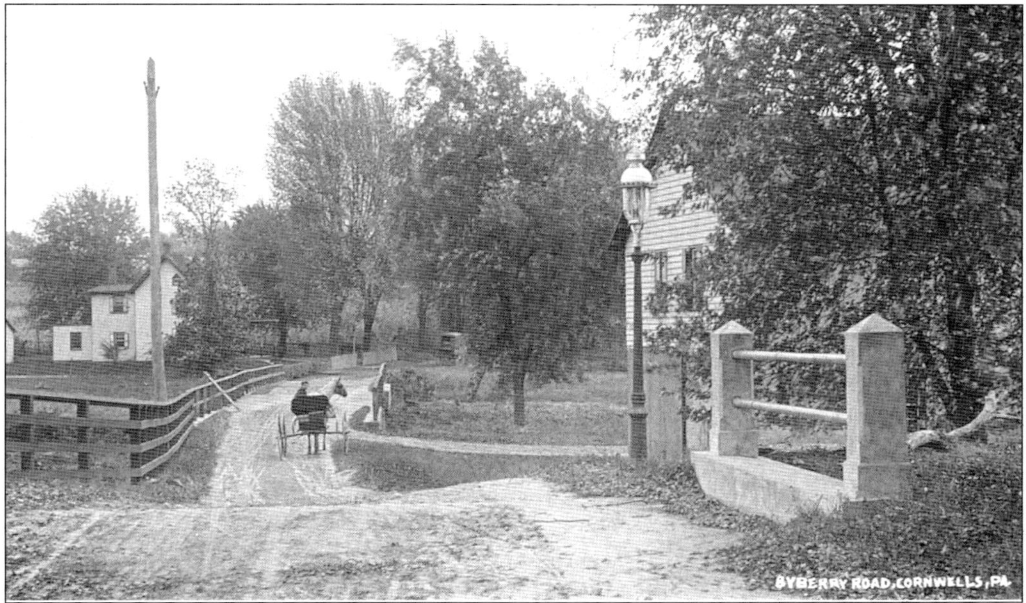

BYBERRY ROAD, CORNWELLS. This 1910 view by William Sliker captures the beautiful rural atmosphere along Byberry Road near Cornwells Heights. Since this area is now heavily developed, the exact location is difficult to determine.

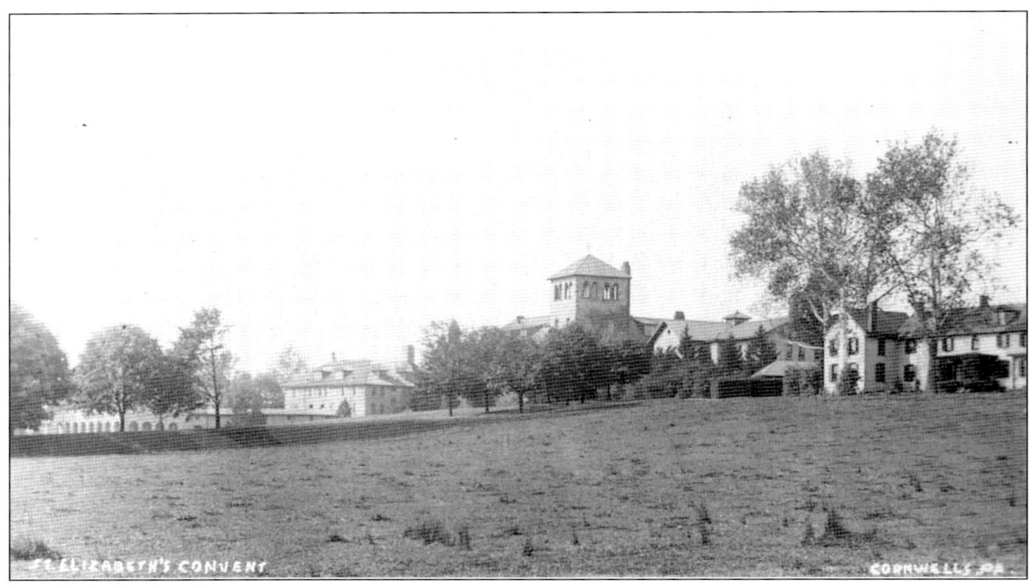

St. Elizabeth's Convent, Cornwells. St. Elizabeth's Convent was founded in 1890 by Sr. Katherine Drexel. The buildings, opened in 1892, are designed in the Spanish Mission style and are quite unique for Pennsylvania. Drexel herself was quite unique. Born to a wealthy Philadelphia banking family, she dedicated her life and her money to helping underprivileged minorities. The convent complex includes a chapel and a school. The buildings shown in this 1915 view remain standing. (Sliker postcard.)

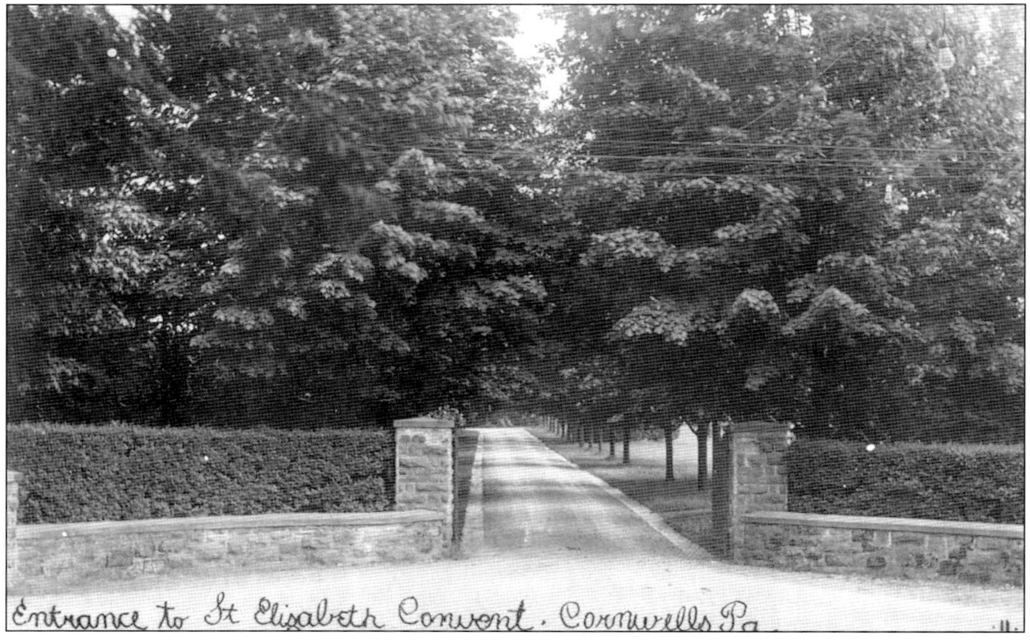

The Entrance to St. Elizabeth's Convent. The beauty of St. Elizabeth's is not just limited to the buildings. Beautiful landscapes as well as scenic driveways and entrances can be found on the property. (Sliker postcard.)

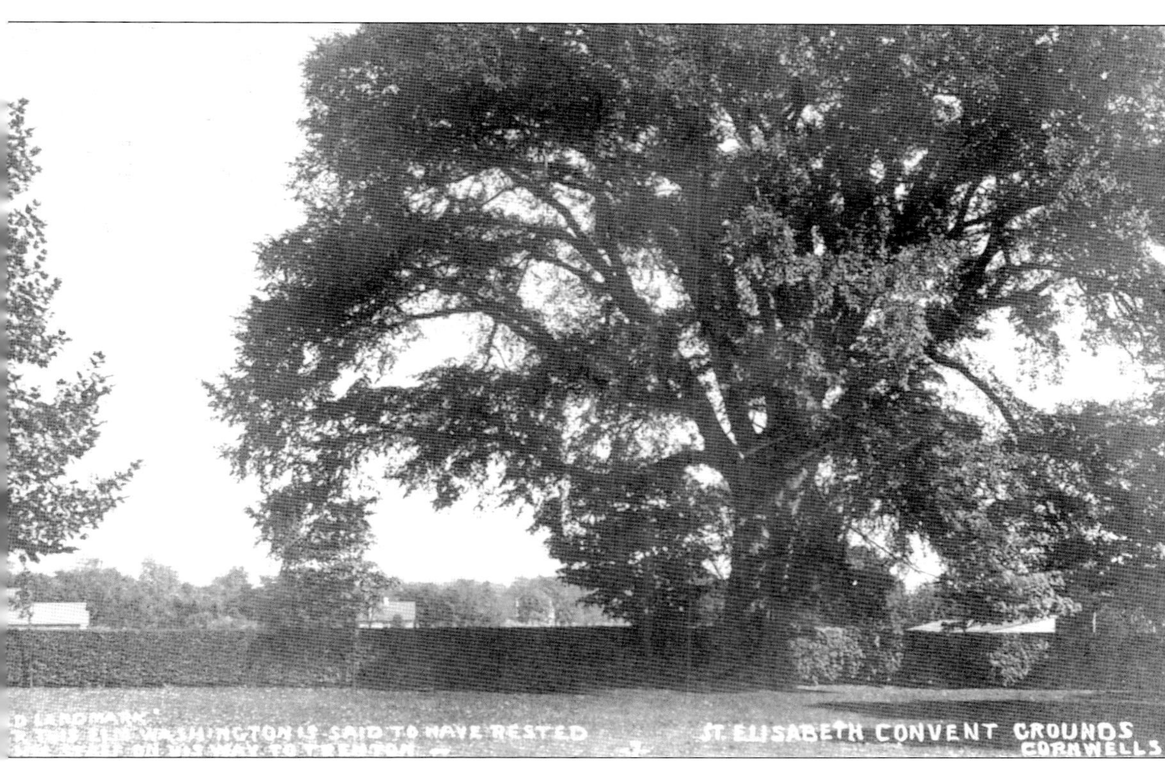

Washington Elm, Cornwells. This magnificent tree once stood on the grounds of St. Elizabeth's Convent along Bristol Pike. As written on the postcard, George Washington supposedly rested under this tree on his way to Trenton. Although he is known to have traveled on the Bristol Pike, legends such as this one are difficult to prove. Whatever the facts may be, historic lore adds a sense of intrigue and mystery to our area. (Sliker postcard.)

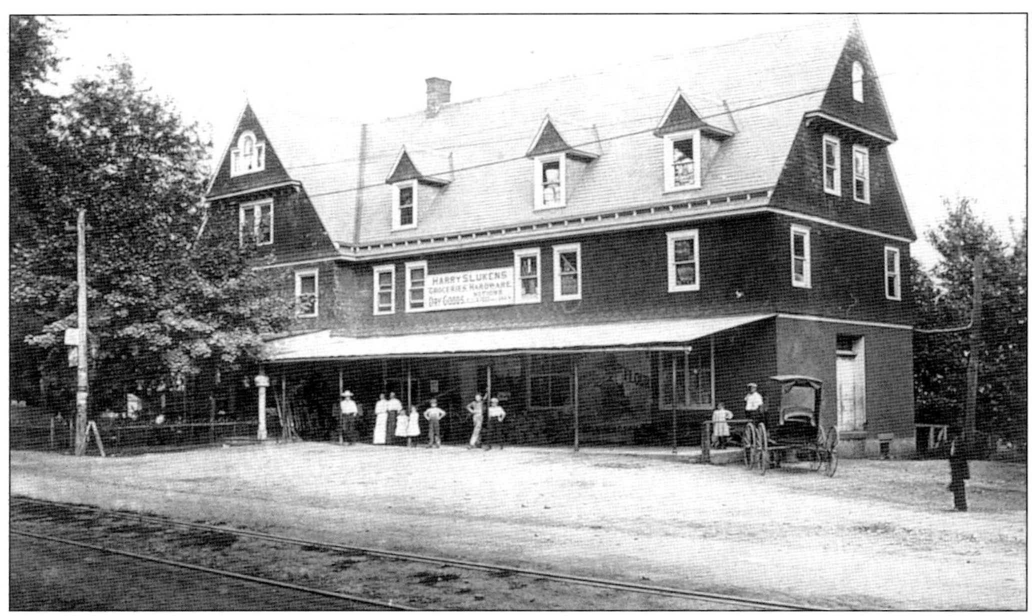

THE LUKENS GENERAL STORE, EDDINGTON. The town of Eddington can trace its roots to 1770, when Richard Gibbs built a farm in southern Bensalem Township and named it Eddington after his home in England. The Eddington store was built in 1895 and stood on Bristol Pike near Street Road. This 1907 view shows the store, then owned by Harry S. Lukens, along the Bristol Pike. The store was torn down *c.* 1960. (Harry Wharton postcard.)

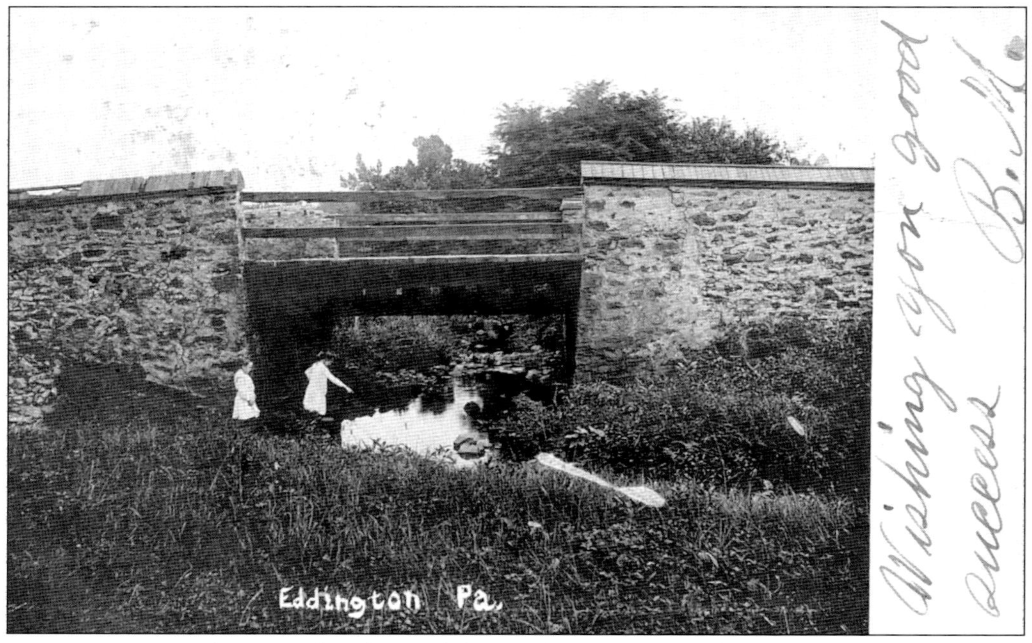

EDDINGTON. Postcard images often depicted the simple, everyday life of a community. This 1906 view shows young children playing near a bridge at a creek in Eddington. (Harry Wharton postcard.)

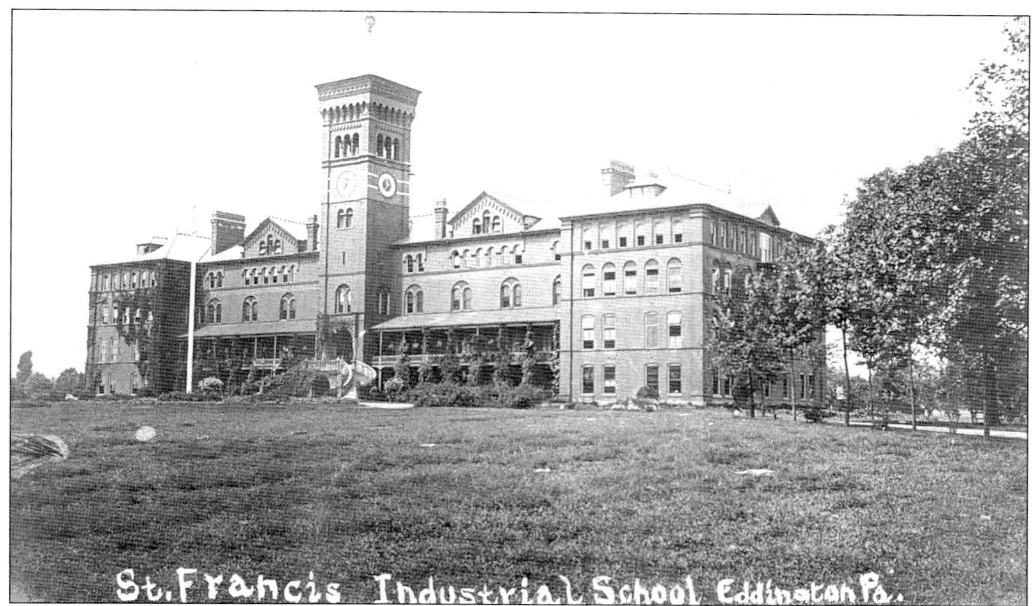

St. Francis Industrial School. Opened in 1888 as a home for orphaned boys, St. Francis Industrial School was developed through the interest of Louise Drexel Morrell and Elizabeth Drexel Smith. They were daughters of the wealthy banker Francis Drexel and sisters of Katharine Drexel of nearby St. Elizabeth's Convent. For almost 100 years, St. Francis, with its distinctive clock tower, was a striking landmark at Street Road and Bristol Pike. It was demolished in 1981, as it had become too costly to maintain. This view is from 1906. (Harry Wharton postcard.)

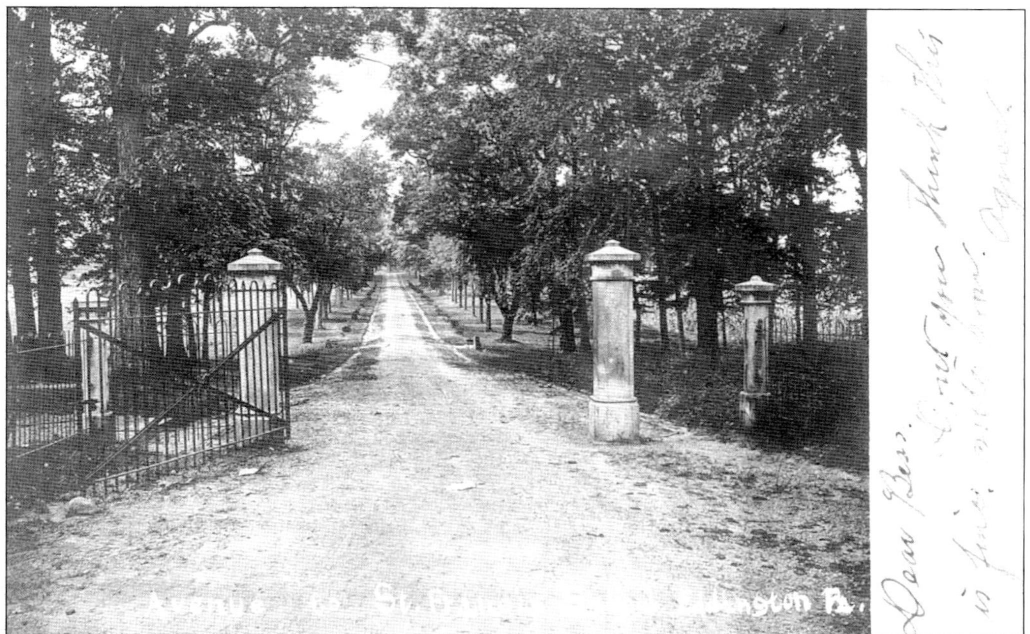

The Avenue to St. Francis School. Although the beautiful school building is gone, much of the grounds, including this drive to the school along Bristol Pike, remain. (Harry Wharton postcard.)

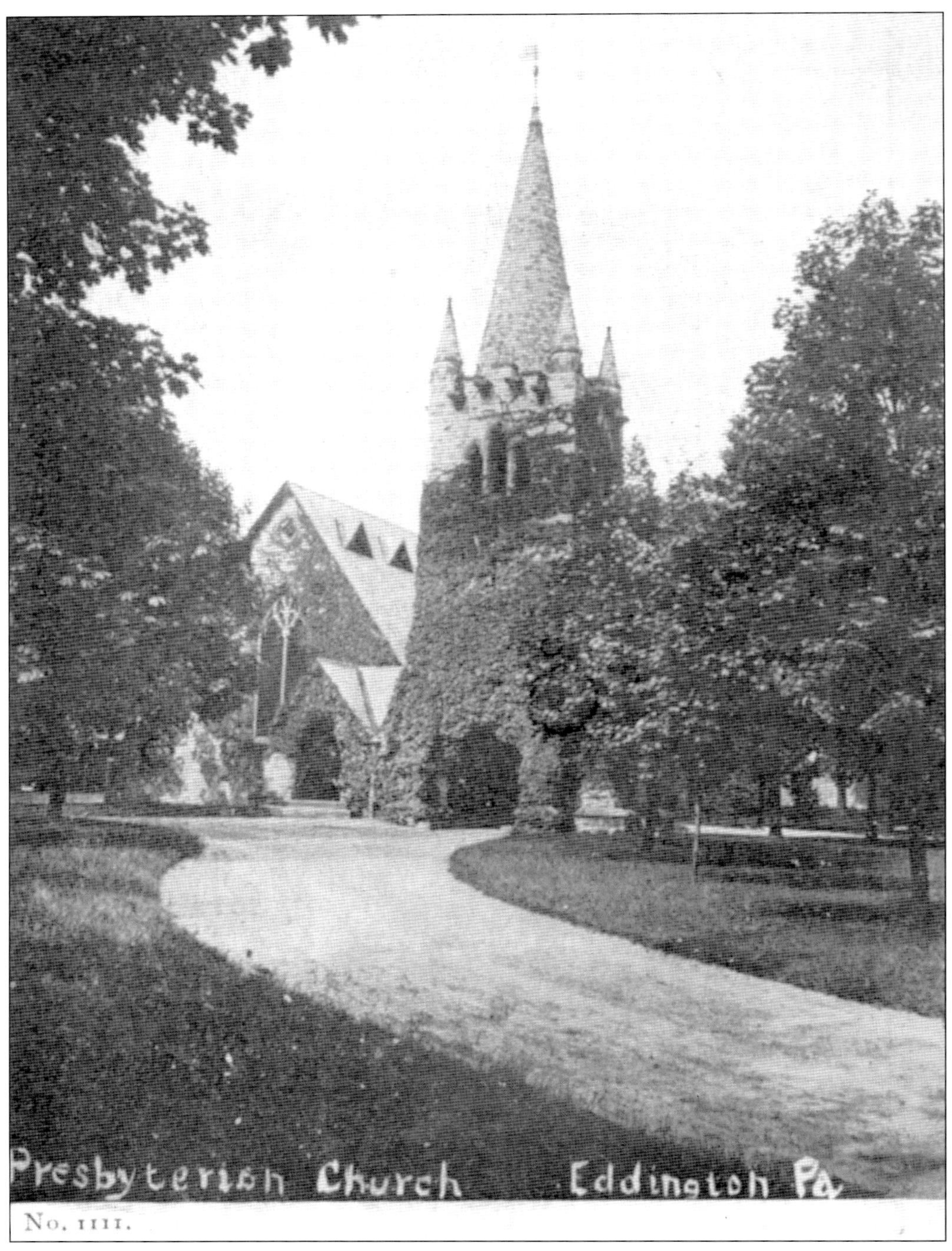

Presbyterian Church, Eddington. The Eddington Presbyterian Church was built in 1885 on Bristol Pike above Street Road. This beautiful stone church incorporated Romanesque and Gothic Revival architectural elements. Of particular interest is the unique steeple tower, which transcends downward to an open archway. This lovely building still stands along busy Bristol Pike in Eddington.

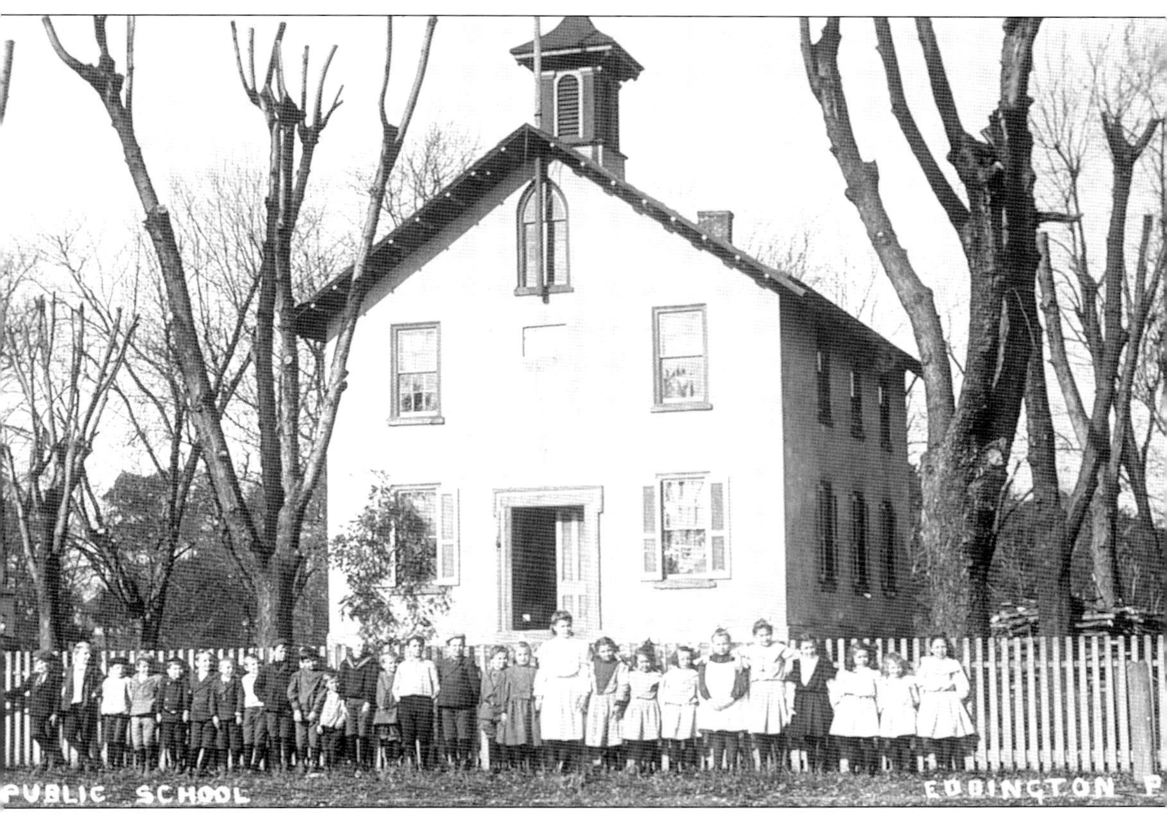

Public School, Eddington. The Eddington Public School was built in 1856 and is located on Bristol Pike above Bensalem Boulevard. Like Andalusia and Cornwells, it is a two-story school. Many early area postcard views of old schools show the entire student population appropriately posed in front of their building. These views in particular are charming snapshots of rural life in lower Bucks County. This school was closed in 1951 and has since housed a variety of businesses. (Hay Photo Postcard Company.)

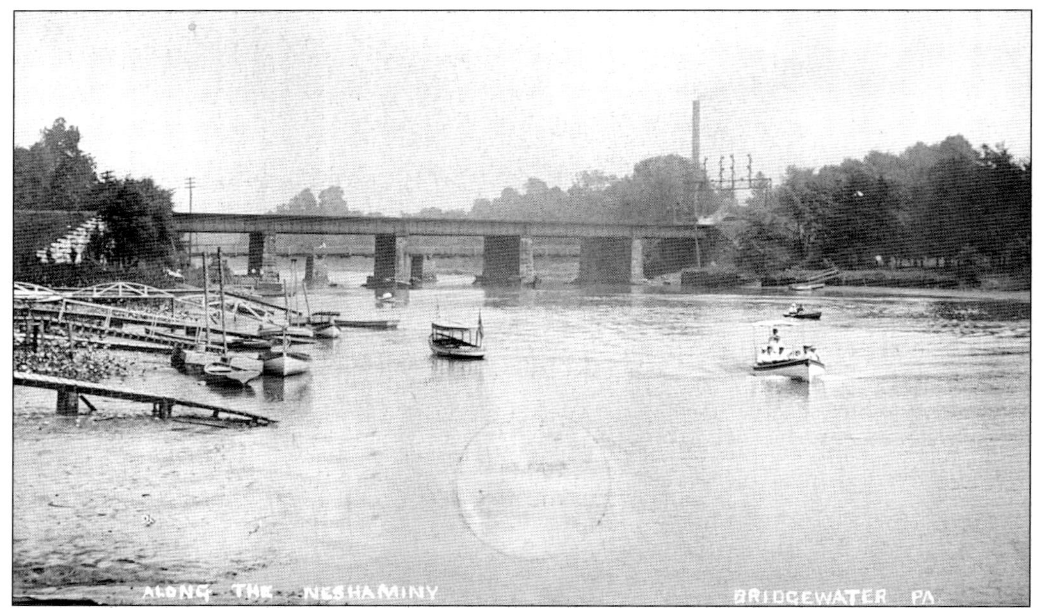

Along the Neshaminy, Bridgewater. This 1910 view looks north on the Neshaminy Creek at Bridgewater. The first bridge seen is the old railroad bridge connecting lines from Cornwells to Croydon Stations. Past that is the old Bristol Pike bridge. These bridges, along with the one at nearby State Road, appear to justify the naming of the area as Bridgewater.

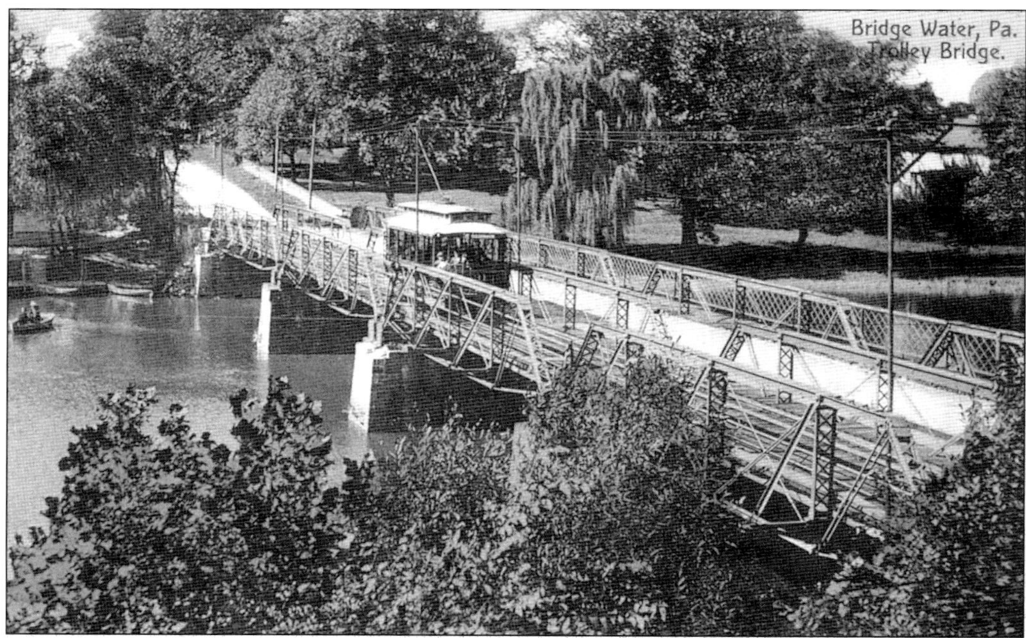

Bridgewater Trolley Bridge. This postcard, mailed in 1909, shows an open-air trolley car crossing the Neshaminy Creek at Bridgewater. A separate bridge was built at this location in the late 1890s alongside Bristol Pike to carry the line that ran from Philadelphia to Bristol.

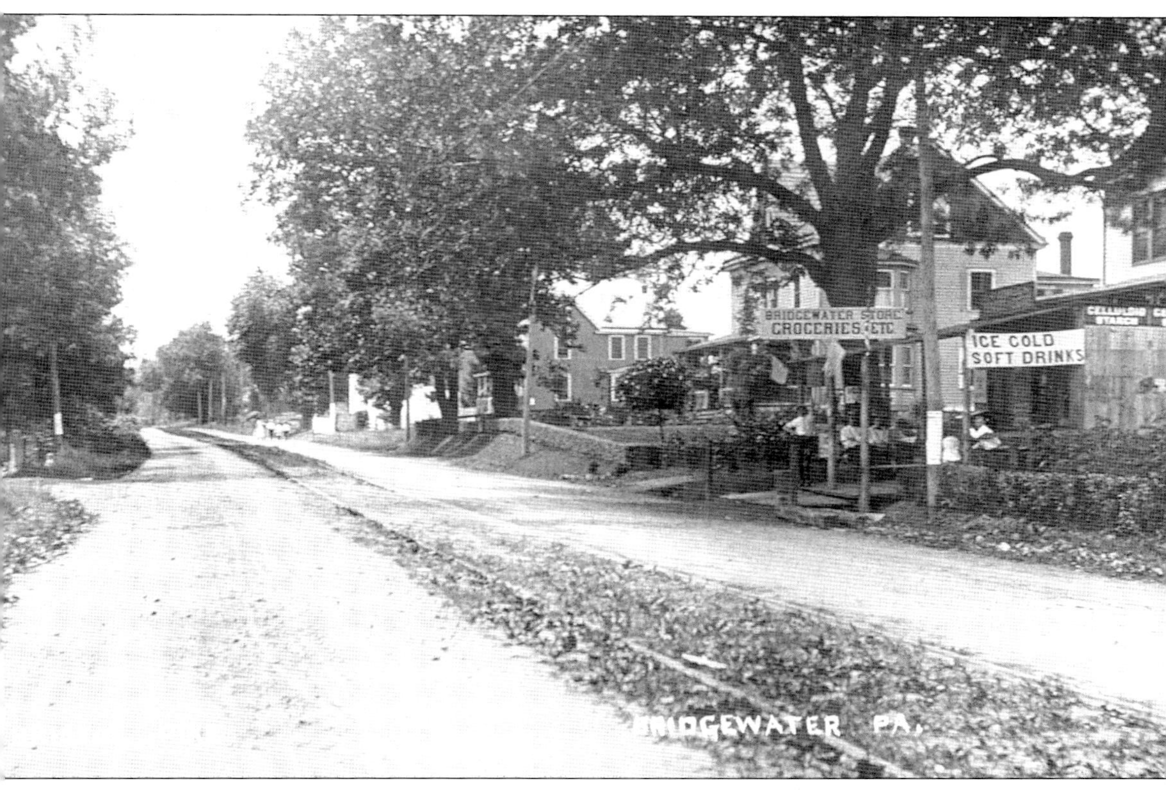

Bristol Pike, Bridgewater. Trolley tracks line the center of Bristol Pike in Bridgewater in this view looking south. A mix of homes and stores line both sides of the old road in this postcard from 1910. The village of Bridgewater is at the junction of Bristol Pike and the Neshaminy Creek. The Bridgewater store is the first building on the right.

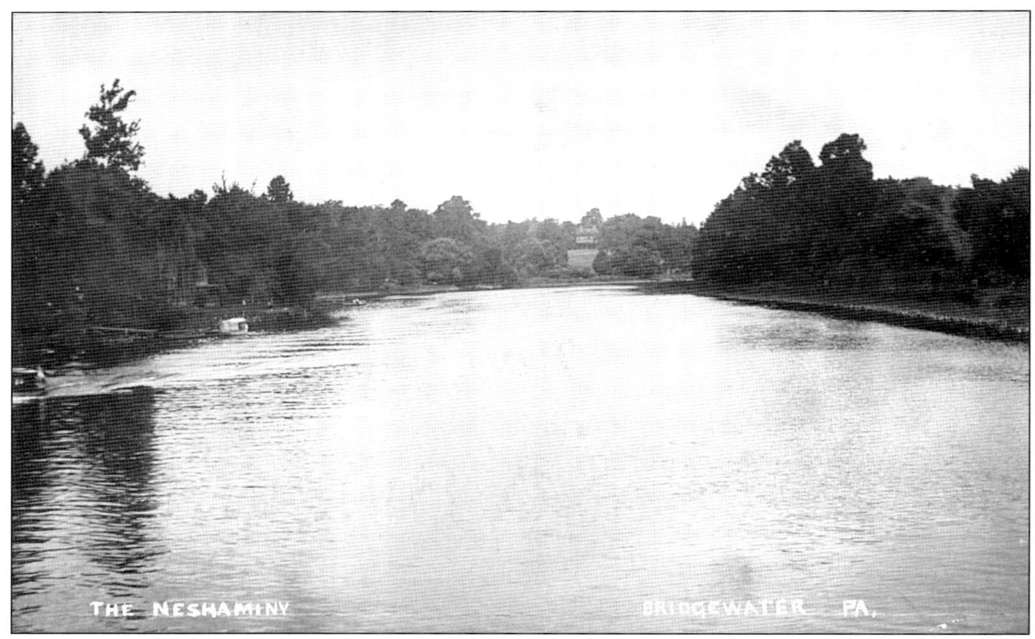

The Neshaminy at Bridgewater. The beautiful Neshaminy Creek is quite wide at Bridgewater. This view is most likely looking north from the Bristol Pike bridge. (Hay Photo Postcard Company.)

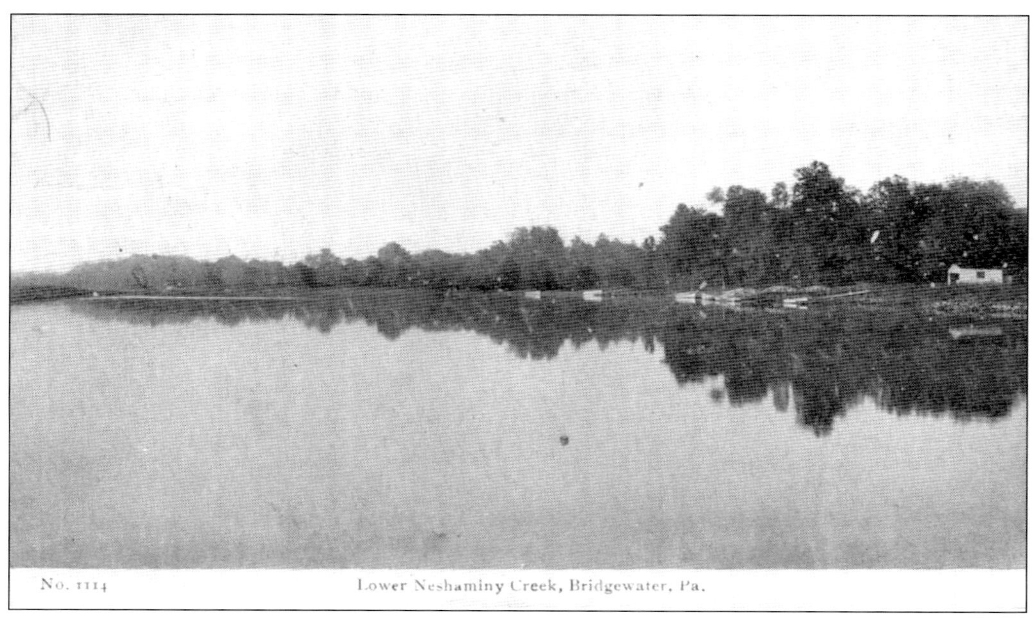

Lower Neshaminy Creek, Bridgewater. The Neshaminy Creek meanders through much of central and lower Bucks County before reaching the Delaware River at Bridgewater. Here the creek is at its widest with relatively calm, tidal water. This is ideal for boating and fishing and has attracted many people for more than two centuries. Neshaminy State Park continues to provide recreational facilities at this location.

Two

FALLS AND BRISTOL

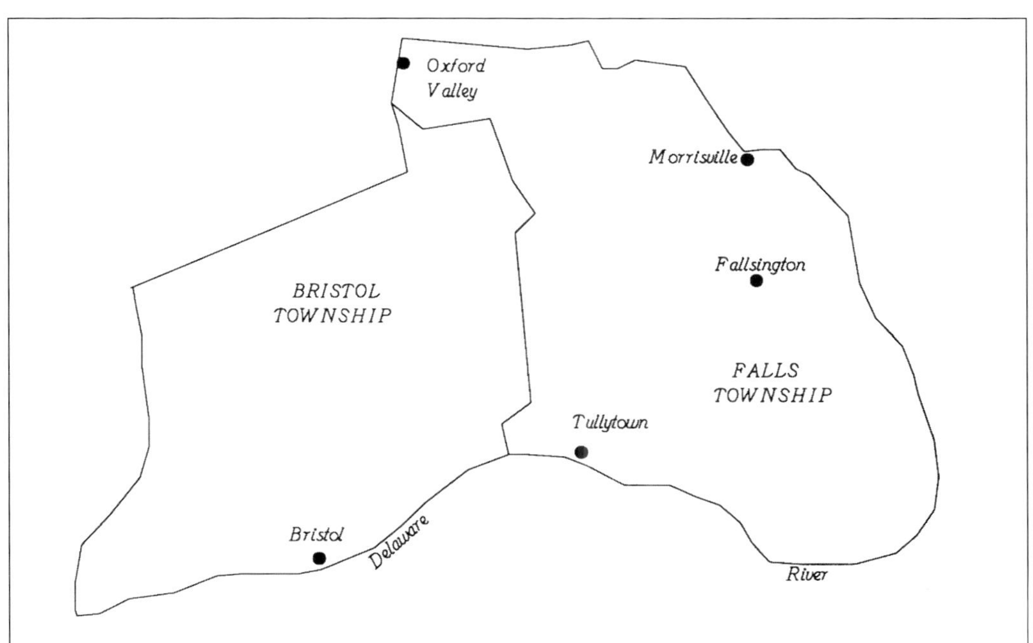

FALLS AND BRISTOL. This chapter will illustrate the lower Delaware River corridor of Bristol and Falls Townships, including Bristol Borough, Tullytown, Fallsington, and Oxford Valley. The region was once the site of William Penn's manor house, Pennsbury, and represents some of the oldest settlements in Bucks County.

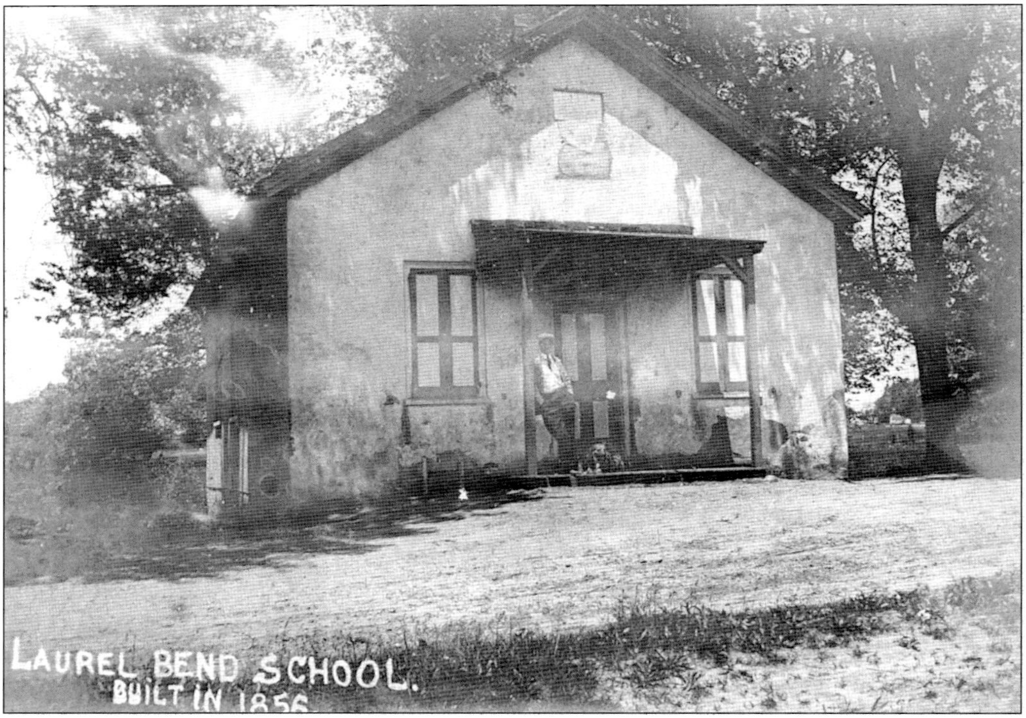

Laurel Bend School. Built in 1856, the Laurel Bend School is located in what is now the Laurel Bend section of Bristol Township on Bath Road. Interestingly, even in this *c.* 1910 view, the school was not in very good repair.

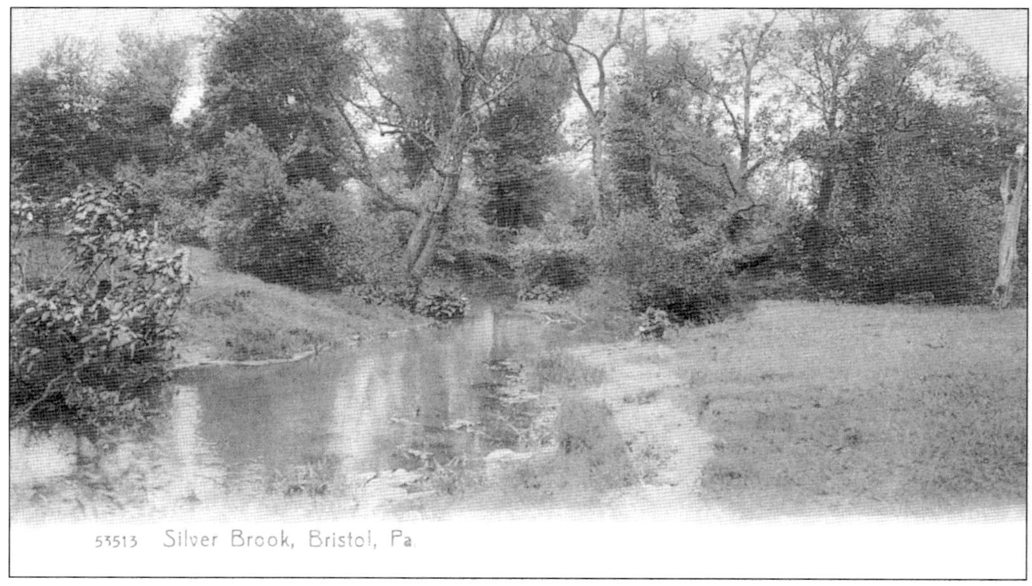

Silver Brook, Bristol. Silver Brook feeds into Silver Lake in Bristol Township above the borough of Bristol. Silver Lake County Park is an important land preserve because much of the county's coastal plain area has been destroyed by development. (Rotograph Company postcard.)

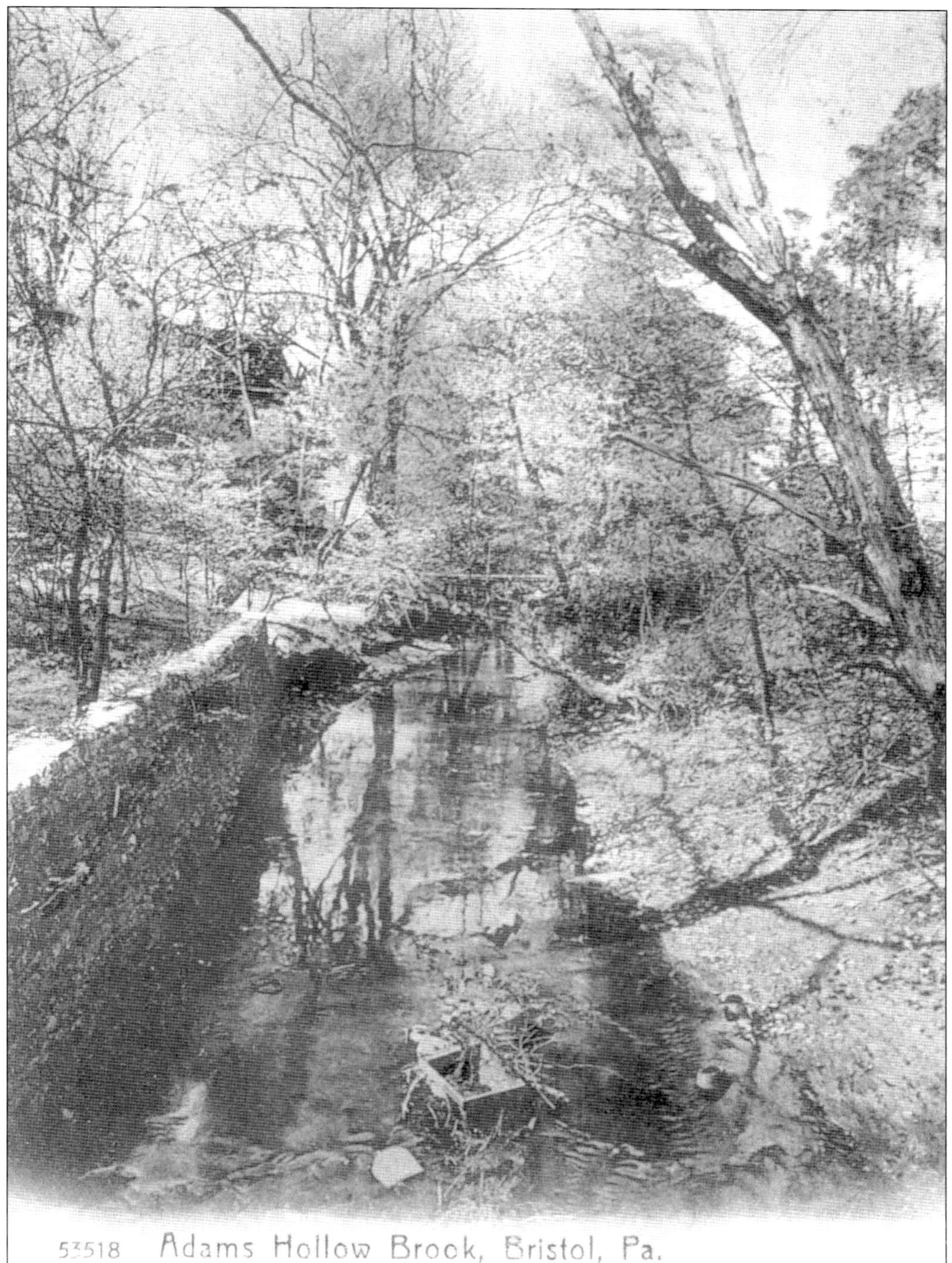

Adams Hollow Brook, Bristol. Bucks County's streams provided wonderful glimpses of the beautiful scenery found throughout the area. Adams Hollow Creek is a small waterway in Bristol, beginning near Silver Lake and emptying into the Delaware River above Jefferson Avenue. (Rotograph Company postcard.)

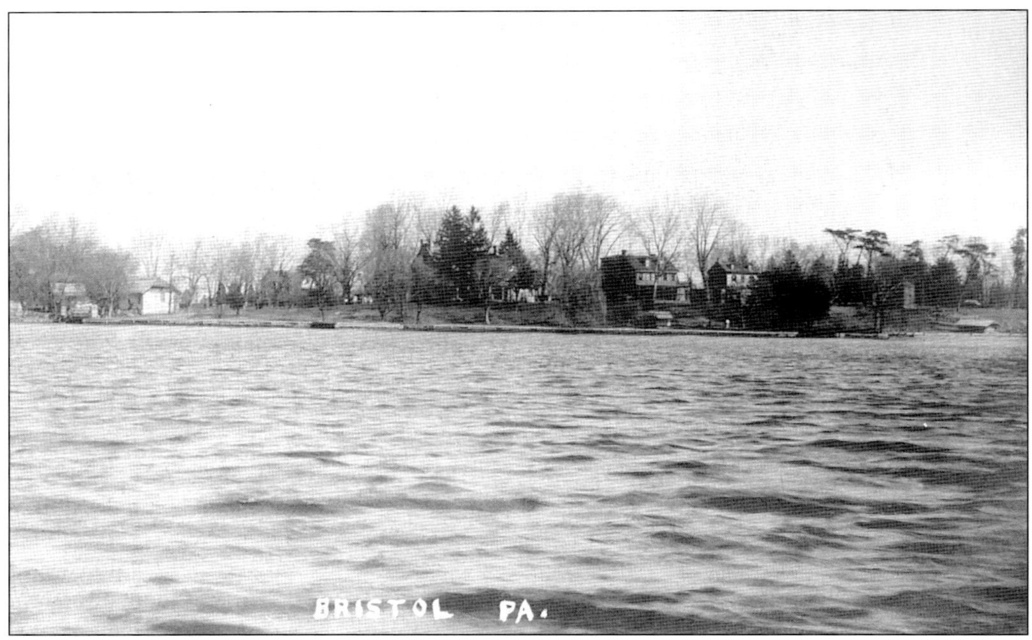

BRISTOL. Bristol was Bucks County's earliest and most important town and was its only true port city. The Delaware River provided easy access to other ports, such as Philadelphia and Burlington, New Jersey. This view shows the Delaware River with a residential section of Bristol in the distance.

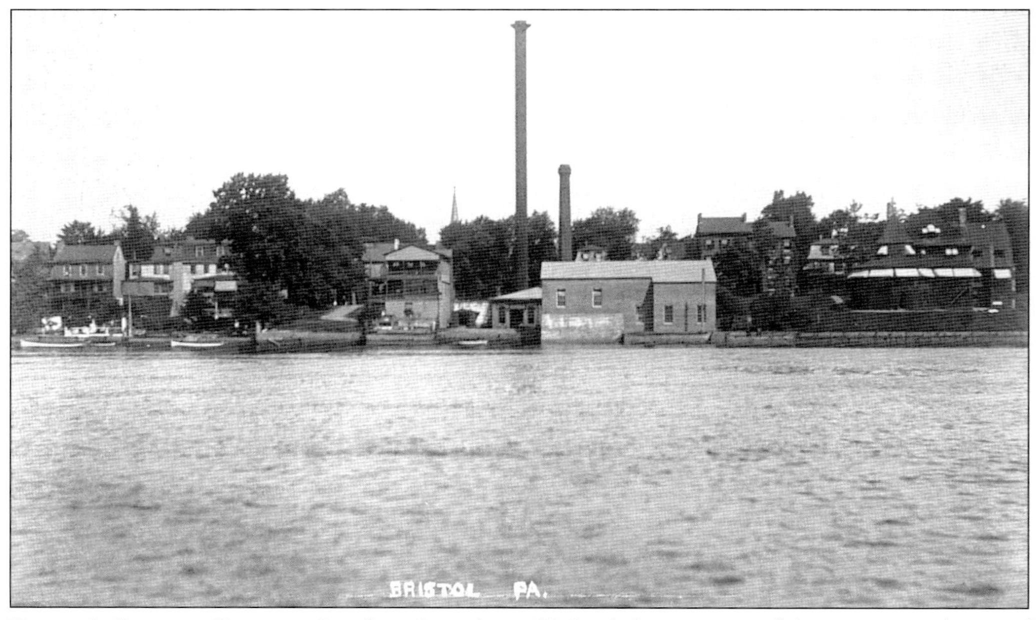

BRISTOL'S BUSINESS DISTRICT. Another river view of Bristol shows more of the commercial area of the town. Note the large smokestacks, indicating an industrial area.

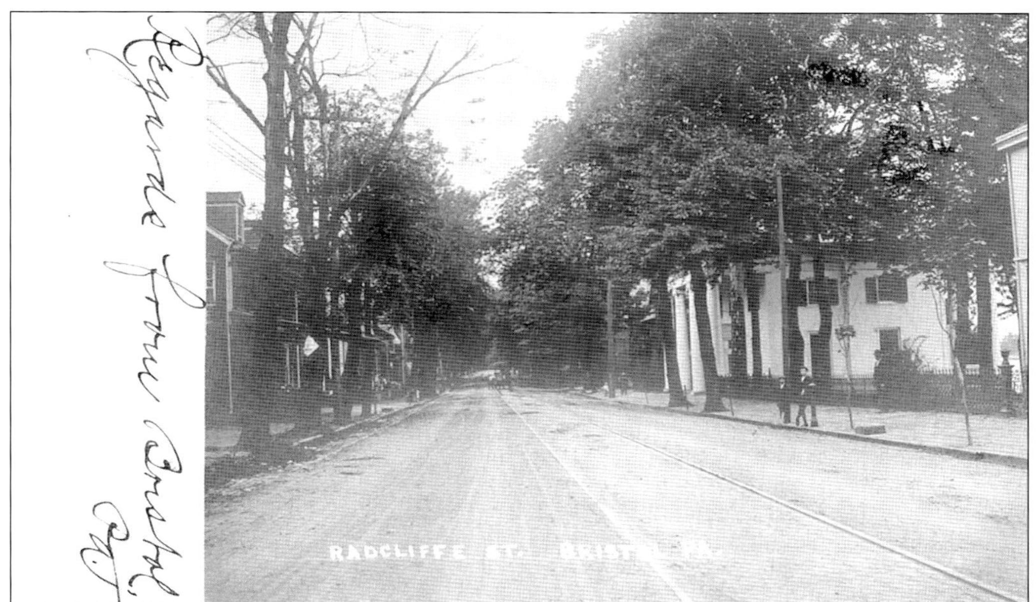

RADCLIFFE STREET, 1906. Radcliffe Street is one of Bucks County's loveliest streets. Beginning at Mill Street, it parallels the Delaware River for several miles before ending at Tullytown. This 1906 view looks north with the old Farmers National Bank on the right.

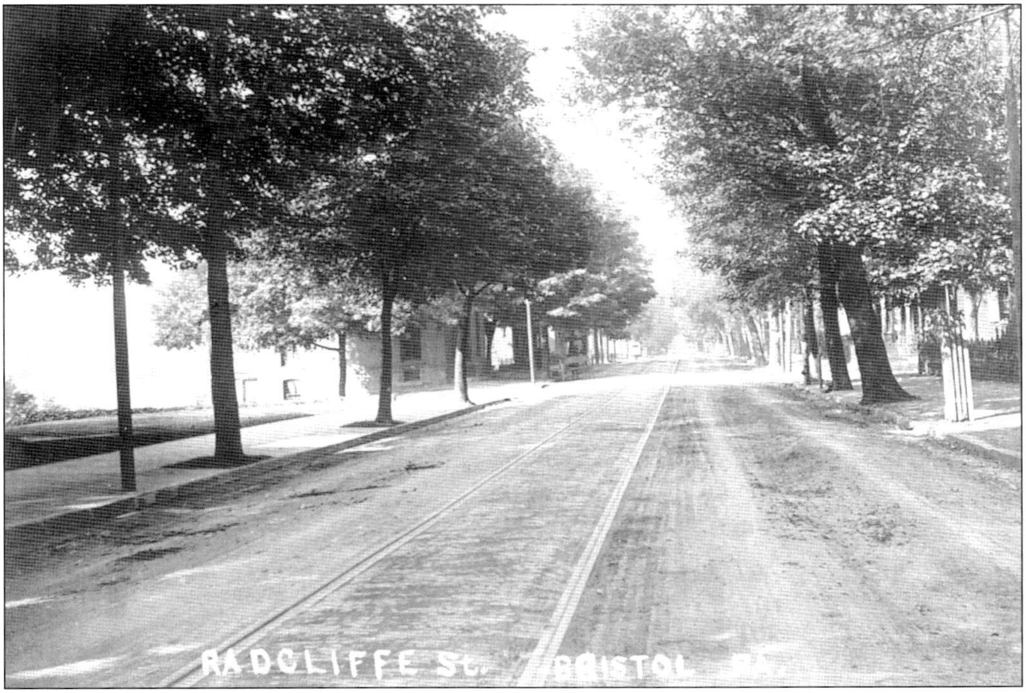

RADCLIFFE STREET. In 1905, Radcliffe Street was a beautiful treelined street with elegant residences and wonderful views of the Delaware River. Today, it remains a picturesque street with an eclectic variety of homes.

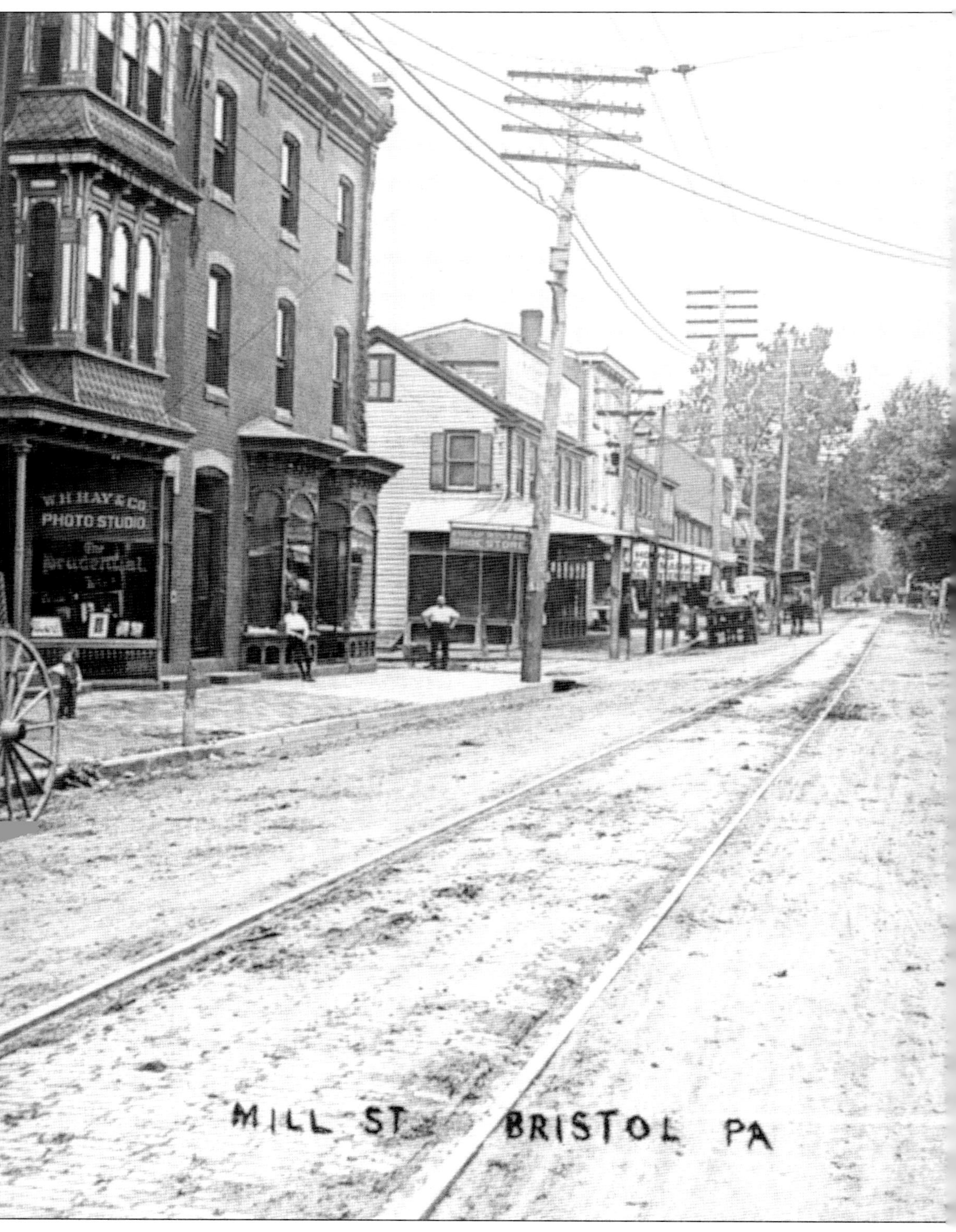
W.H. HAY & CO.
PHOTO STUDIO
SHOE STORE
MILL ST BRISTOL PA

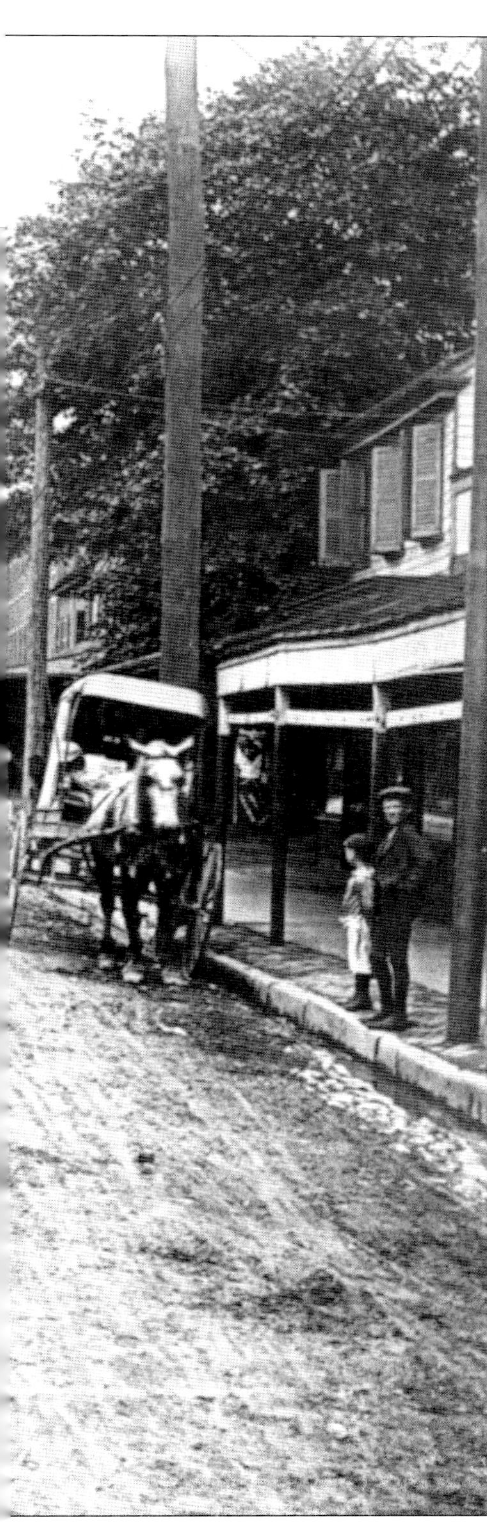

MILL STREET, BRISTOL. While Radcliffe Street contained the finest homes in lower Bucks County, Mill Street had the busiest shopping district. This 1908 view shows the variety of establishments on Mill Street. Of noteworthy interest is the first store on the left behind the carriage wheel. The window sign reads, "W.H. Hay & Co. Photo Studio." The Hay Photo Studio published many postcards of lower Bucks County. Many of them are illustrated in this book, including this one. Perhaps they were doing a little self-advertising.

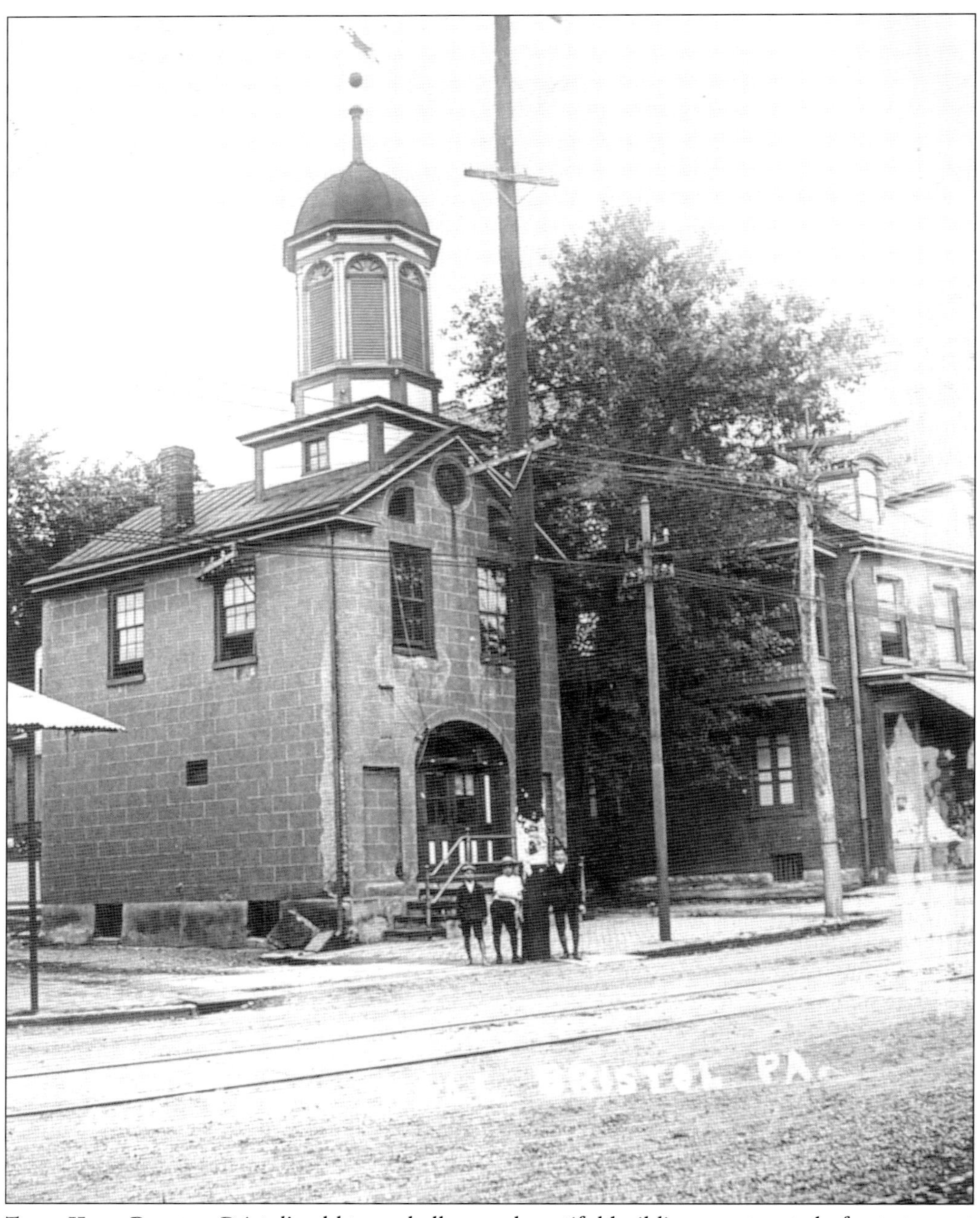

Town Hall, Bristol. Bristol's old town hall was a beautiful building constructed of cut stone at Market and Radcliffe Streets. The crowning cupola was particularly handsome. Built in the 1830s, the small building became inadequate and was torn down in 1938, when a larger building was constructed at another location. (Hay Photo Postcard Company.)

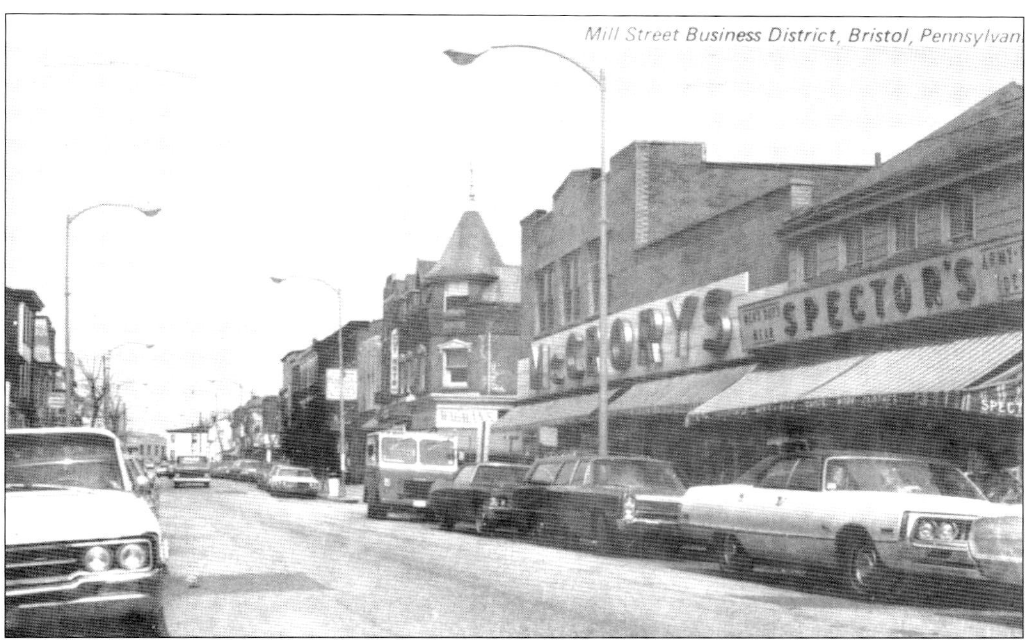

MILL STREET, BRISTOL. In the 1970s, Mill Street still contained many small stores, including McCrory's and Spector's. Both stores were in business for many decades, but the construction of large shopping malls and changing shopping patterns caused these stores to close in the 1980s.

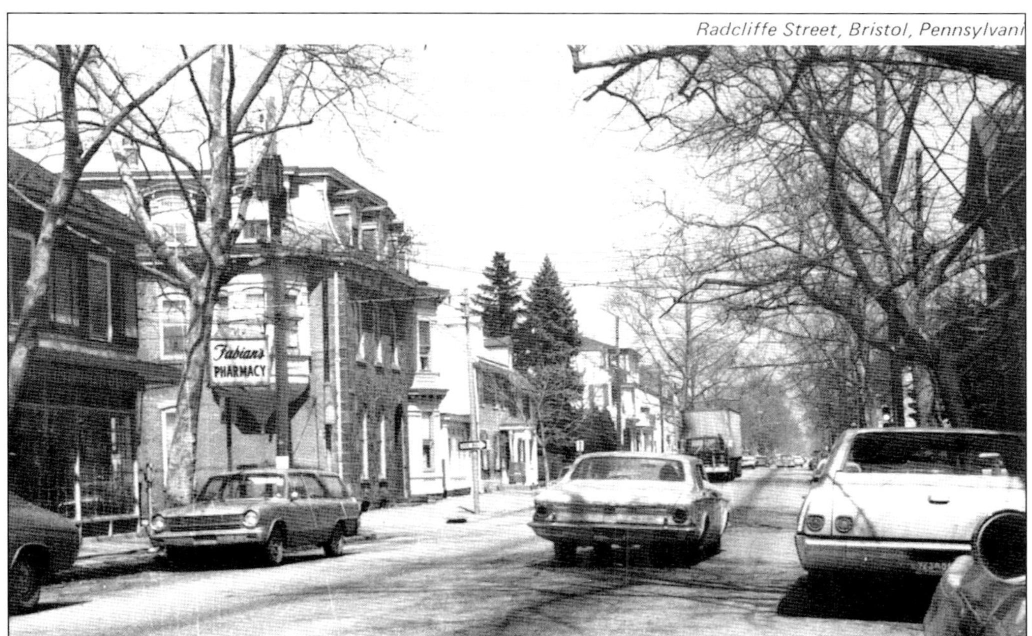

RADCLIFFE STREET, BRISTOL. This somewhat modern view of lower Radcliffe Street in the 1970s shows the attractive mix of commercial and residential buildings. To the left is Fabian's Pharmacy, where the author purchased this postcard in the 1980s. After many years in business, the pharmacy recently closed.

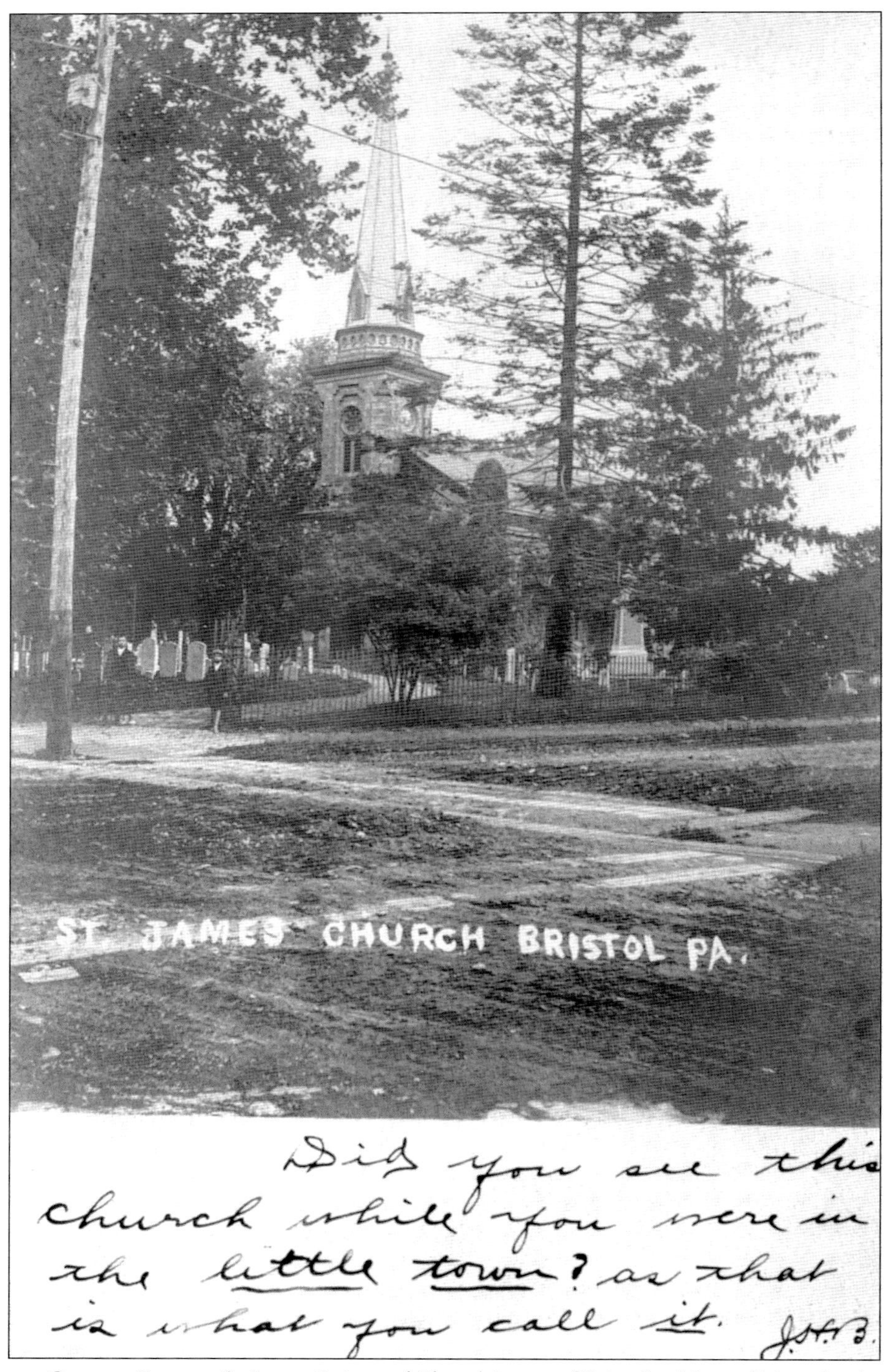

St. James Church, Bristol. St. James Episcopal Church is one of Bristol's oldest religious institutions. The congregation dates to 1712, while the building dates only to the 1850s. Its tall steeple and old cemetery make it a beautiful place in old Bristol. This postcard was mailed in 1905.

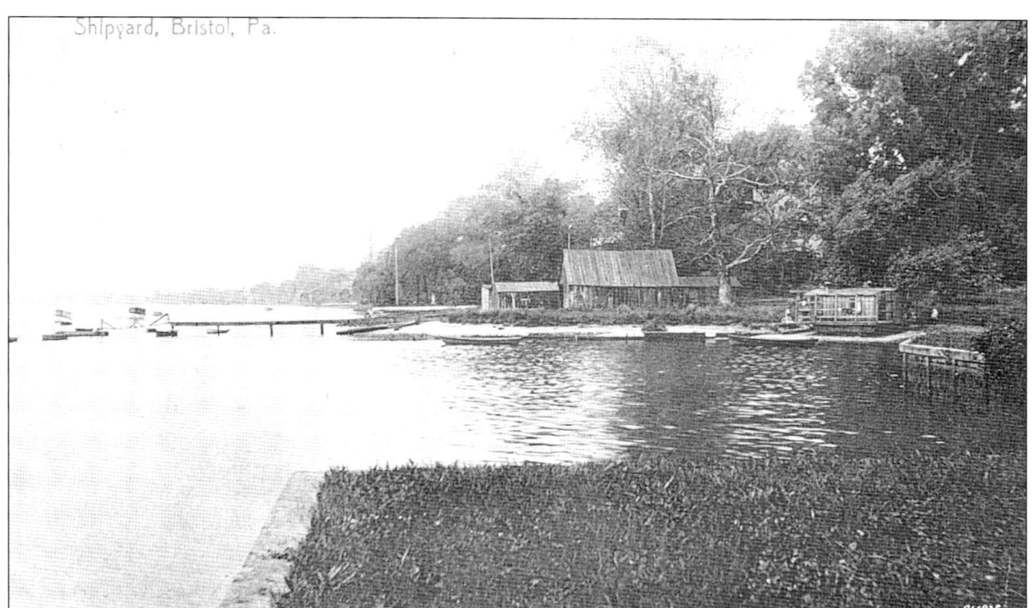

The Shipyard, Bristol. Before automobiles, the Delaware River was a major influence on Bristol's development. The relationship between the borough and the river is evident in this 1910 postcard showing a small and somewhat secluded shipyard dock. (J.K. Streeper postcard.)

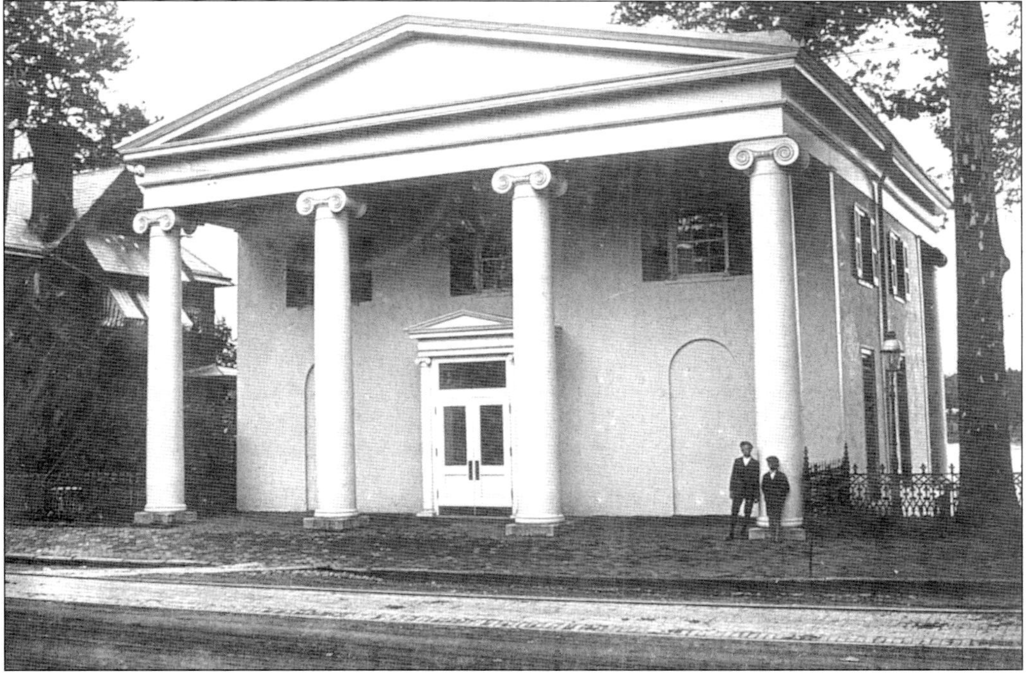

The Bank, Bristol. Radcliffe Street has always been lined with fashionable, upscale homes along the Delaware River. This building was originally completed in 1818 as a home for prominent Philadelphia businessman John Craig. The beautiful Greek Revival building was purchased by the Farmers National Bank of Bucks County in 1833.

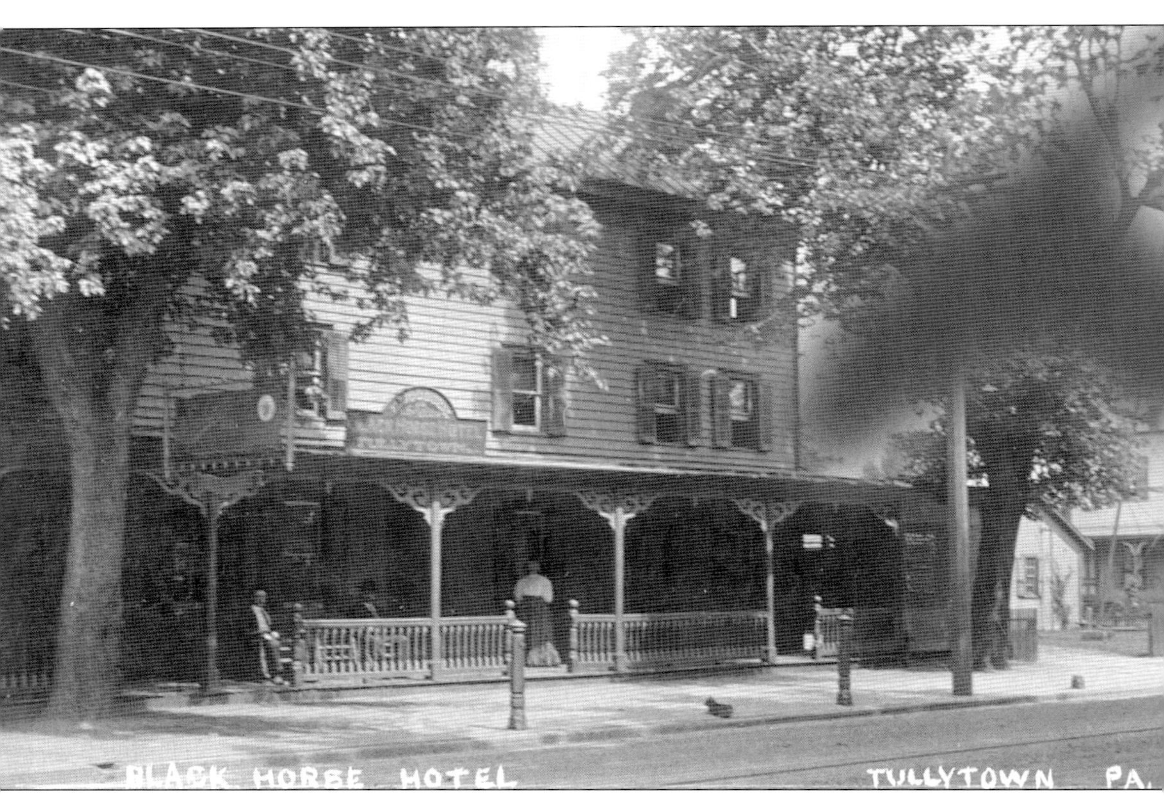

THE BLACK HORSE HOTEL, TULLYTOWN. The Black Horse Hotel was situated on the stagecoach route, Kings Highway, at the halfway point between Bristol and Trenton. It was first licensed in 1796 by John Tully. The village surrounding the hotel became Tullytown and was incorporated as a borough in 1891.

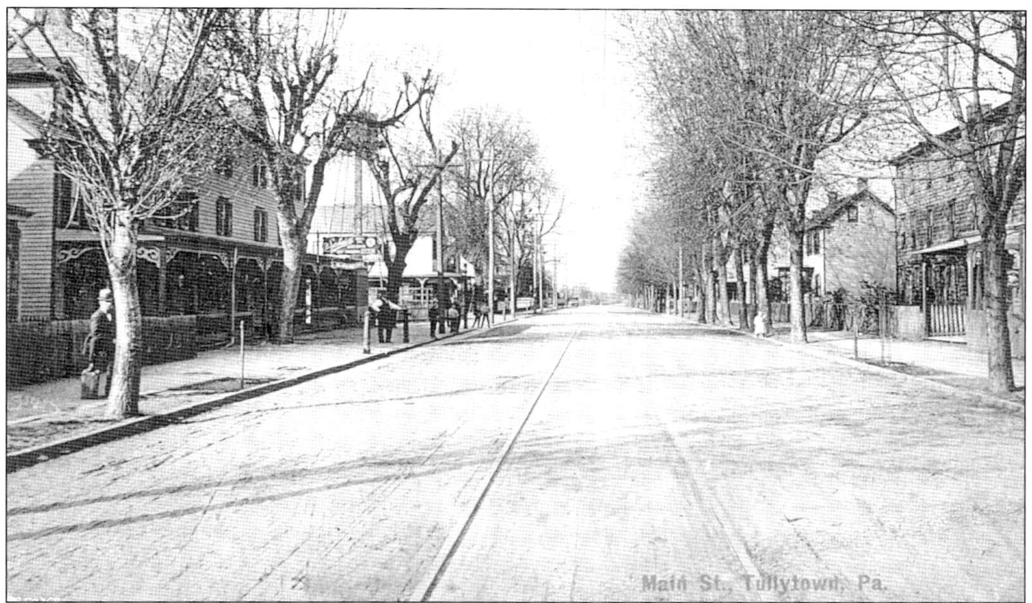

MAIN STREET, TULLYTOWN. This 1912 view of Main Street in Tullytown looks north toward the Martin's Creek Bridge. The Black Horse Hotel is on the left. Today, Tullytown is a mix of older and newer well-kept homes. (J.K. Streeper postcard.)

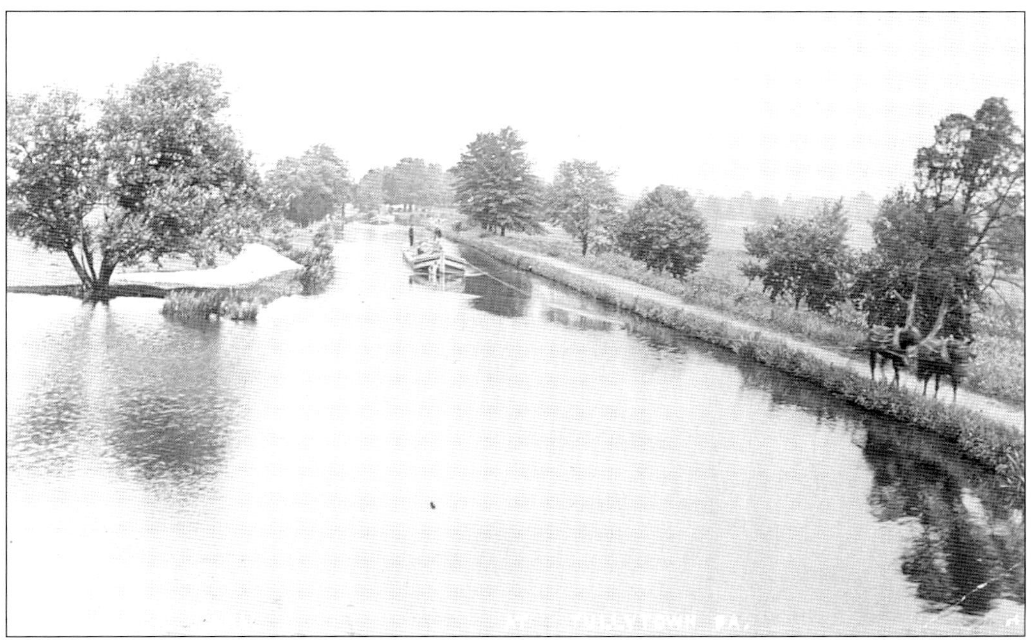

LEHIGH CANAL, TULLYTOWN. The official name is the Delaware Division of the Pennsylvania Canal, although many local residents refer to it as the Delaware Canal. Opened in 1832, it connected the hill regions at Easton to the tidal waters of the Delaware at Bristol. This 1908 view shows the lower end of the canal near Tullytown. The towpath, complete with mules pulling a barge, is on the right. The canal closed to commercial traffic in 1931. (Hay Photo Postcard Company.)

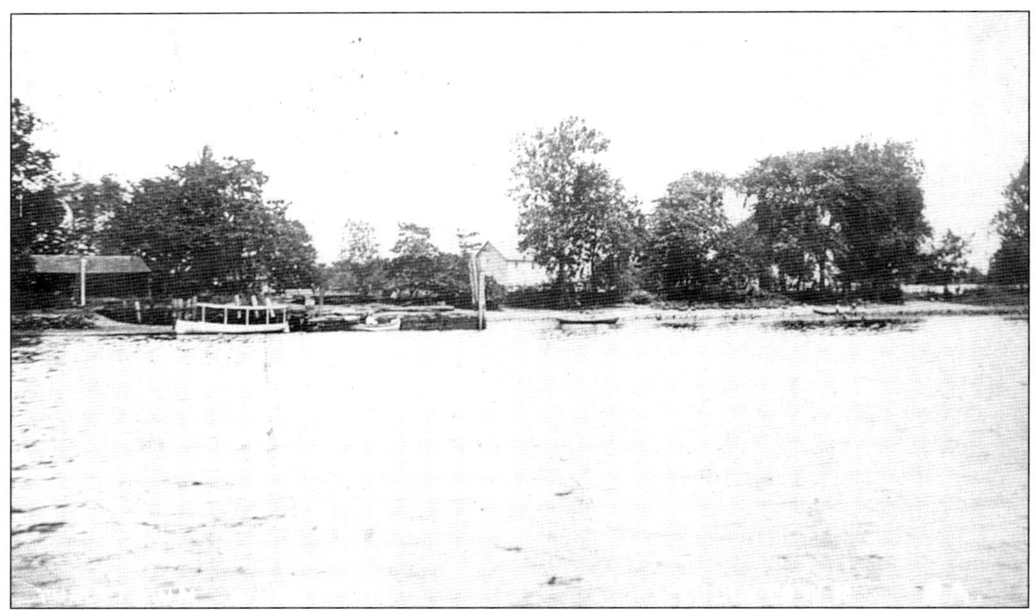

The Tullytown Wharf. The tidal waters of the Delaware River at Tullytown offered a variety of activities and industries to the people who inhabited the area. This 1912 view shows a small wharf on the Delaware in a very rural setting. From the looks of the wharf, it appears that this spot was intended for pleasure boating and fishing.

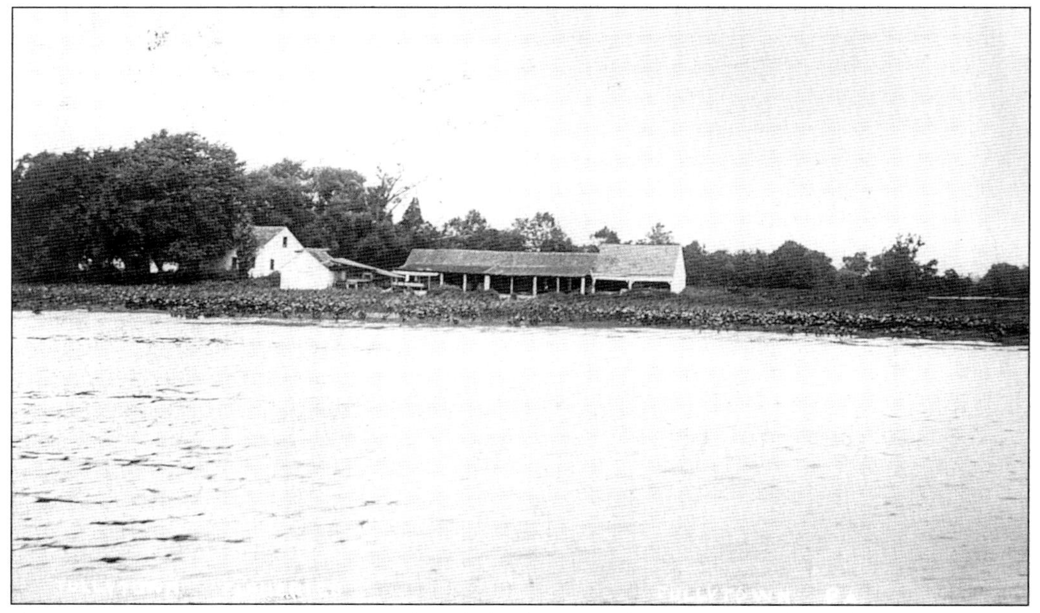

Tullytown Fisheries. On an 1891 atlas of the lower Delaware River, the Tullytown area had numerous fisheries along this waterway. Compared to Bristol, with its commercial and industrial buildings along the river, Tullytown's waterfront was quite rural, with buildings surrounded by coastal plain vegetation and trees. The U.S. Steel Company and several landfill sites have destroyed some of this sensitive coastal plain region of Bucks County.

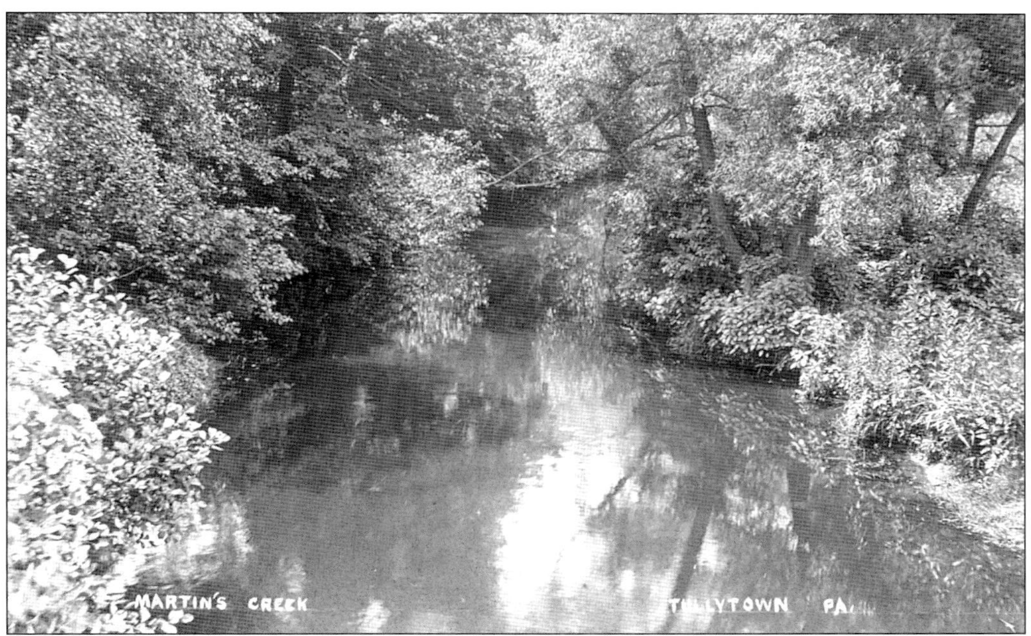

MARTIN'S CREEK, TULLYTOWN. Martin's Creek is a small stream that begins near Fallsington, crosses the Delaware Canal, and empties into the Delaware River at Tullytown. This view shows a shady, picturesque spot along the creek in 1908.

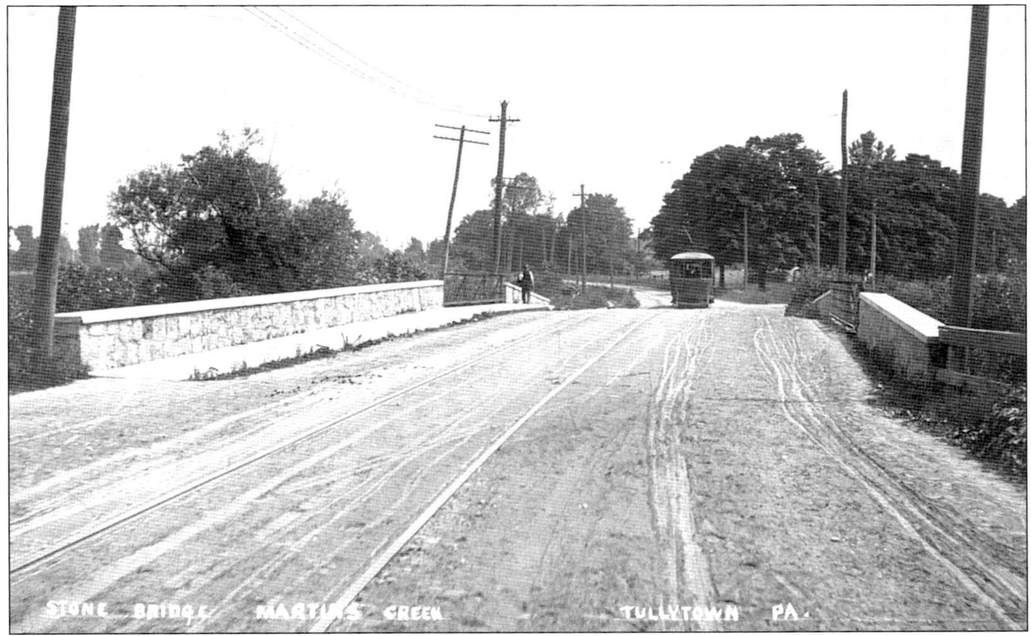

STONE BRIDGE, MARTIN'S CREEK, TULLYTOWN. The trolley line at Bristol was extended through Tullytown to Morrisville in 1903. Here, a trolley is about to cross an old bridge over Martin's Creek in Tullytown, *c.* 1907. This bridge along Main Street has been replaced.

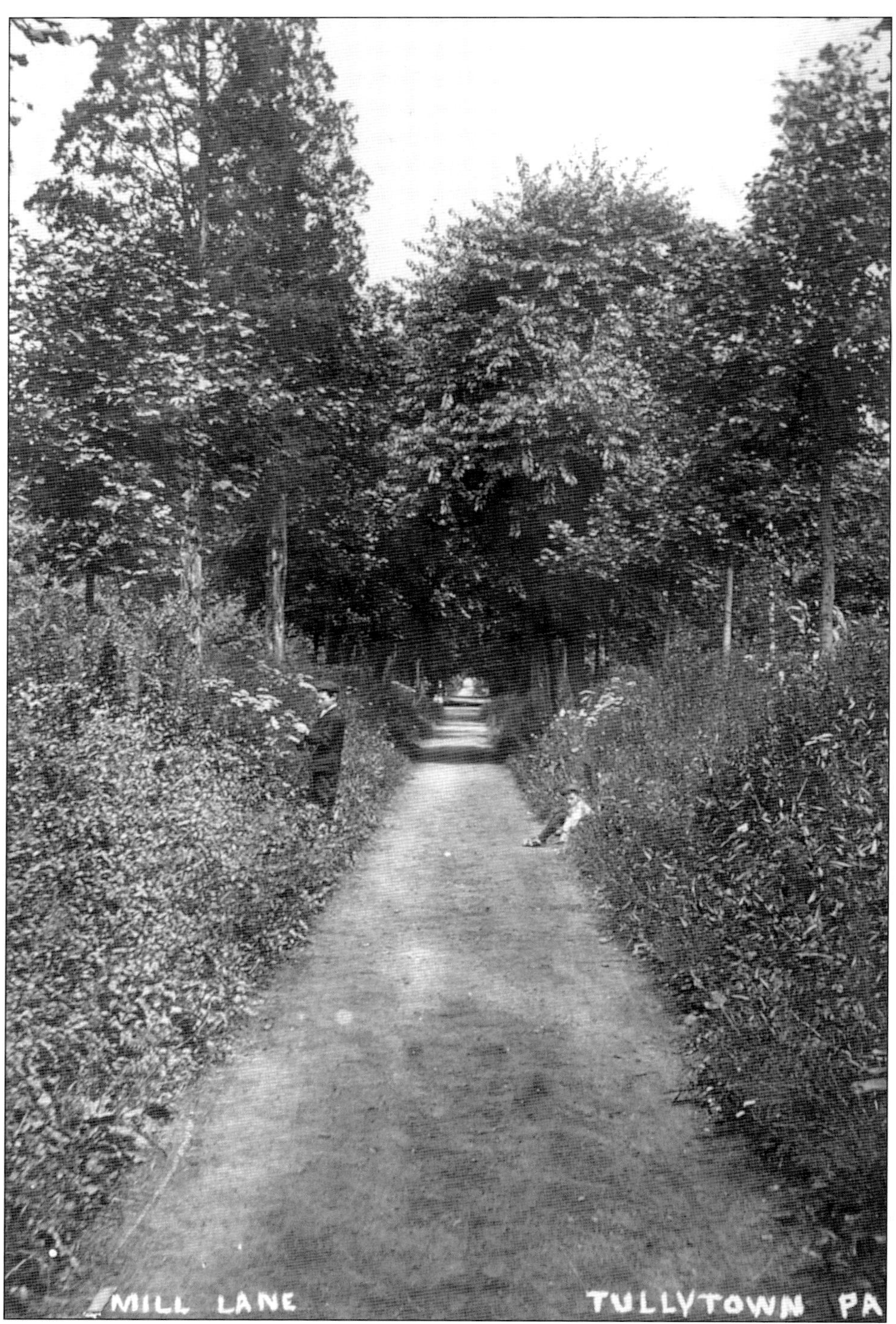

MILL LANE, TULLYTOWN. The beauty of Bucks County is illustrated quite well on many old postcards. This picturesque country lane with abundant trees and children at play captures the essence of early-20th-century life in lower Bucks County. Portions of Mill Lane still exist in Tullytown.

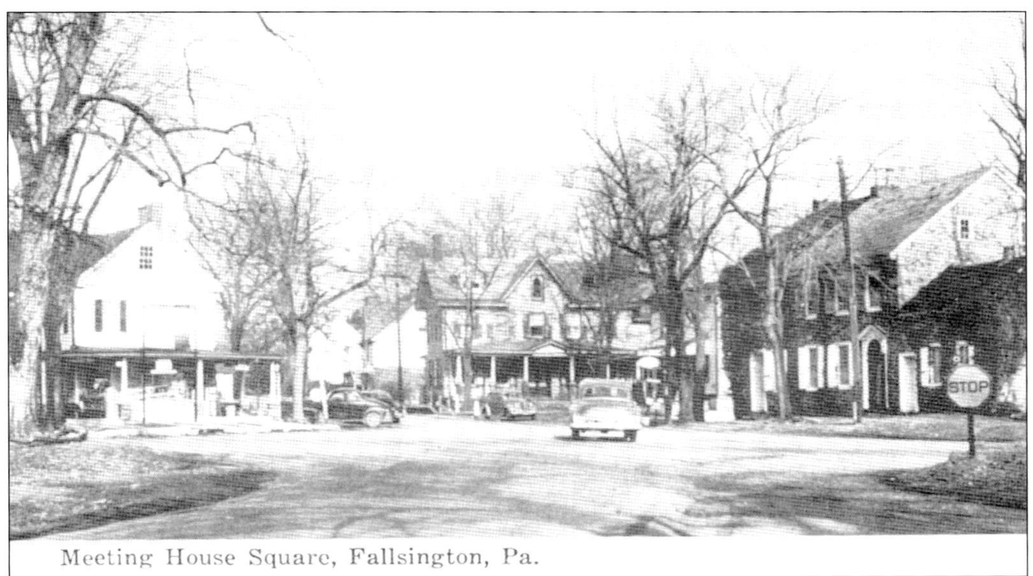

Meeting House Square, Fallsington, Pa.

MEETINGHOUSE SQUARE, FALLSINGTON. This early-1950s view shows the center of Fallsington before its reclamation as a historical village. Fallsington dates to the 1690s and was an early center for Quaker worship. To the left is the old Stagecoach Tavern, which was obliterated by numerous additions. To the right is the beautiful Burges-Lippincott House. Today, both structures are restored to their original appearance.

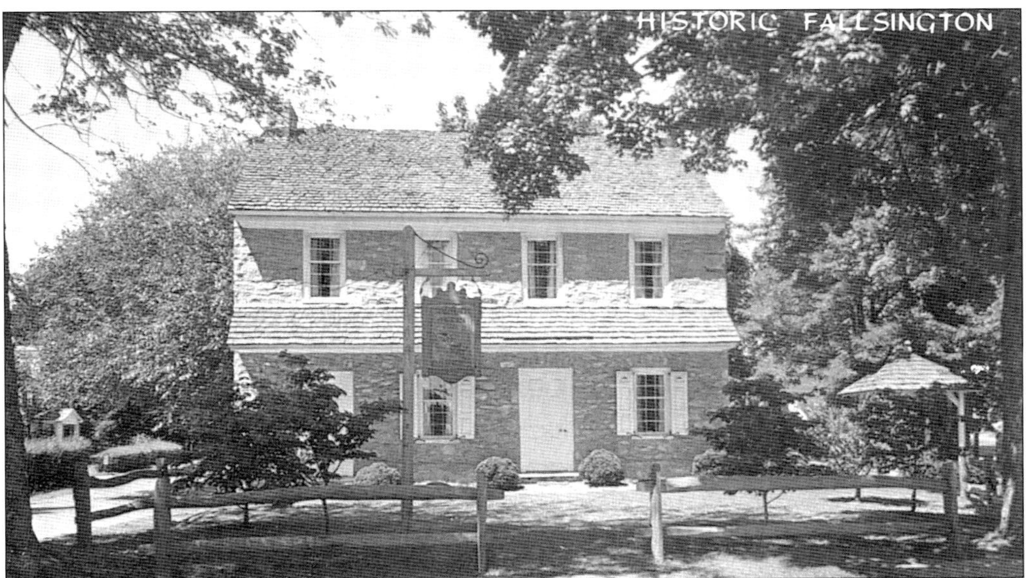

STAGECOACH TAVERN, FALLSINGTON. Prominently situated on the north side of Meetinghouse Square, the Stagecoach Tavern is one of Fallsington's best-known buildings. The tavern, which was built in the 1750s along the old stagecoach route, had been known as the National Hotel in the 1800s. By the early 1900s, the building (with numerous additions) had been used as a jail, a post office, and a hardware store before being completely renovated back to its original appearance in the 1960s.

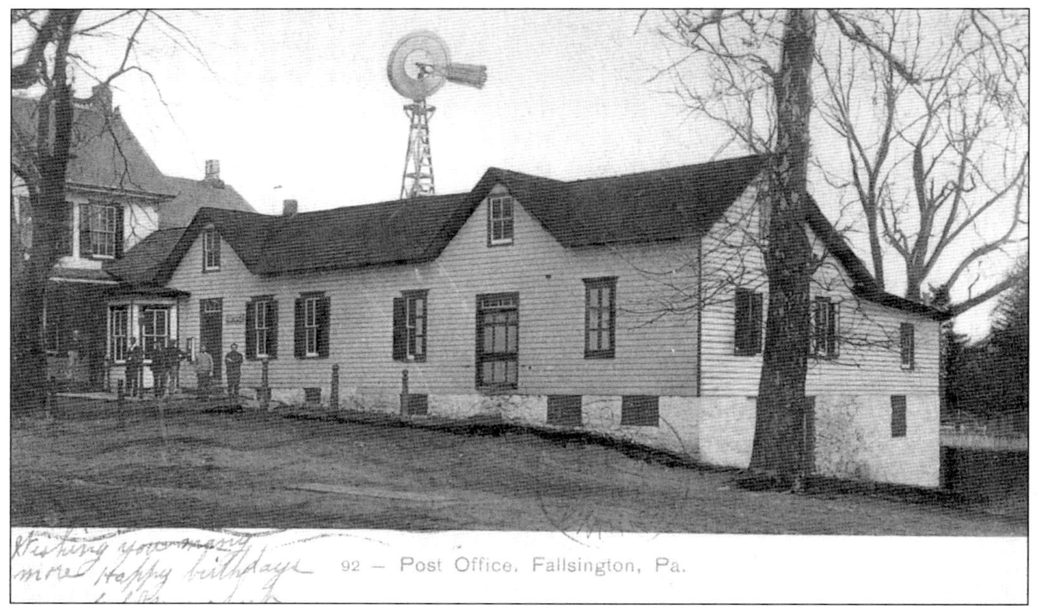

The Post Office, Fallsington. This building was also a general store and stood on Meetinghouse Square opposite the Stagecoach Tavern. Built in the early 1800s, it was destroyed by fire in 1910. A new building was built on the site and currently houses the headquarters of the local historical society and a gift shop. The house to the right is still standing on Yardley Avenue. This postcard was mailed in 1906.

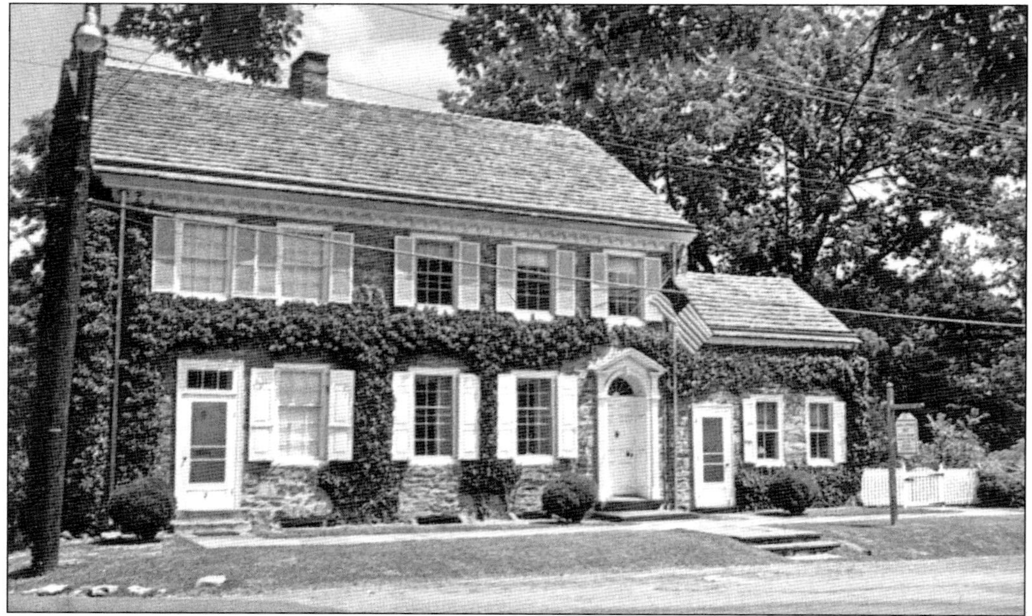

Burges-Lippincott House, Fallsington. Built in 1809, this house faces Meetinghouse Square in Fallsington and is an outstanding example of late-Colonial and early-Federal architecture. Beautiful Bucks County stone and handsome woodwork throughout the house make this a very picturesque dwelling. Today, Fallsington is a restored colonial village in Falls Township.

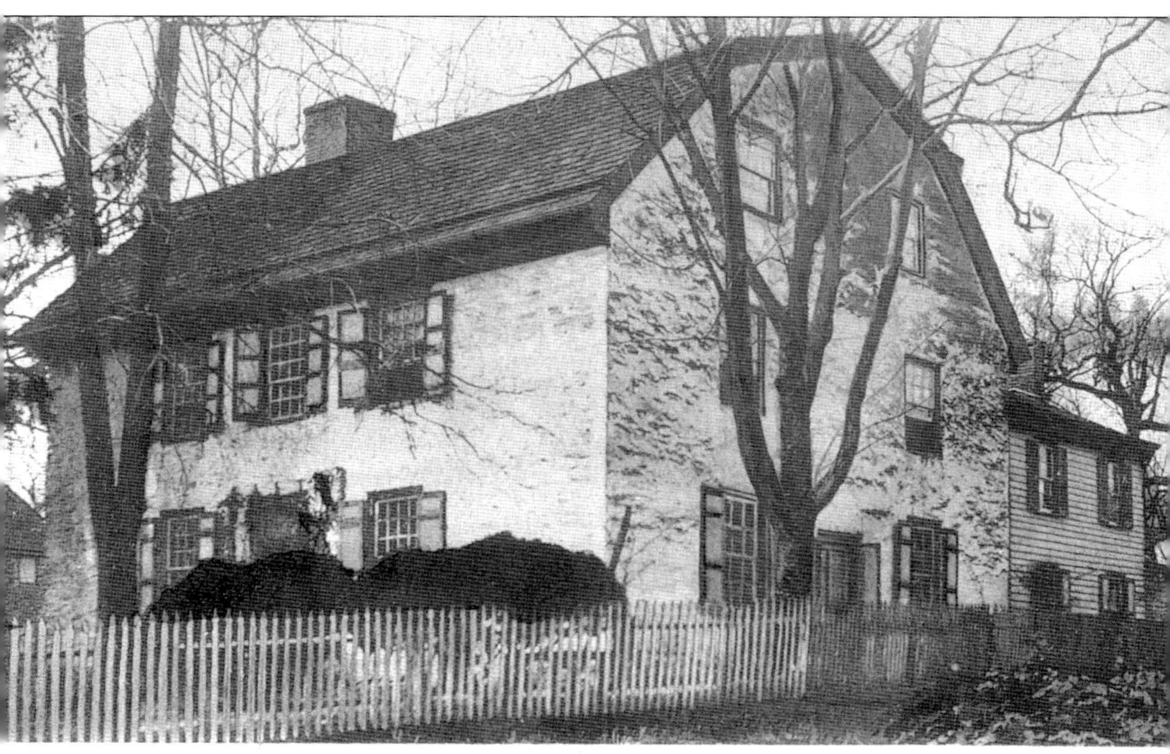

FALLSINGTON. This building, located on the south side of Meetinghouse Square, was built in 1728 as a Quaker meetinghouse. It was constructed to meet the demands of a growing Quaker population in the village at the time. An earlier, smaller meetinghouse was built in 1690. This building went through various uses, as other meetinghouses were built in the village. Today, the building is known at the Gambrel Roof House, it has been beautifully restored and is privately owned.

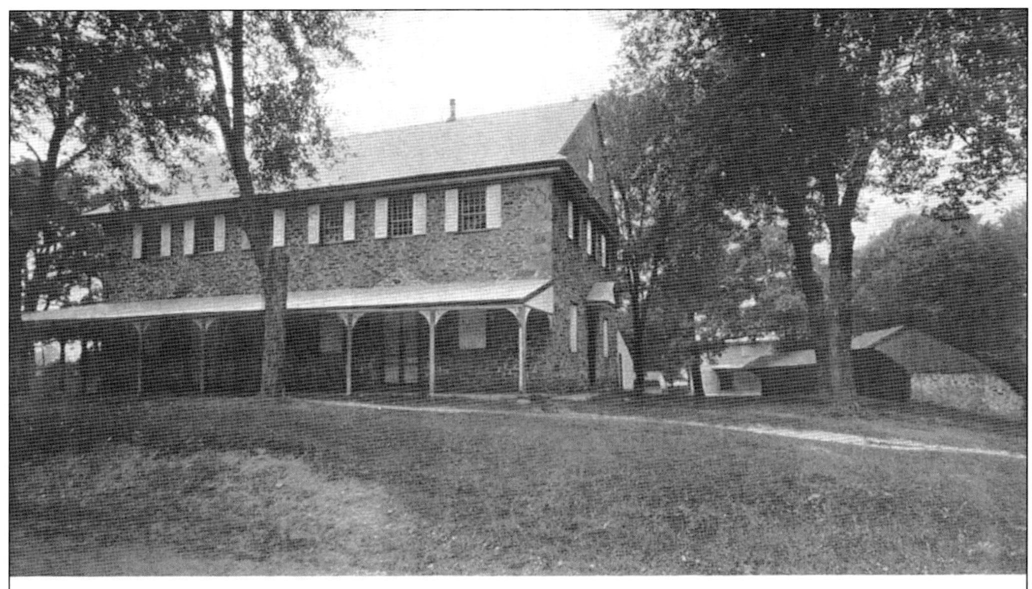

The Fallsington Friends Meetinghouse, Fallsington. Built in 1789, this was the third meetinghouse to be built in Fallsington. It is typical of the large, two-story meetinghouses found also in Middletown, Wrightstown, Solebury, and Buckingham. Although the building still stands virtually unchanged, it no longer serves as a religious facility. It has been used as a childcare facility for many years. (Arnold Brothers postcard.)

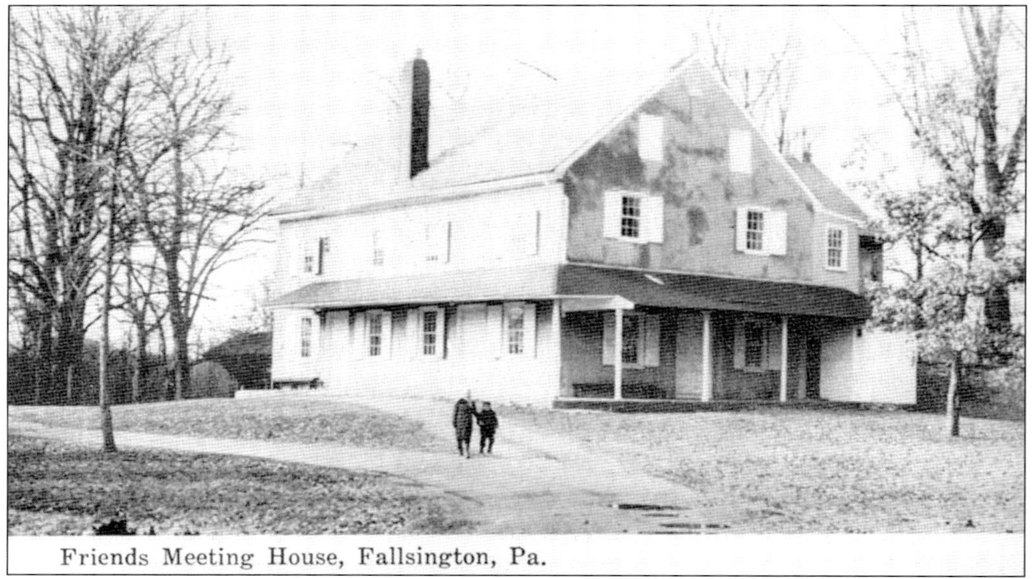

Friends Meetinghouse, Fallsington. This was the forth and final Quaker meetinghouse built in Fallsington. Dating to 1841, the Falls Monthly Meeting of Friends is the only active Quaker facility in the village. It is located directly behind the 1789 meetinghouse. This Charles Seeman postcard dates from the 1950s.

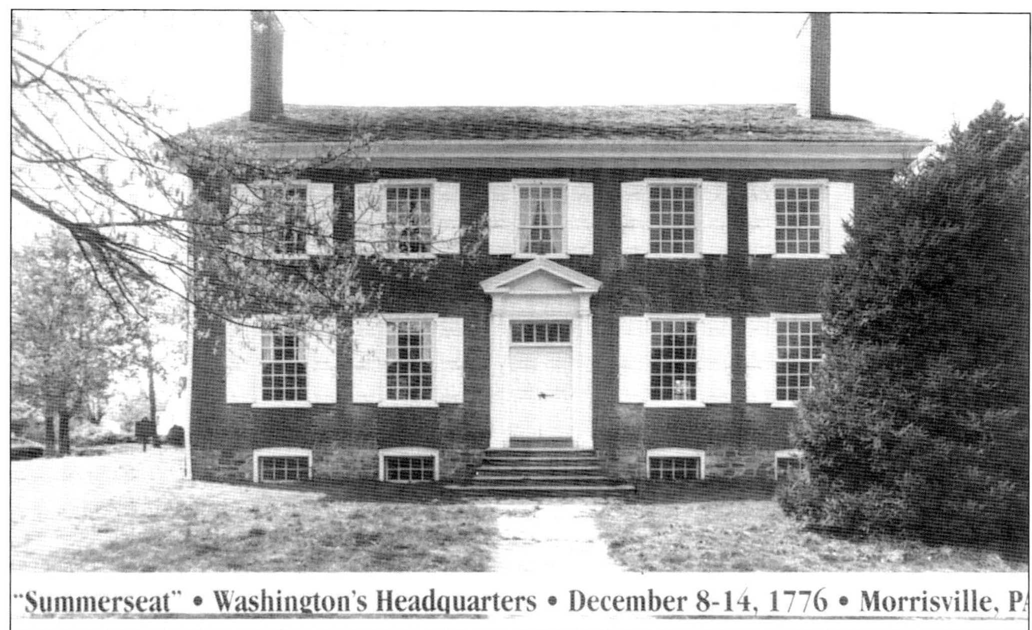

SUMMERSEAT MANSION, MORRISVILLE. The centerpiece of Morrisville Borough, Summerseat was the home of Robert Morris, a prominent figure in colonial times and a signer of the Declaration of Independence. Dating to the mid-1700s, Summerseat is significant because of its service as a headquarters for George Washington during the Revolutionary War. It is a unique Georgian-style structure with one side made of brick and the other side made of stone. Morrisville was named after Robert Morris.

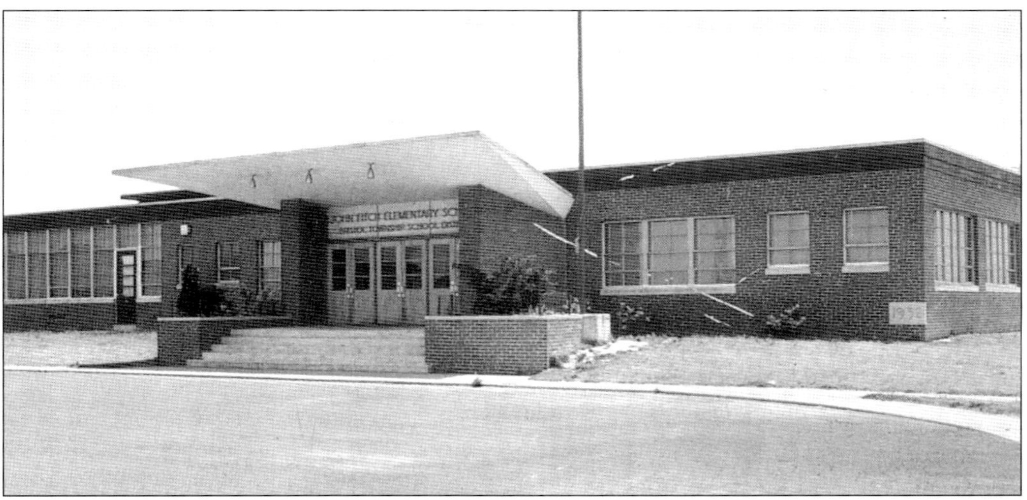

LEVITTOWN. In the early 1950s, the biggest change occurred to the Bucks County landscape—the creation of Levittown. More than 5,500 acres of farmland was purchased by William Levitt. Eventually, more than 17,000 homes—along with shopping centers, churches, and schools—were built. It was, if nothing else, a self-contained suburb extending into four municipalities. This 1950s postcard shows the John Fitch School in Levittown, built in 1952. Fitch tested steamboat theories in a Davisville pond and on the Delaware River.

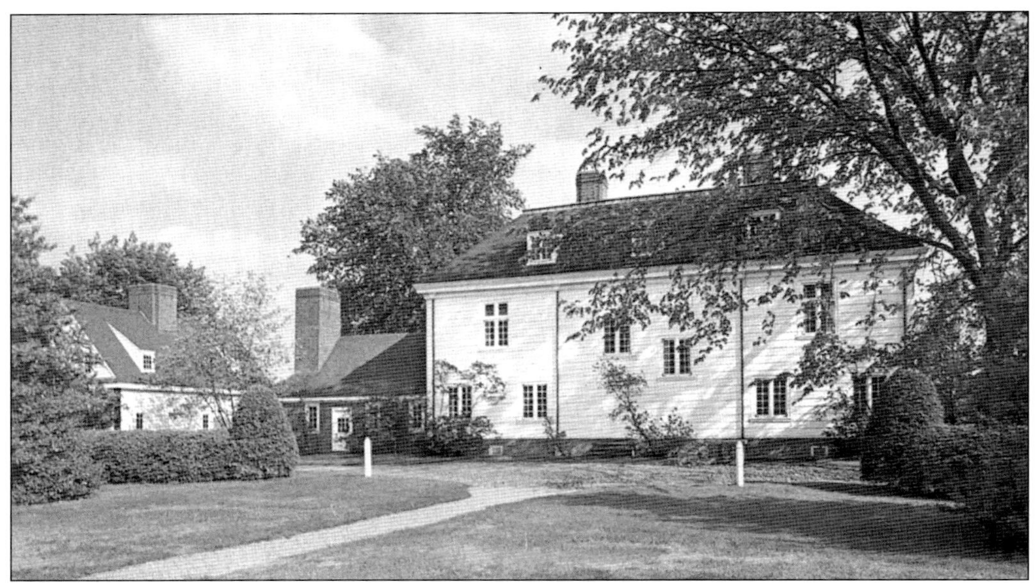

Pennsbury Manor. William Penn, founder of Pennsylvania, chose a site along the Delaware River below the great bend and the falls to build his country manor house in 1683. His plantation in Falls Township became known as Pennsbury Manor. Penn spent little time at Pennsbury; after his death, the house was neglected and was eventually torn down. In the 1930s, the entire Pennsbury Manor complex was re-created using Penn's original notes and records. This view shows the rear of Pennsbury Manor.

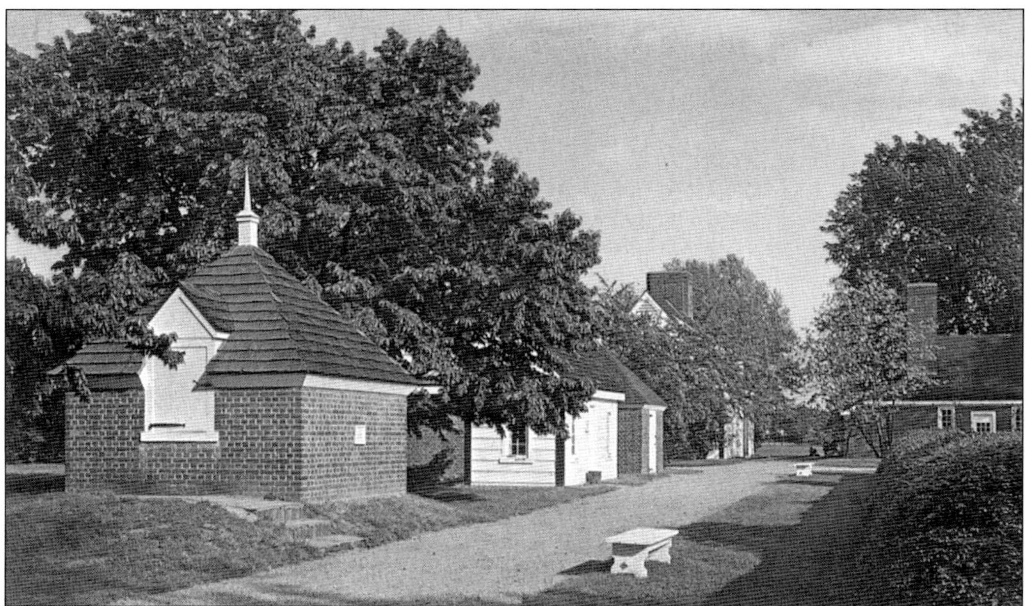

Pennsbury Manor. The museum at Pennsbury offers visitors a view of the entire re-created plantation that William Penn inhabited. Livestock, colonial demonstrations, as well as numerous outbuildings can be seen at this site. Shown here is the icehouse, the office, the smokehouse, and the bakehouse.

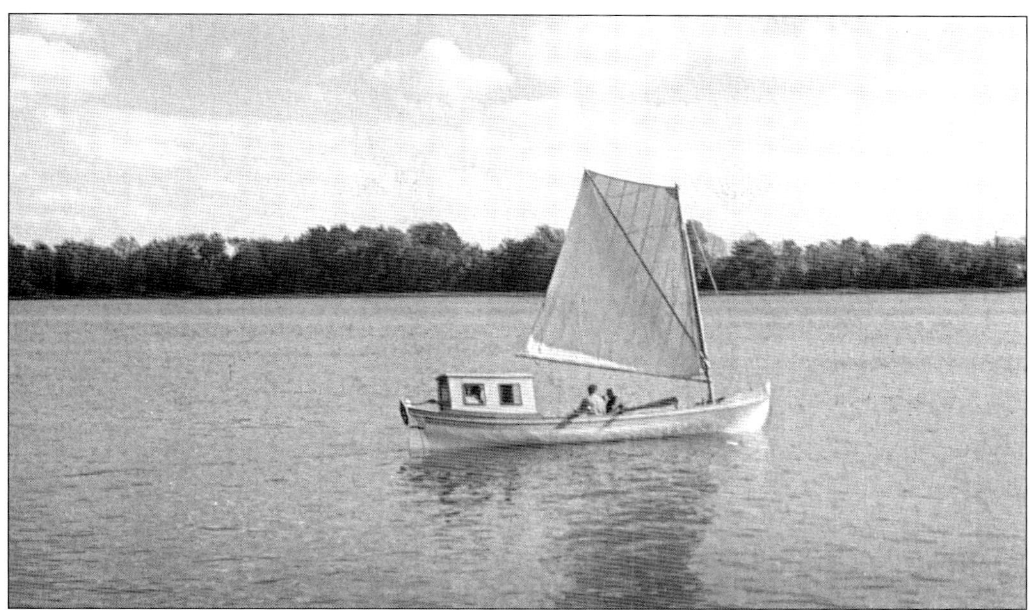

Pennsbury Manor. This is a replica of William Penn's boat sailing on the Delaware River near Pennsbury Manor. The boat can be seen on permanent display at the museum. For a man as important and prominent as Penn, the boat is not impressive in size or style.

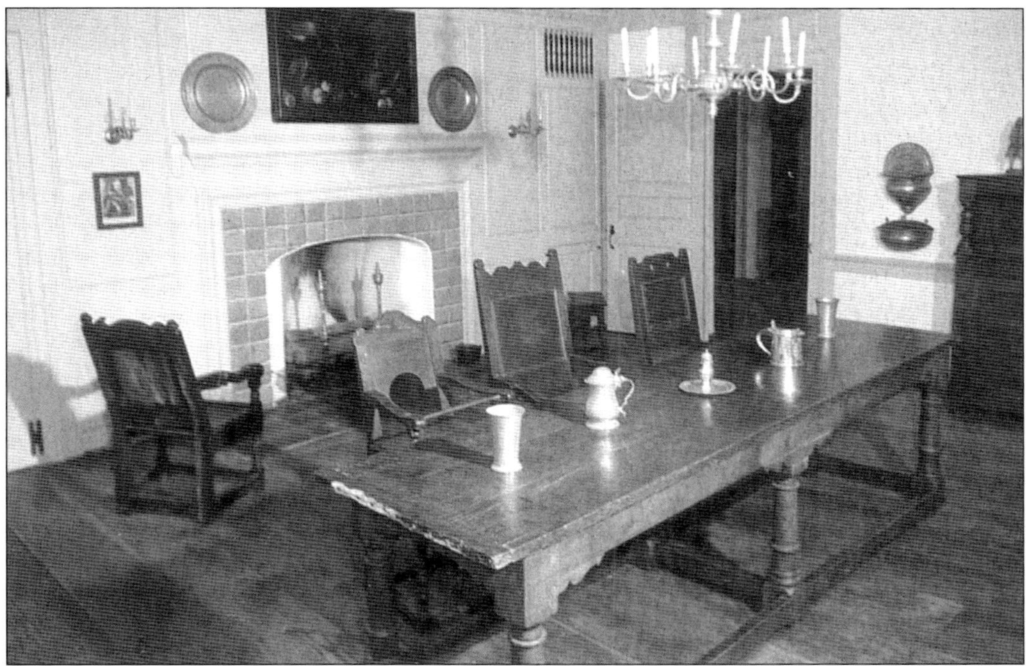

The Dining Room, Pennsbury Manor. At Pennsbury Manor, visitors can get a real visual experience of how Pennsylvania's founder and most prominent individual lived. Although the buildings have been re-created, several pieces at the manor are authentic antiques dating to the late 1600s. This view shows the architectural features and furniture of the dining room.

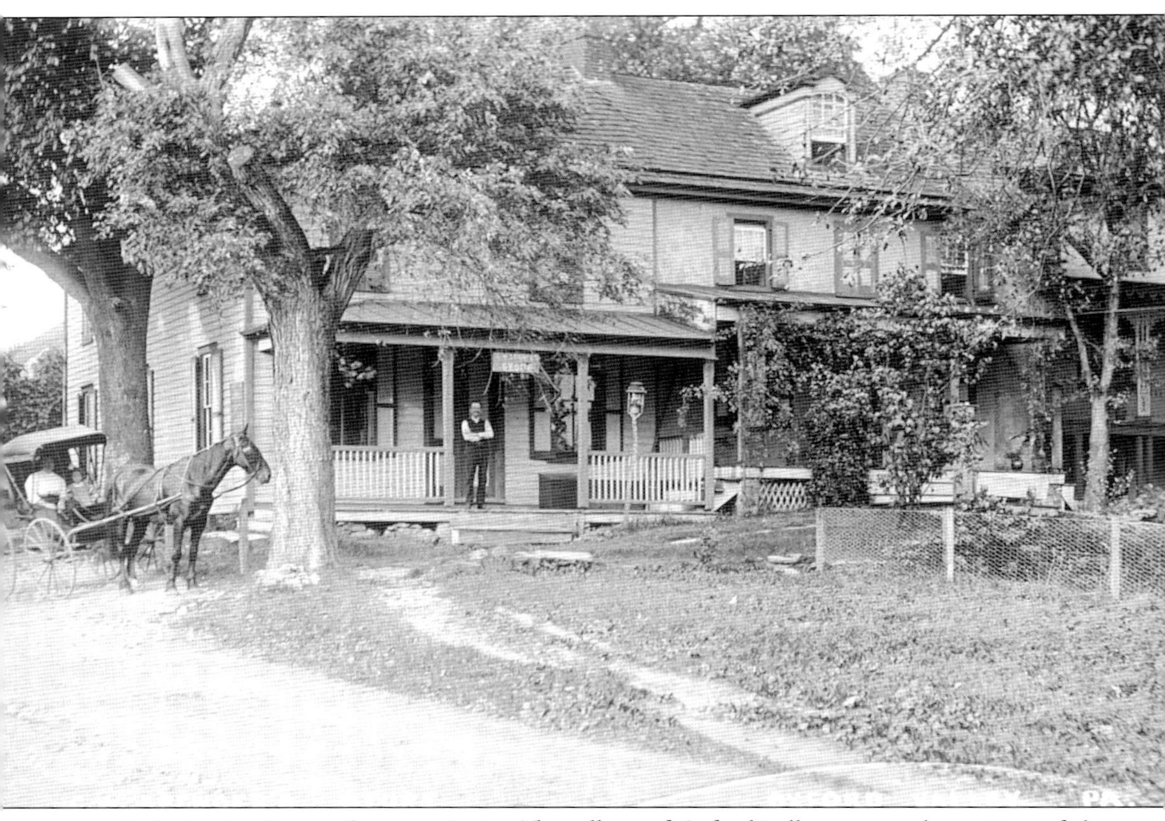

C.W. Spencer's Store, Oxford Valley. The village of Oxford Valley was in the vicinity of the crossroads of Old Lincoln Highway and Oxford Valley Road. Near this intersection once stood Spencer's Store. General stores were the center of activity in small, rural villages and sold a variety of items. This wonderful vignette from *c.* 1908 shows a woman and girl in a horse and carriage alongside the store. (Hay Photo Postcard Company.)

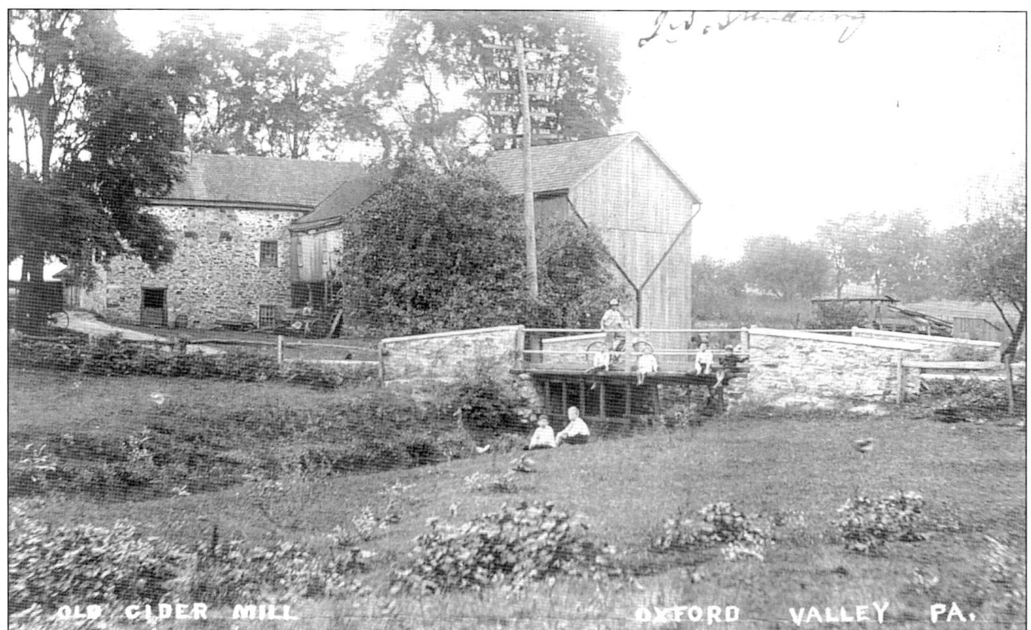

THE OLD CIDER MILL, OXFORD VALLEY. A picturesque spot where children played was near this old stone mill on Queen Anne Creek at Oxford Valley in Middletown Township. Today, this area is occupied by the Oxford Valley Mall and the Sesame Place complex.

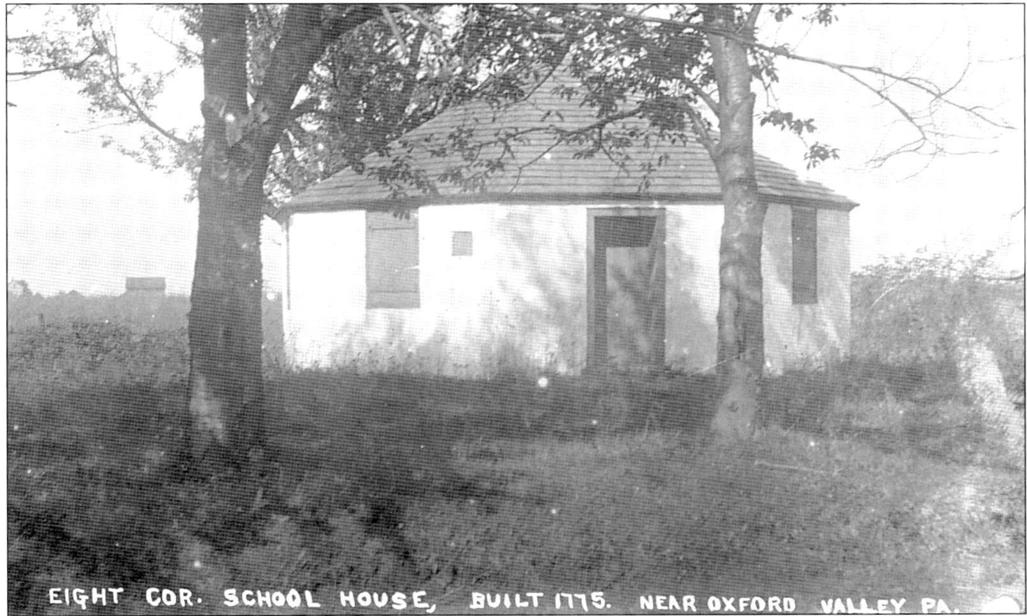

EIGHT-SIDED SCHOOLHOUSE, OXFORD VALLEY. This school, one of three built in the area, was located on Oxford Valley Road north of Lincoln Highway. Built in 1775, it is said to be the first eight-sided schoolhouse. Sadly, the school had been allowed to deteriorate, and only the foundation exists today. Some have proposed plans to rebuild the school as part of a development deal.

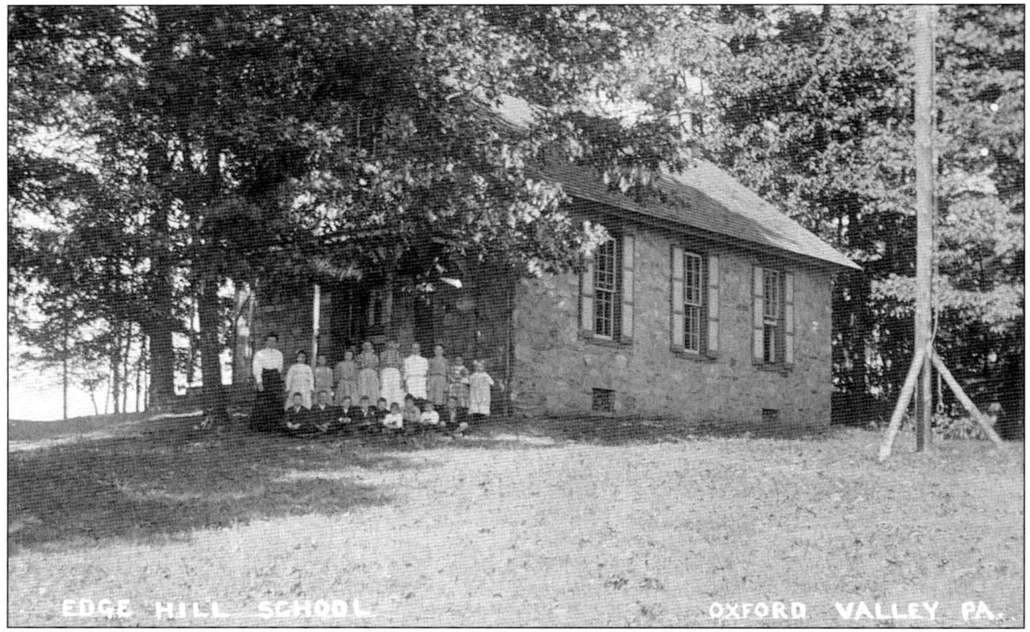

EDGE HILL SCHOOL, OXFORD VALLEY. This school was built in the mid-1800s and is located on Old Lincoln Highway east of Woodbourne Road in Middletown Township. The building served as an office for a used car dealership. In August 2000, the building was damaged by a fire.

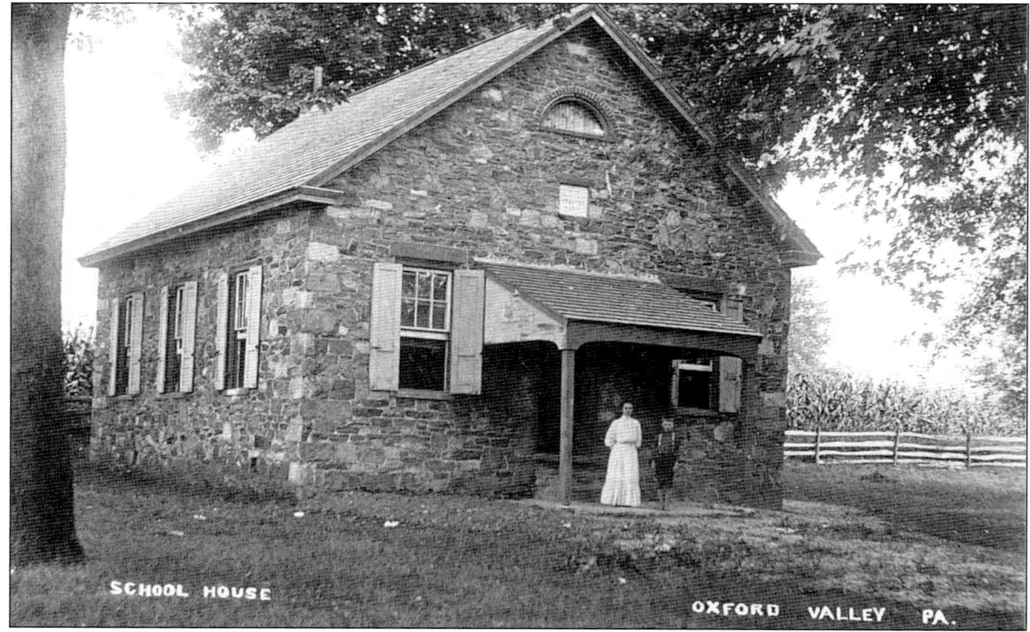

SCHOOLHOUSE, OXFORD VALLEY. This school stood in Falls Township on the south side of Lincoln Highway, east of Oxford Valley Road. Built in 1854, it was torn down in 1969 and replaced by an Arby's Restaurant.

Three

Up the Neshaminy Creek

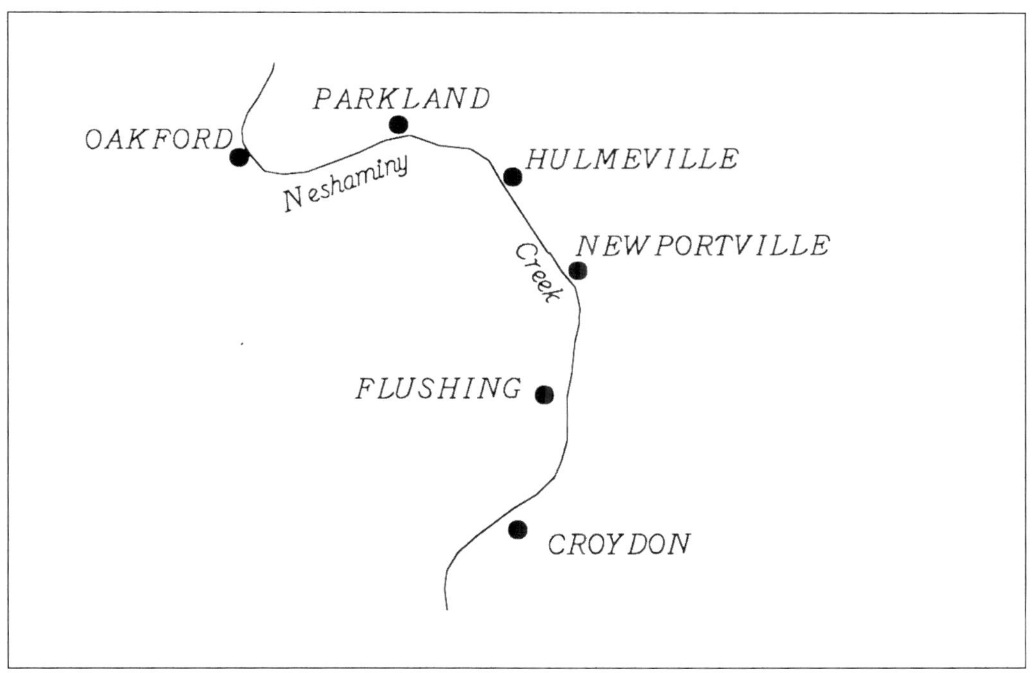

Up the Neshaminy Creek. This chapter illustrates the influence of the Neshaminy Creek in lower Bucks County from the time of the first mills in the 1700s to the recreation and resort towns of the early 1900s. Starting at Croydon, the chapter follows the Neshaminy Creek north toward Oakford.

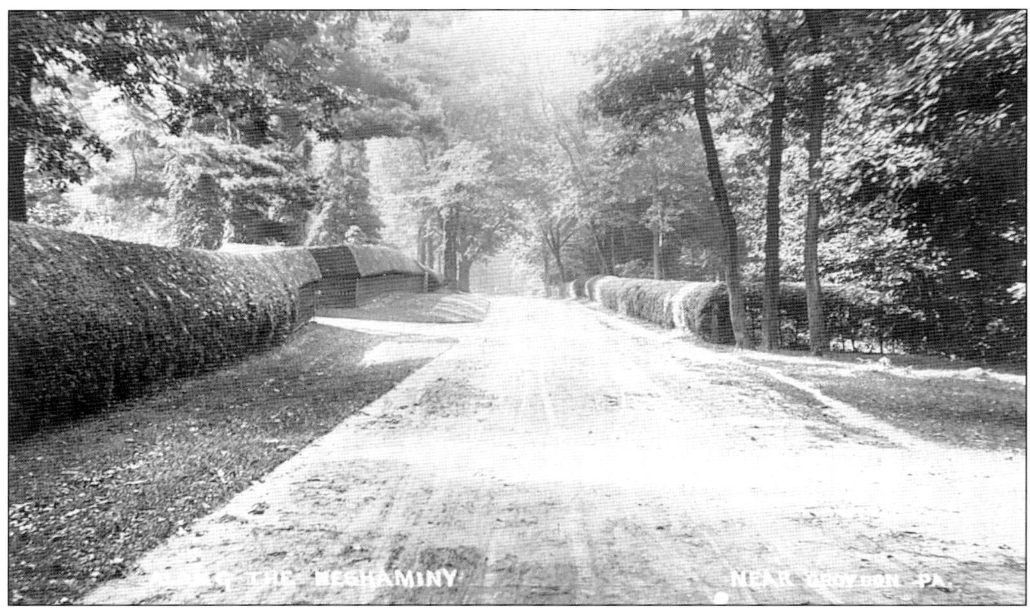

Along the Neshaminy, Croydon. Croydon is a village and a station stop on the old Pennsylvania Railroad line in Bristol Township, immediately north of Bridgewater. Today, the area has a large residential population and is heavily commercialized. This Wharton postcard from 1907 captures a rather scenic though unidentified area near the Neshaminy Creek.

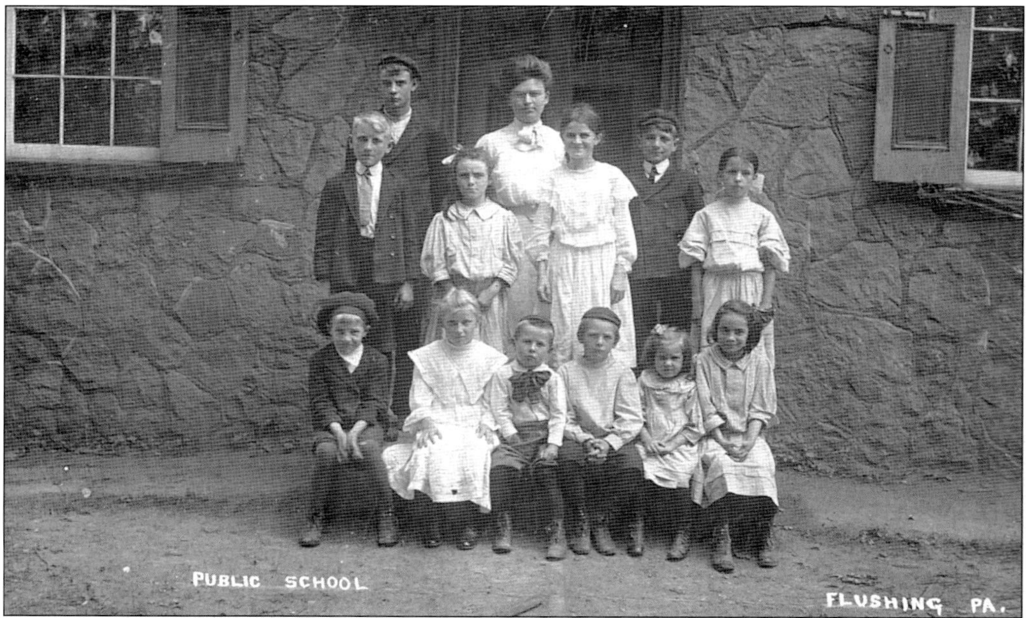

Public School, Flushing. Flushing was a small village in Bensalem Township along the Neshaminy Creek between Newportville and Bridgewater. The village consisted of a few buildings, including this schoolhouse, built in 1876. This 1910 view illustrates the small student population as well as the diverse ages of the pupils. On the reverse side of the postcard is written, "Miss Belle Scott, Teacher." (Hay Photo Postcard Company.)

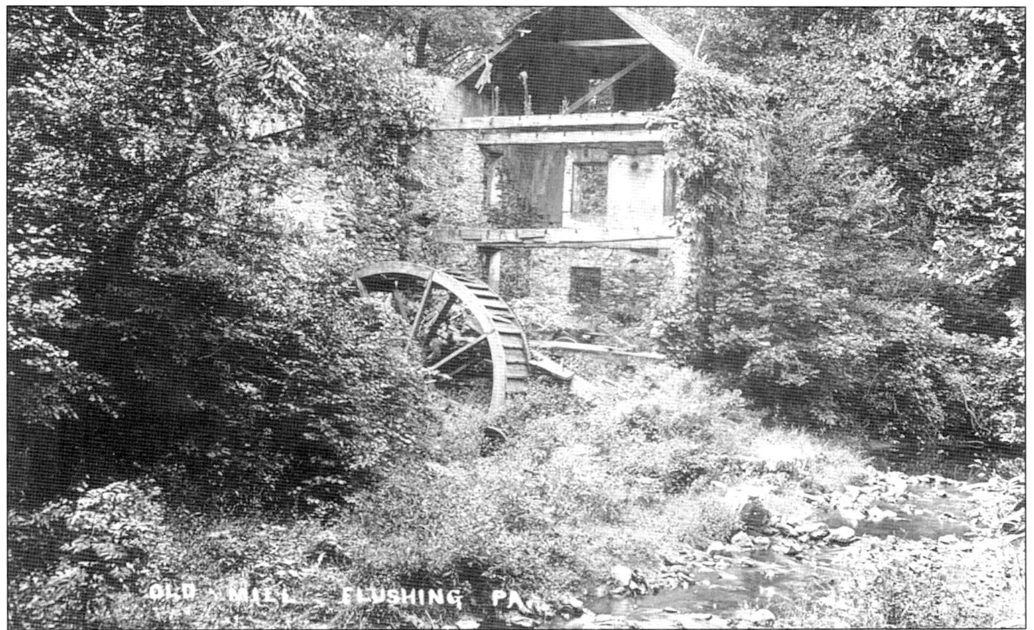

Old Mill, Flushing. In 1907, all that remained of the old Flushing mill was the ruins of the building and waterwheel. Today, nothing remains of this mill, located near Flushing Road and the Neshaminy Creek. (Hay Photo Postcard Company.)

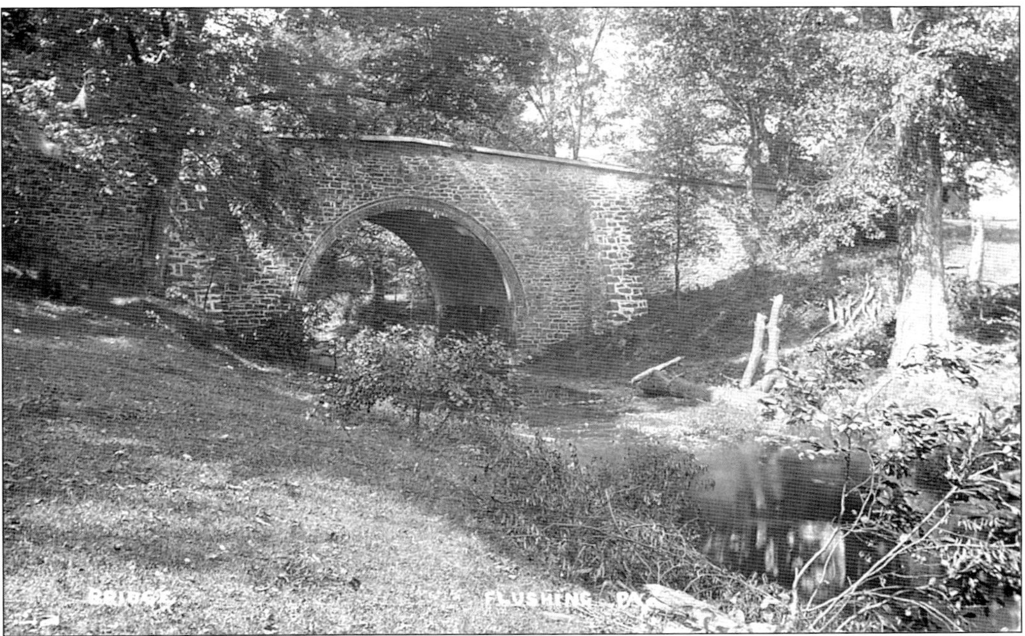

A Bridge, Flushing. A small stream flows through eastern Bensalem Township and empties into the Neshaminy Creek at Flushing. This beautiful stone arch bridge crossed the creek at Flushing. The bridge has been rebuilt and replaced, but the old shade trees and picturesque creek remain. (Hay Photo Postcard Company.)

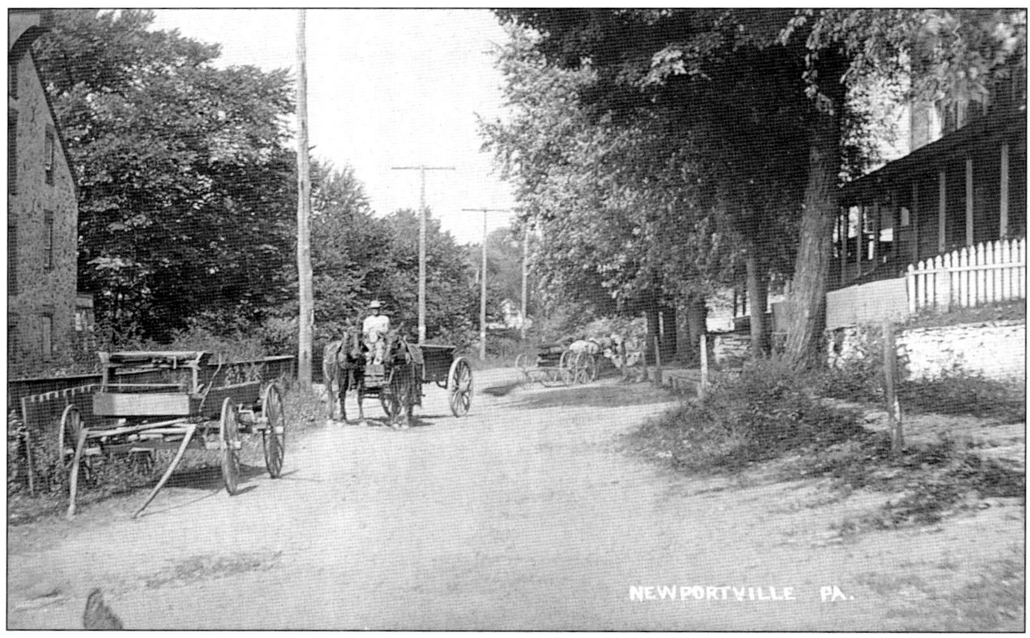

NEWPORTVILLE. The village of Newportville is an old settlement along the banks of the Neshaminy Creek in Bristol Township. This 1909 view shows a typical summertime activity in Newportville. The old mill is to the left and the buildings on the right along Lower Road have been torn down. Today, Newportville contains a number of structures dating from the 1700s and 1800s.

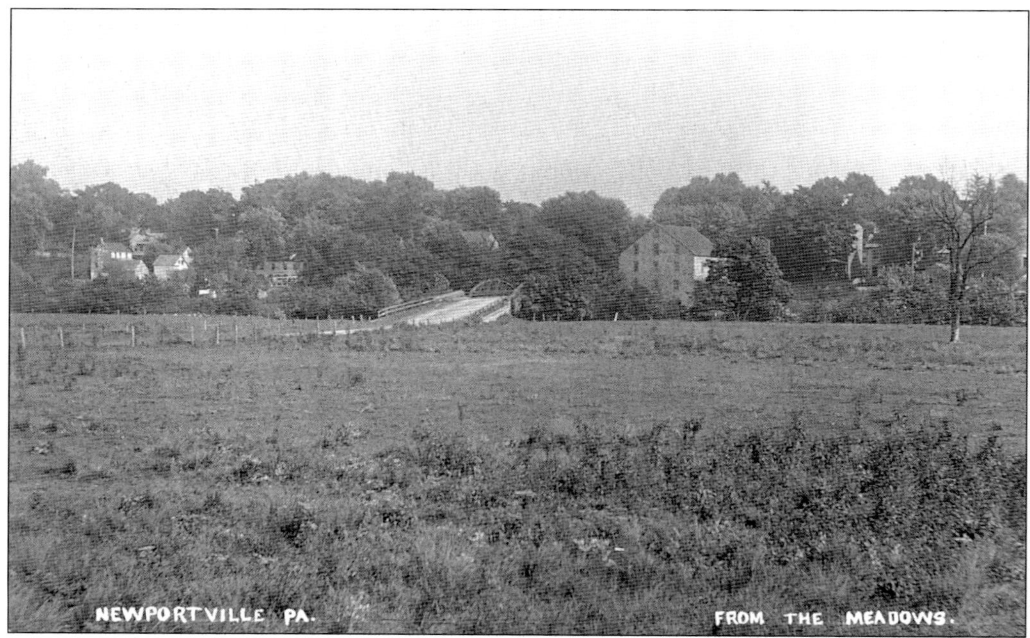

NEWPORTVILLE. This 1908 view of Newportville looks east from Bensalem. The old Newport or Falls Road bridge over the Neshaminy has been replaced and the large stone mill is also gone. Houses and stores now occupy the land in the foreground.

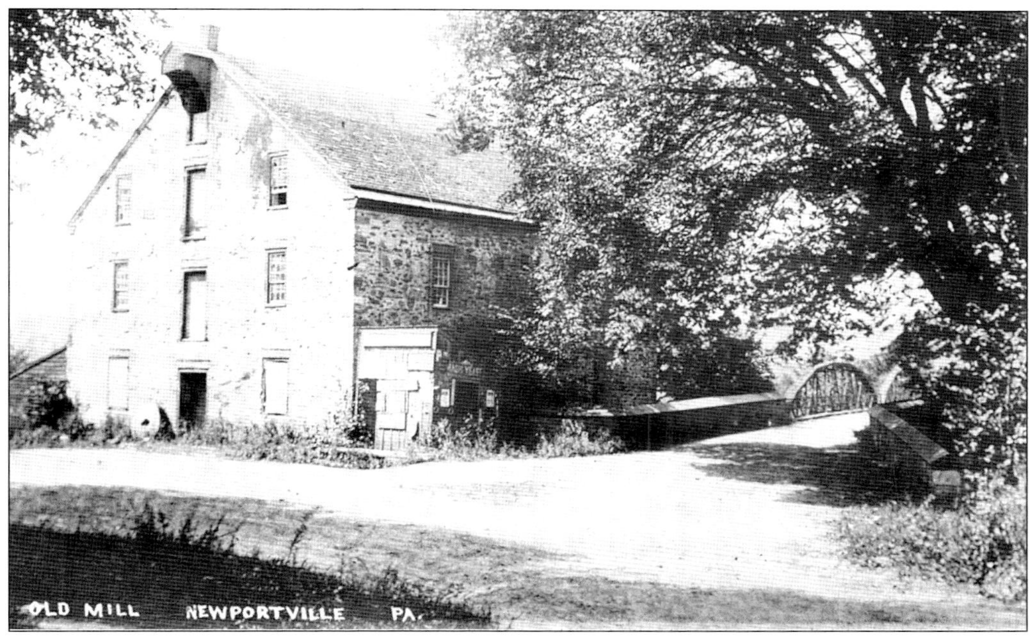

The Old Mill, Newportville. This view shows an old mill on the Neshaminy Creek in Newportville at the junction of New Falls and Lower Roads. The bridge over the Neshaminy can be seen to the right of the mill. Both the mill and bridge have been torn down.

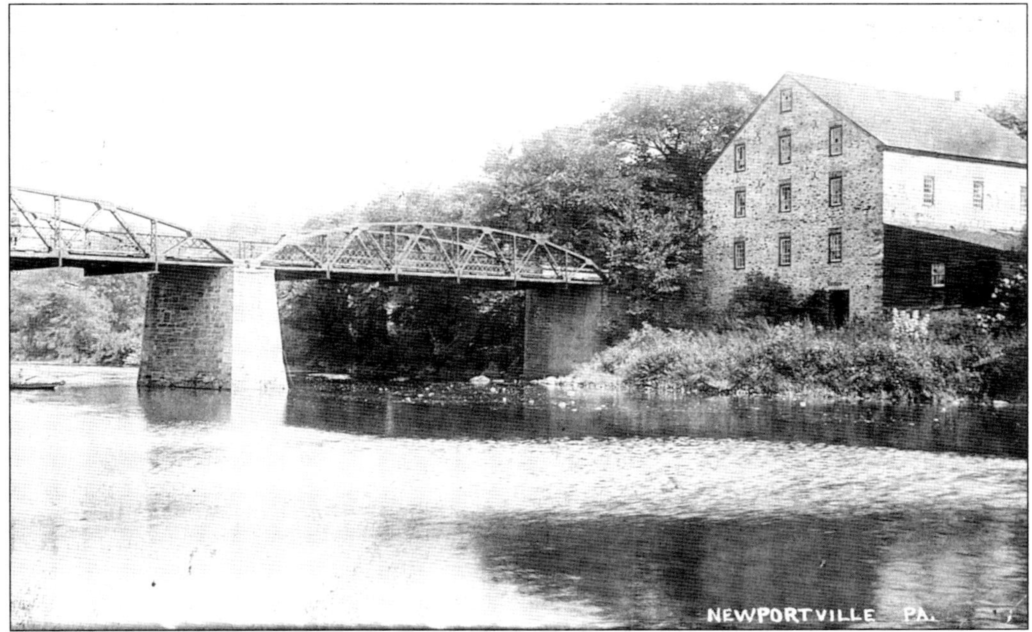

Newportville. This is a closer look at the old Newportville Bridge and the very large mill as viewed from the Neshaminy Creek in 1910. Mills along the wide Neshaminy tended to be larger than those found on smaller streams, due to the power the stream could provide. This mill appears to have five floors.

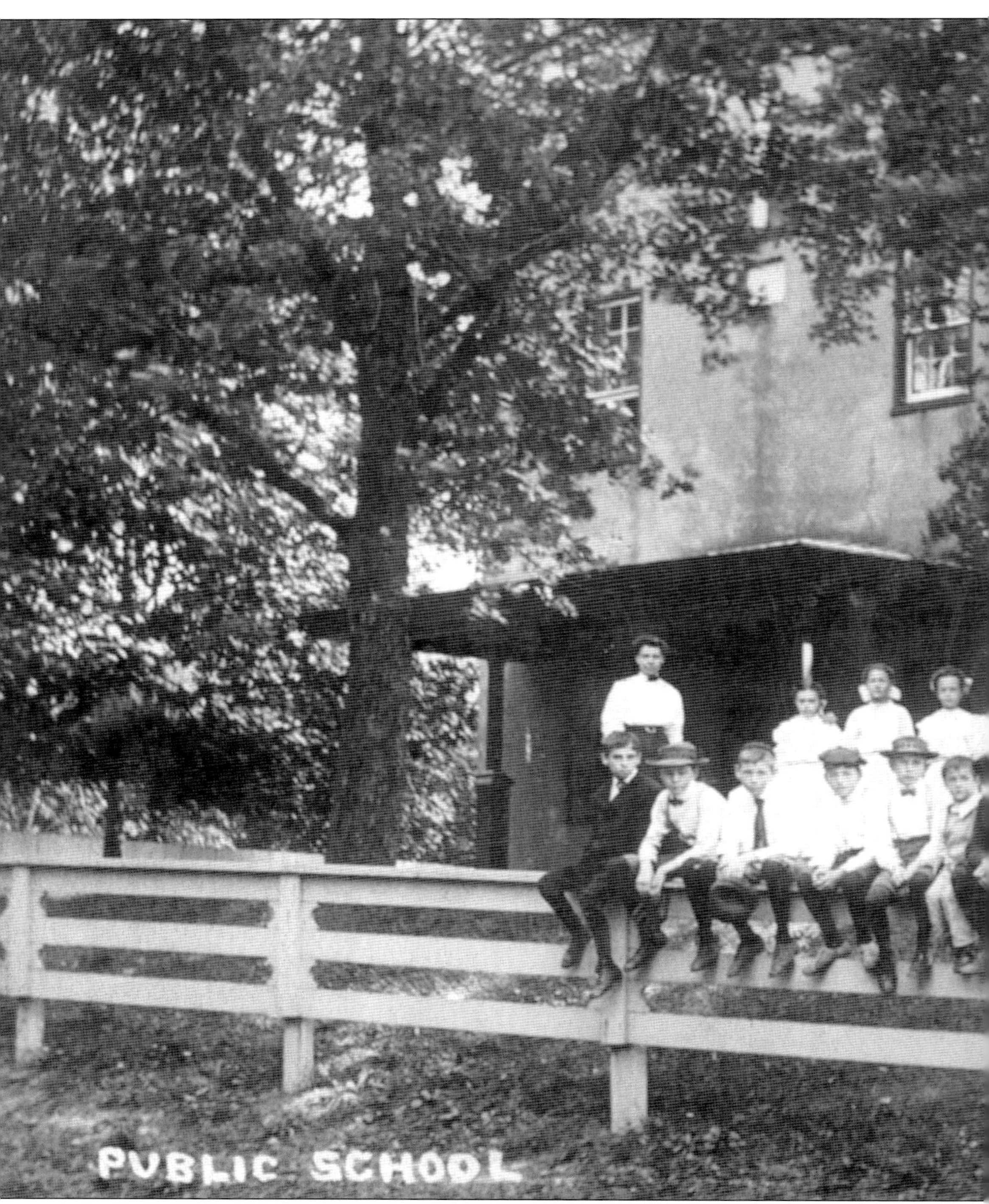

Public School, Newportville. Newportville School was a two-story, two-room building. This school is larger than most in the Bristol Township area, indicating a larger student population in Newportiville. This is a wonderfully posed picture with the young boys sitting on the school

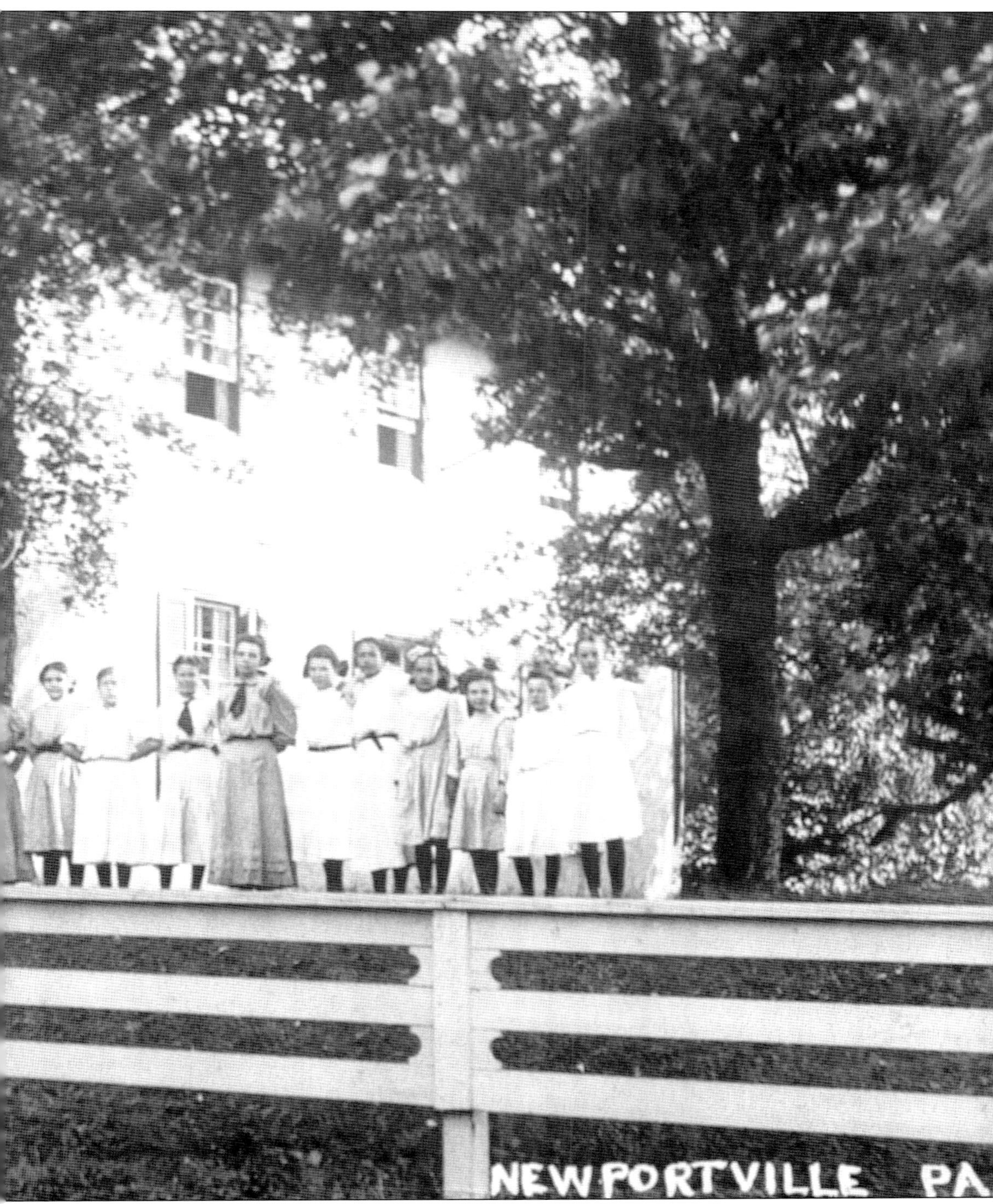

fence, separated from the girls. An interesting aspect of this postcard is that the girls appear to be standing on top of the fence when they are actually standing on a hill near the school.

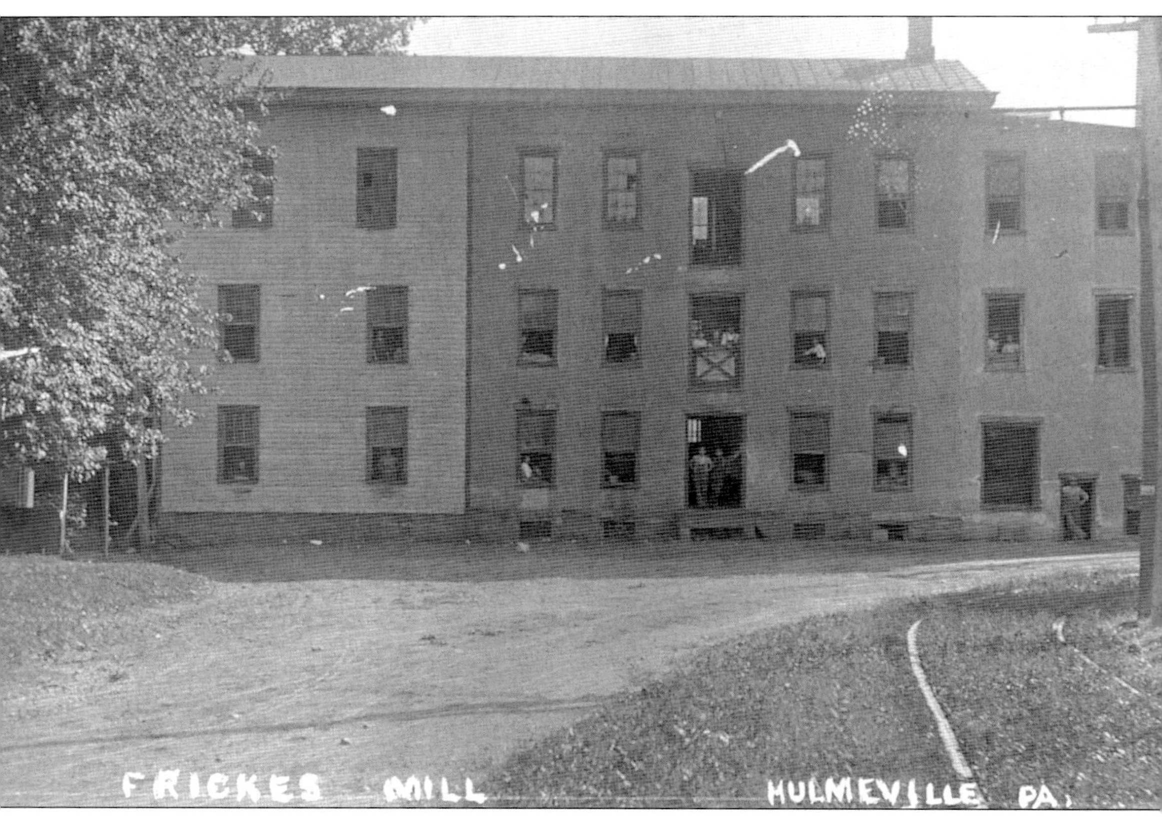

Frickes Mill, Hulmeville. Hulmeville Borough is situated on the banks of the Neshaminy Creek. Although the borough was incorporated in 1872, many buildings in Hulmeville are much older. There have been mills at this site since 1725, although this building dates from the late 1800s. Currently, the mill on Hulme Street contains a flea market.

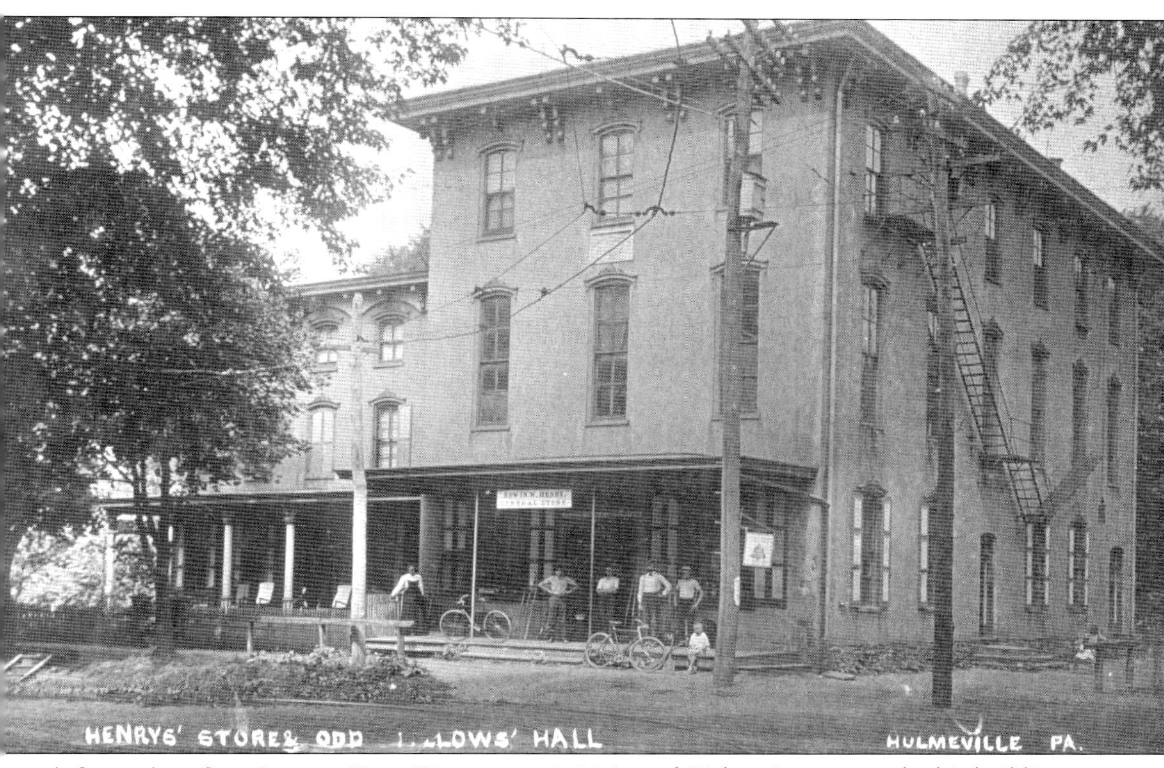

A Store And Odd Fellows Hall, Hulmeville. At Main and Hulme Streets stands this building, originally known as Johnson's Hall. Built in 1871, the building has served as a general store and meeting hall throughout its existence. Of particular interest are the fine arched window trimmings found throughout the structure. The building continues to be used for offices and residences; its appearance is quite similar to this 1910 view.

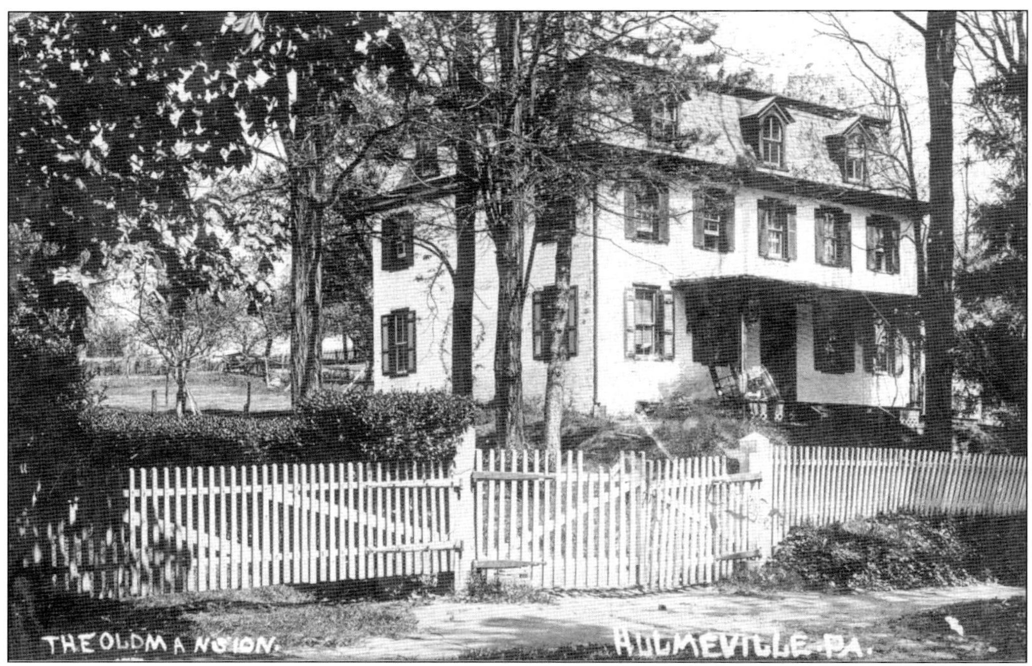

The Old Mansion, Hulmeville. This old home with a fine mansard roof can still be seen on Green Street in Hulmeville, complete with old shade trees. The property dates to the late 1700s. This view is from 1910.

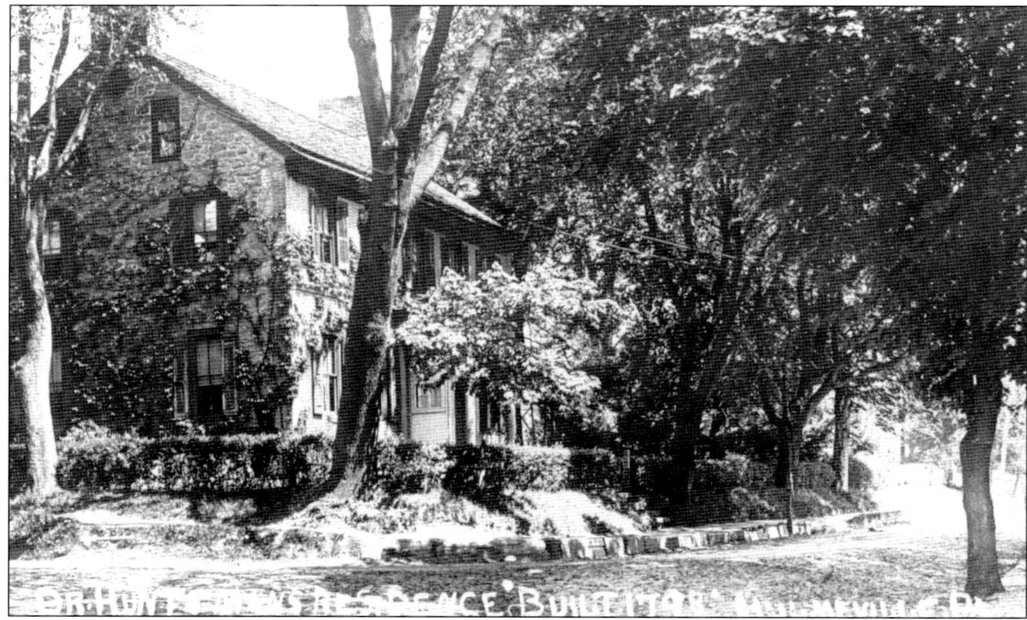

Hulmeville. The borough of Hulmeville has many old and interesting buildings along Main Street, but some of the side streets also contain historic structures. This home, built in 1798, stands on a shade-covered Green Street. It was the home of Dr. Huntsman at the time of this 1908 postcard.

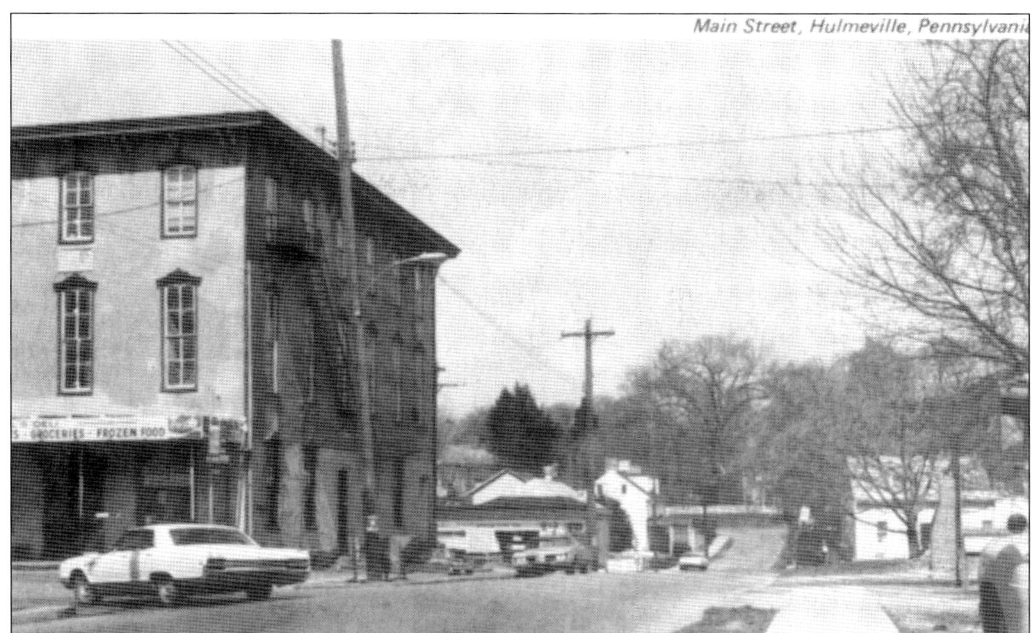

MAIN STREET, HULMEVILLE. This early-1970s view shows Main Street at Hulme Street in Hulmeville. To the left is Johnson's Hall, which contained a food store at the time. Hulmeville has not changed much since then, and a similar view can be seen today.

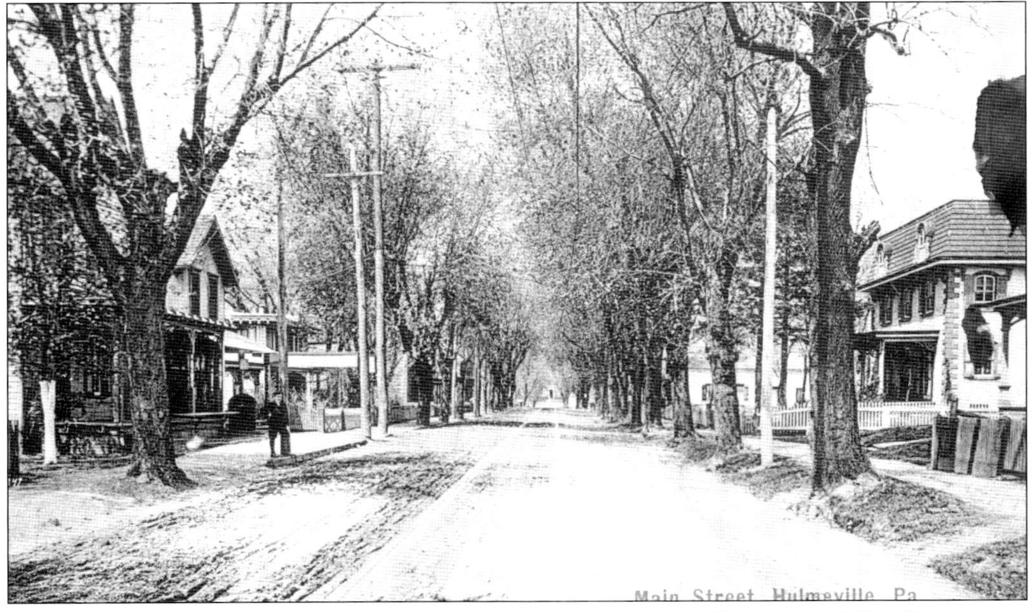

MAIN STREET, HULMEVILLE. Hulmeville's character is captured well in this 1909 J.K. Streeper postcard. Large trees and interesting architecture from different periods dominate Main Street. The large mansard-roof house on the right, as well as most others, are still standing and are well maintained in this tiny borough.

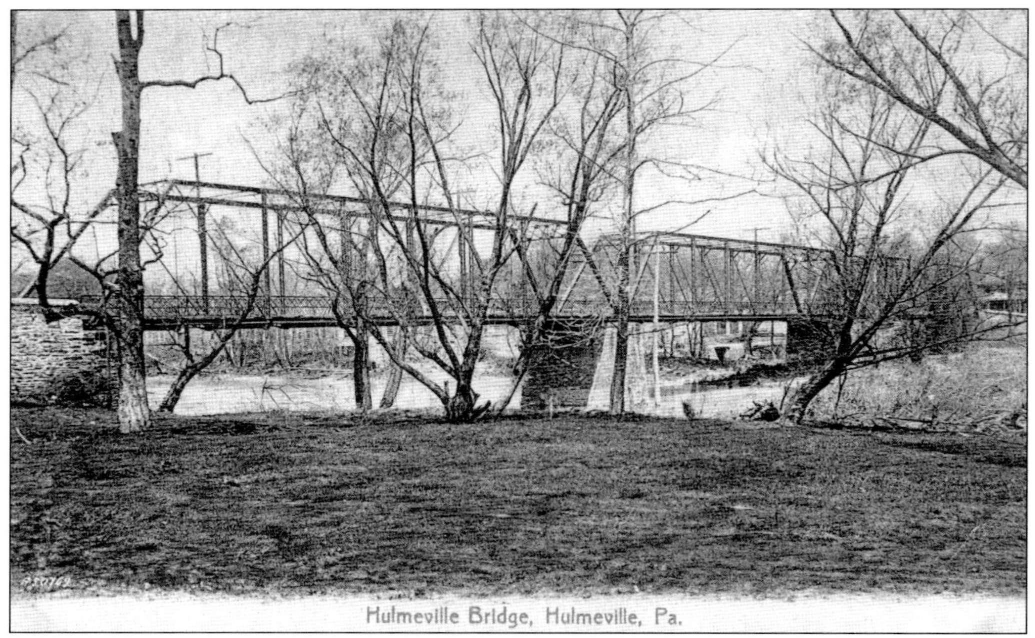

HULMEVILLE BRIDGE. This iron bridge carried Hulmeville Road over the Neshaminy Creek between Bensalem and Hulmeville. Built in 1899, it replaced an earlier bridge constructed of wood. The iron bridge became obsolete with increased traffic and was replaced with a concrete bridge in 1918. (J.K. Streeper postcard.)

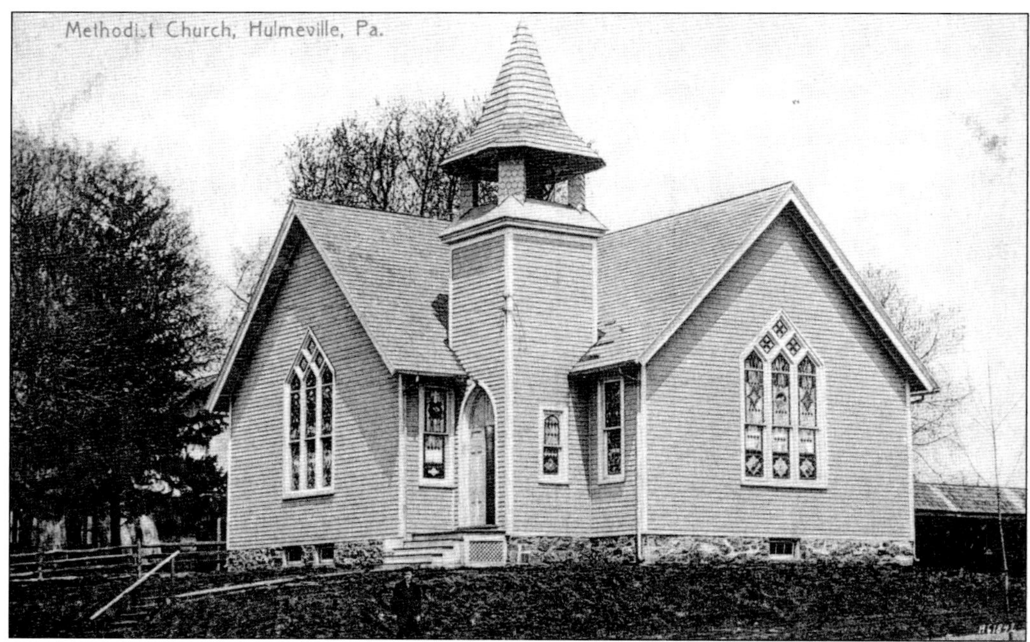

METHODIST CHURCH, HULMEVILLE. The Methodist Church in Hulmeville dates to 1840, when the first church was built south of town. This building, built in 1904, is located on Main Street. Its appearance has changed little over the years. (J.K. Streeper postcard from 1912.)

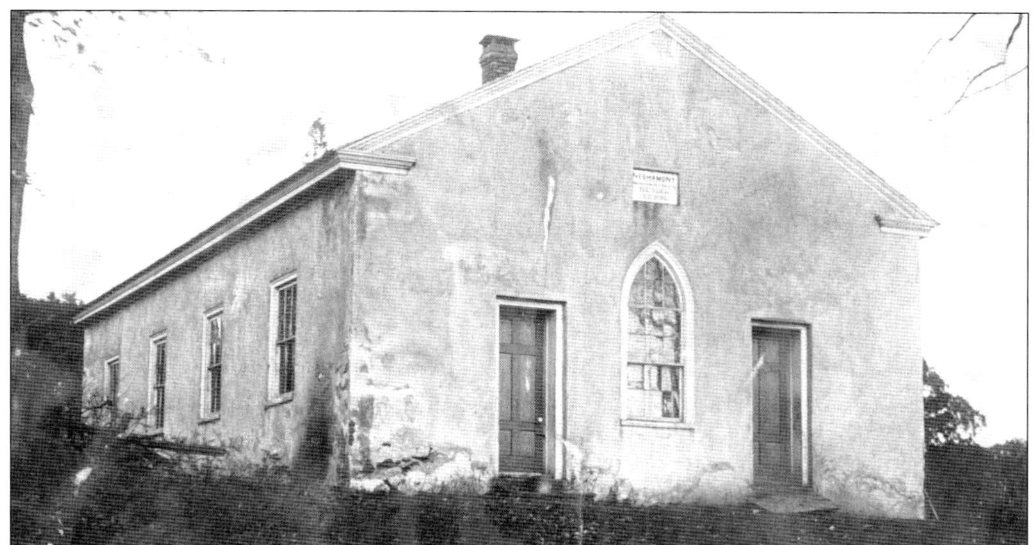

Neshaminy Methodist Church. Built in 1840 as the "Neshamony" Methodist Church, this structure is located in a wooded area at the lower end of Main Street and was the church's original building. As Hulmeville developed, the congregation built a newer church farther up Main Street in the borough. The long, Gothic-style window flanked by doors on both sides is a bit of odd architecture for an old country church. The structure is now part of a garage complex with the entire front plastered over.

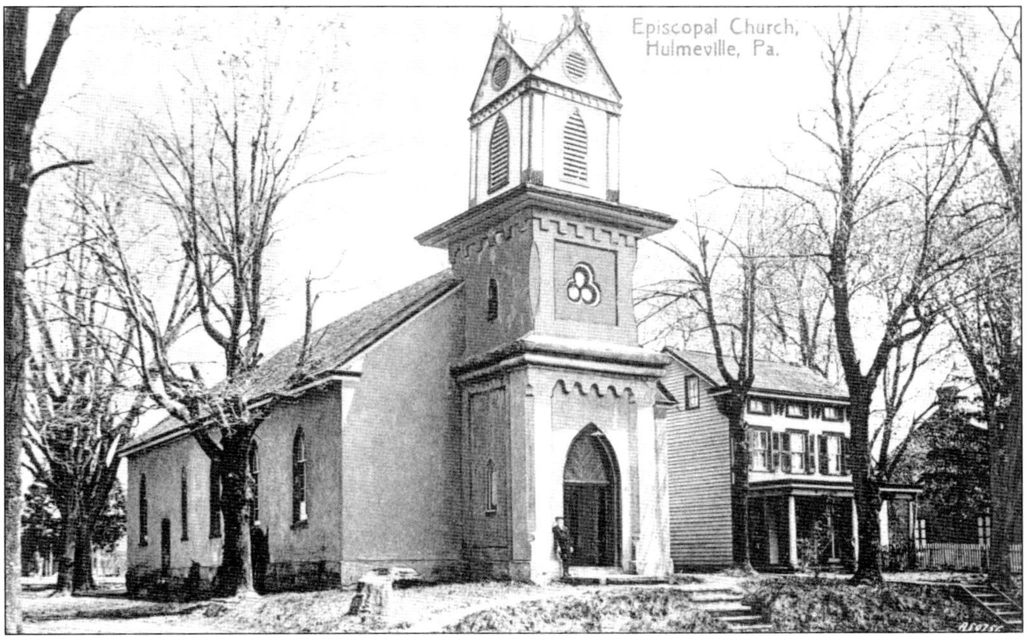

The Episcopal Church, Hulmeville. The Grace Episcopal Church is a beautiful building on Main Street in Hulmeville. It was created from a parent church, St. James, in nearby Bristol. This building, more than 100 years old, has gone through some changes and no longer has the ornate Gothic-style steeple. (J.K. Streeper postcard from 1912.)

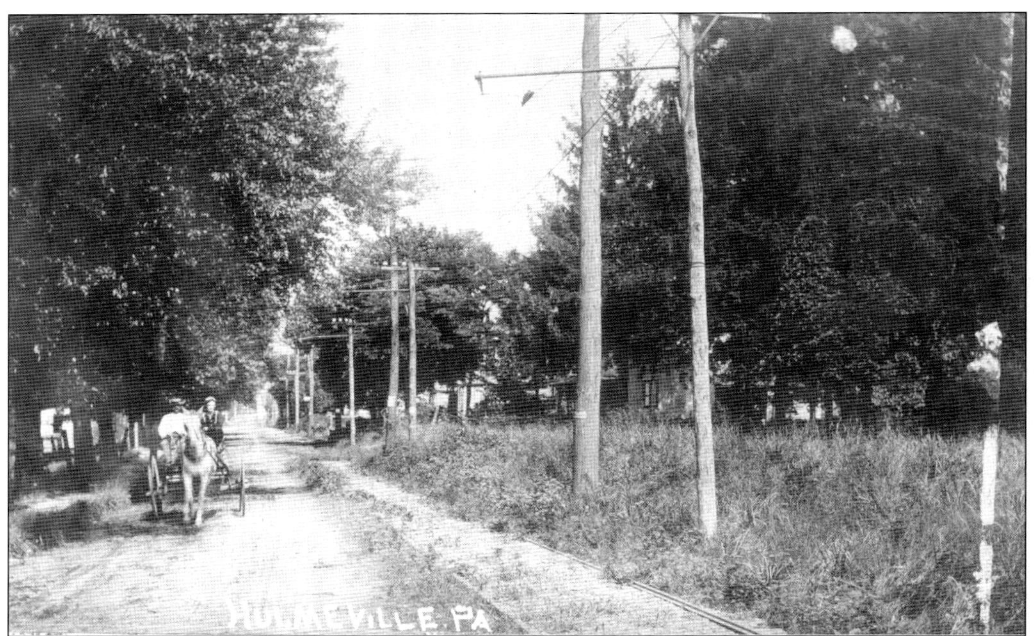

Hulmeville. This *c.* 1910 view shows the typical transportation of that time, along Main Street in Hulmeville. What appears to be the old school is the first building near the trees on the right side of the road. Notice the trolley tracks from the route that came from Bristol.

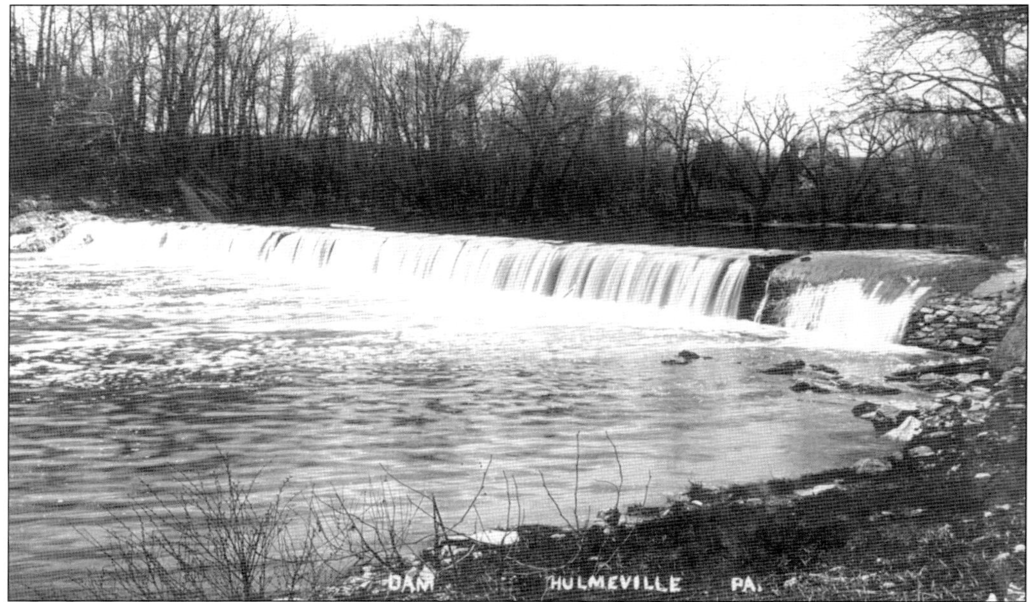

Hulmeville Dam. In the late 1800s, a small picnic park was established along the Neshaminy Creek in Hulmeville. A pavilion, refreshment stand, and several picnic groves were created, but the highlight of the park was the Neshaminy Creek. A dam was created on the creek for the enhancement of boating, swimming, and fishing.

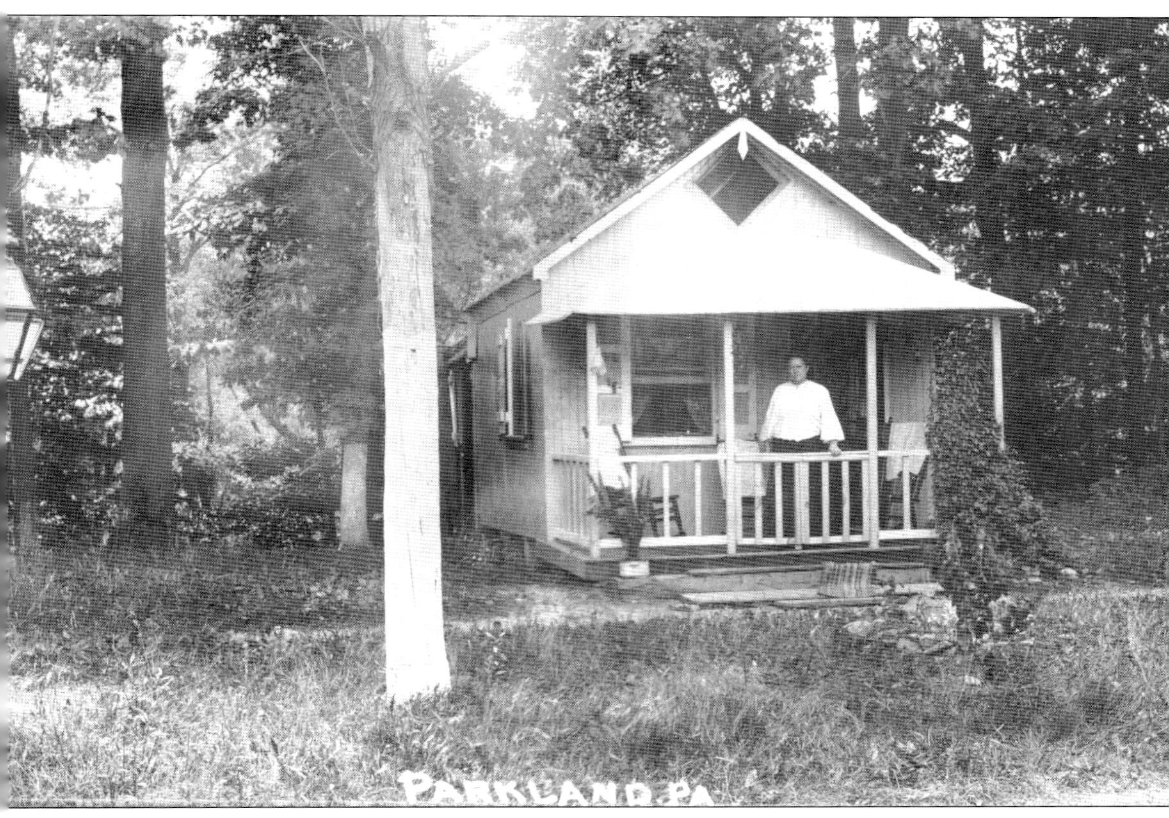

Parkland. This postcard mailed in 1908 states, "We are staying at this cottage. It is lovely here." This is a typical summer cottage along the Neshaminy Creek in Parkland. Many people from Philadelphia vacationed along the Neshaminy in the early 1900s. (Wharton postcard.)

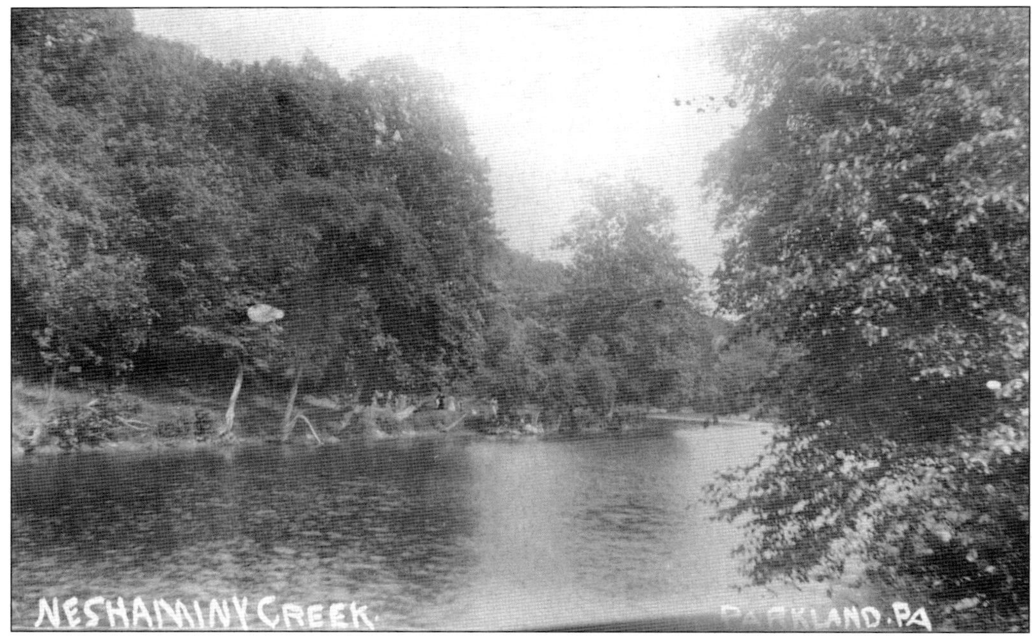

NESHAMINY CREEK, PARKLAND. The Neshaminy Creek in Parkland provided recreation for many people who spent the summer season along its banks. Boating and swimming in clear, cool water was the main attraction. Faintly visible in the center distance is a gathering of people and a canoe on the shore. (Wharton postcard.)

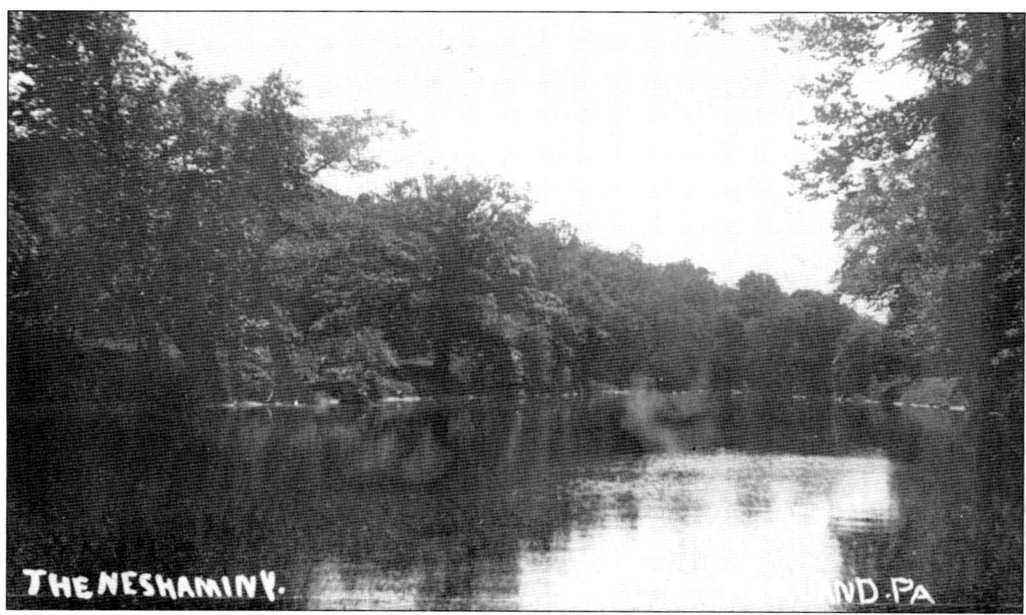

THE NESHAMINY, PARKLAND. This is another pretty spot on the peaceful Neshaminy Creek at Parkland. (Wharton postcard from 1908.)

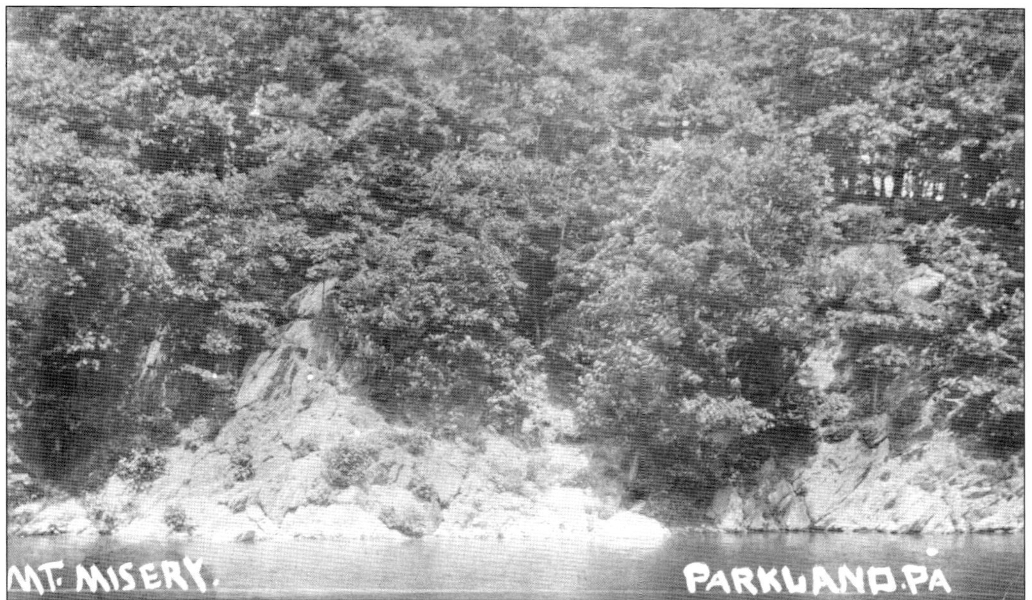

Mount Misery, Parkland. Interesting rock formations and steep hills dominate a small area on the Neshaminy Creek at Parkland. The Neshaminy carves out quite a little gorge in the vicinity from Oakford to Hulmeville. The origin of the name Mount Misery appears to be a mystery over 100 years old. Perhaps something tragic occurred at this spot. The author spent summer days along the creek in this vicinity. (Wharton postcard.)

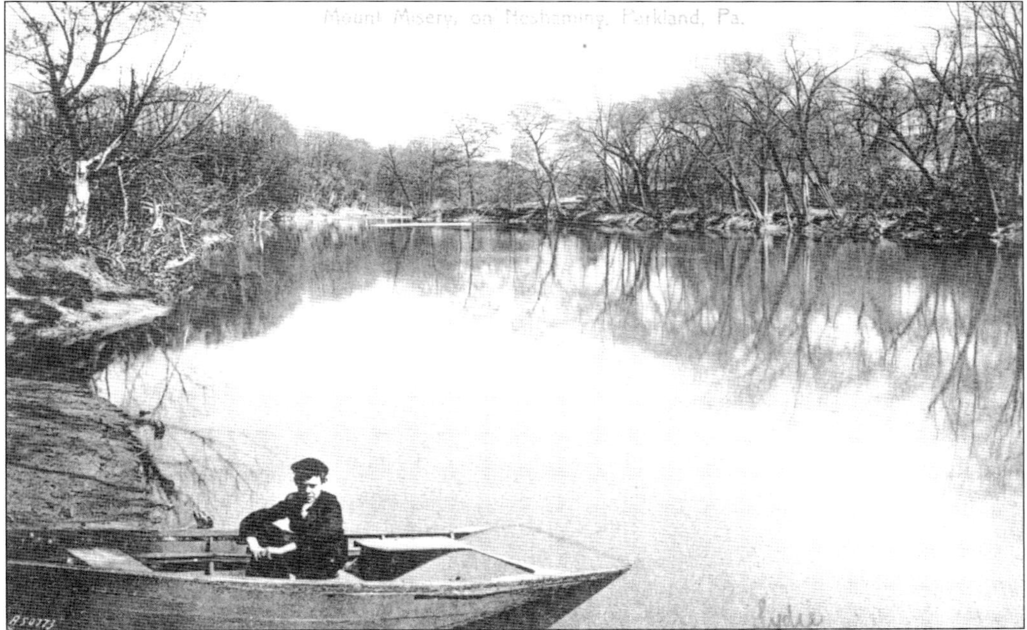

Mount Misery. The tranquil, clear waters of the Neshaminy Creek have always been a draw to children. In this *c.* 1908 view, a young lad prepares to venture out on a small boat on a sunny winter day. (J.K. Streeper postcard.)

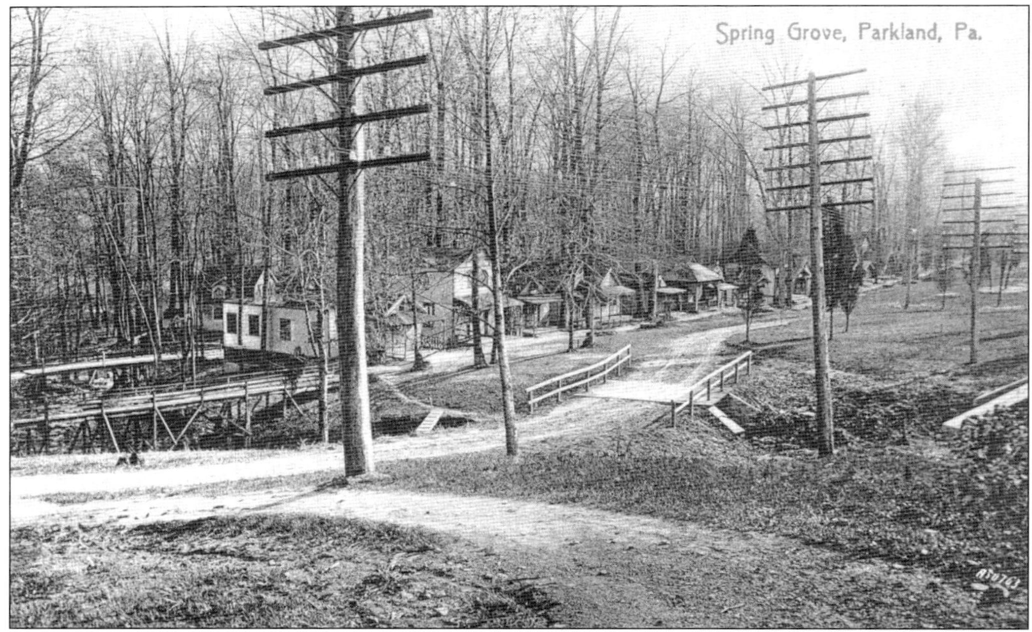

SPRING GROVE, PARKLAND. This 1909 postcard illustrates the many attractive cottages and bungalows that were built in the Parkland area. Many of these summer vacation homes later became year-round residences. (J.K. Streeper postcard.)

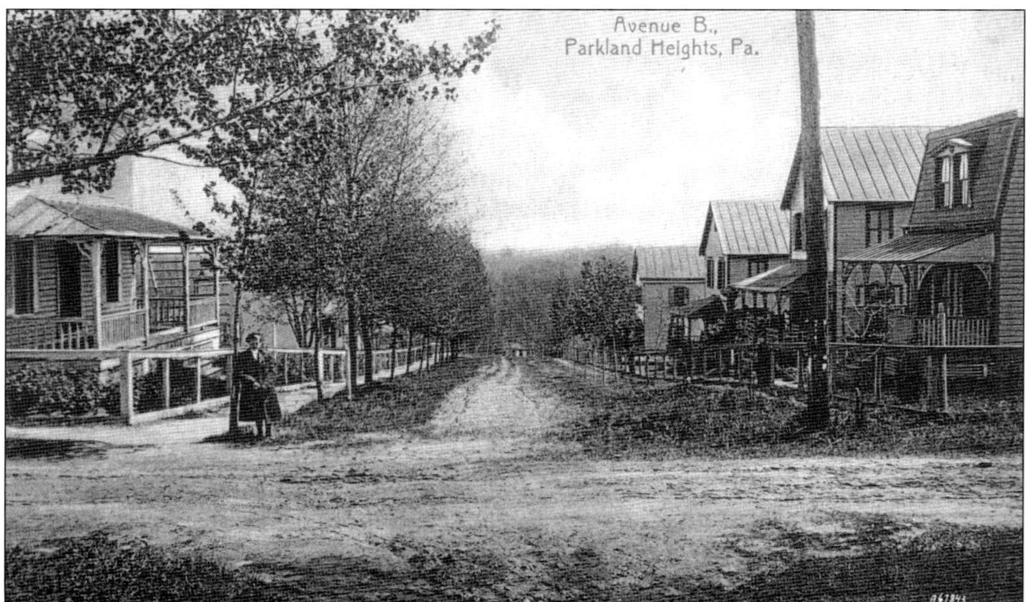

AVENUE B, PARKLAND. The small residential section of Parkland consisted of small, framed houses. In Parkland, streets were named after the alphabet. Avenues A through E run north-south. In this 1909 view looking south, Avenue B slopes down the hill toward the Neshaminy Creek. These homes, built *c.* 1900, still stand in Parkland along with newer ones. (J.K. Streeper postcard.)

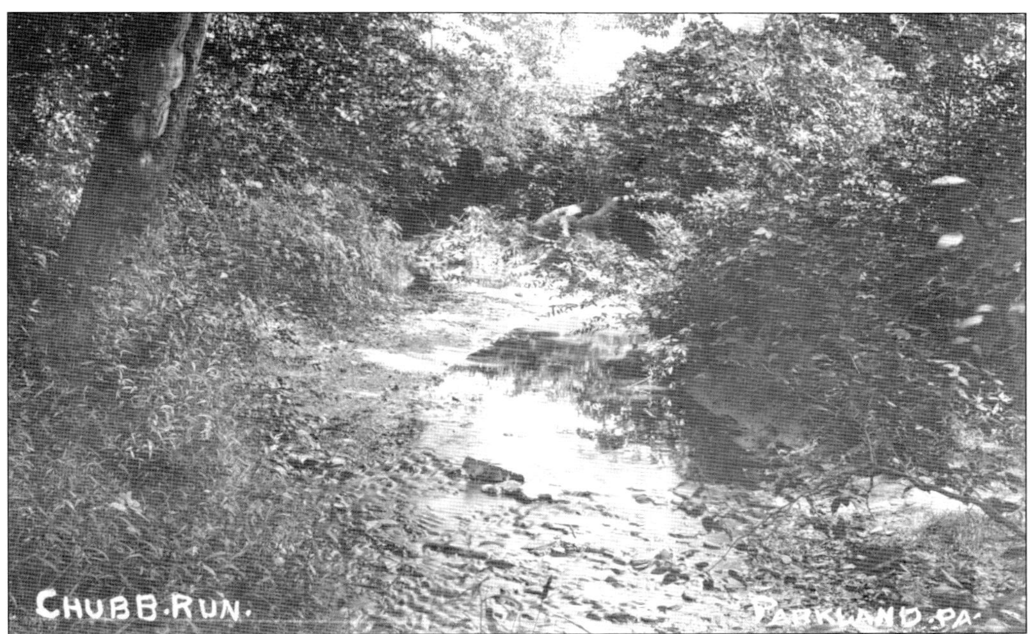

CHUBB RUN, PARKLAND. Chubb Run is a small stream that empties into the Neshaminy Creek at Parkland. As seen here, it was quite a picturesque spot.

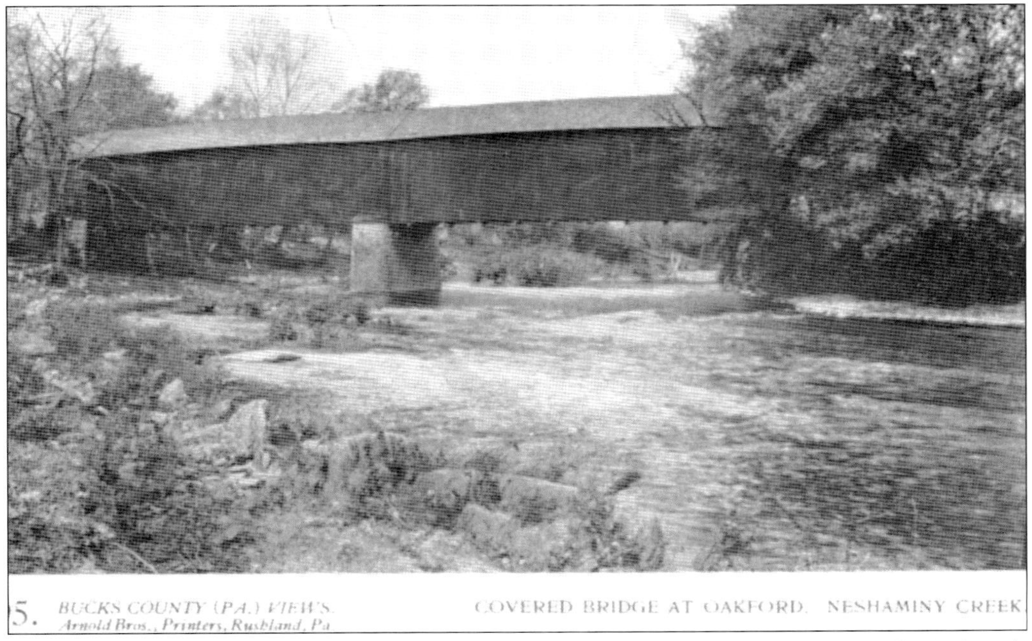

COVERED BRIDGE, OAKFORD. Bucks County once had numerous covered bridges, of which only a dozen remain. None have survived in lower Bucks County, with the exception of the rebuilt covered bridge in Tyler State Park. The bridge in Oakford carried Old Lincoln Highway over the Neshaminy Creek between Bensalem and Middletown. Built in 1845, it was replaced in the 1920s by a concrete bridge. (Arnold Brothers postcard.)

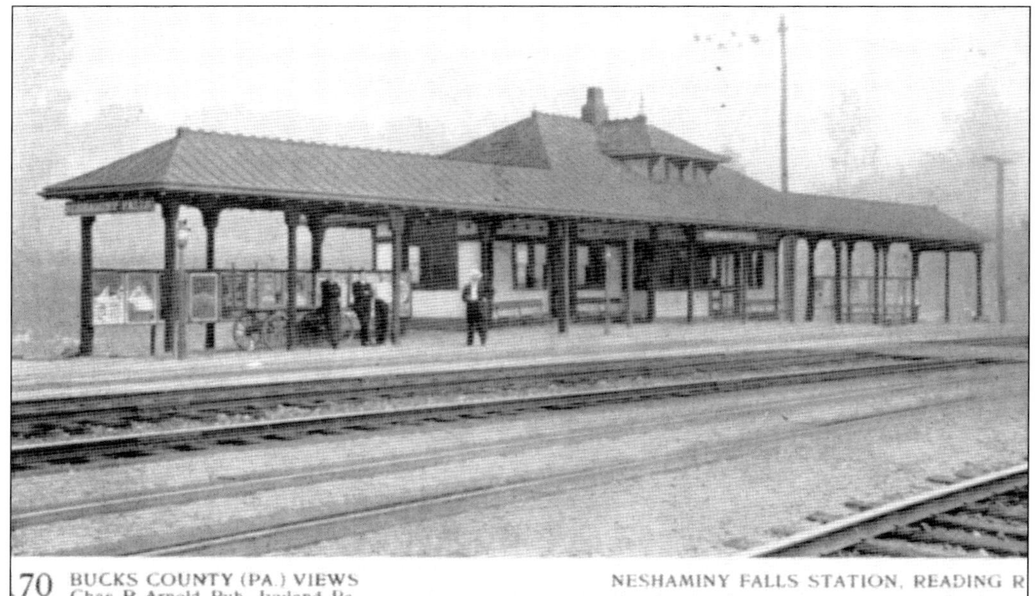

Neshaminy Falls Station. Neshaminy Falls was a village where the old Reading Railroad line crossed the Neshaminy Creek. A man-made dam across the Neshaminy created a falls, thus establishing the name. A very early but short-lived amusement park was built on a scenic site, with forests, rocks, and springs near the creek. This Arnold Brothers postcard shows the attractive station at Bristol Road in the early 1900s. A modern station building now occupies this site.

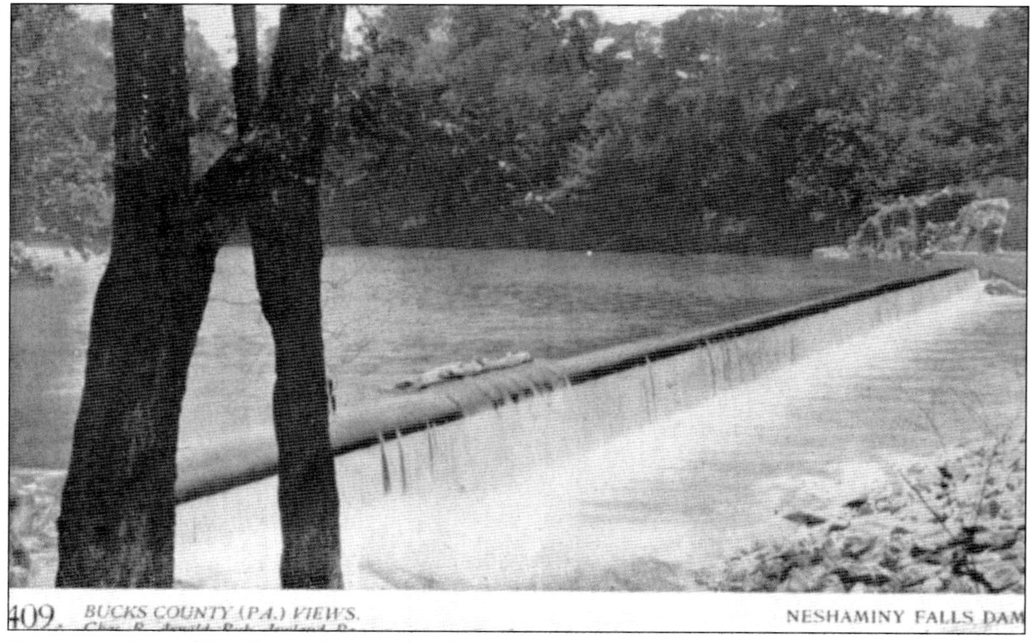

Neshaminy Falls. The dam at Neshaminy Falls was quite wide. It created a placid recreation area for boating and swimming above the falls. (Arnold Brothers postcard.)

Four

ALONG THE STREET ROAD CORRIDOR

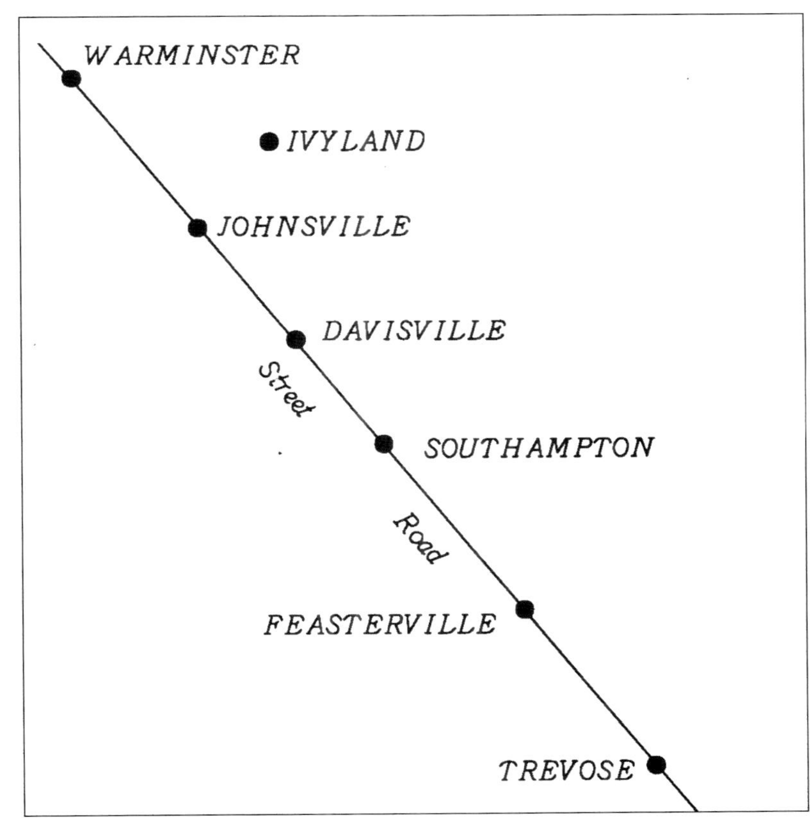

STREET ROAD. This road played a vital part in the development of southwestern Bucks County in the 1700s and 1800s. This chapter captures the many villages along or near Street Road from Trevose, westward to Warminster.

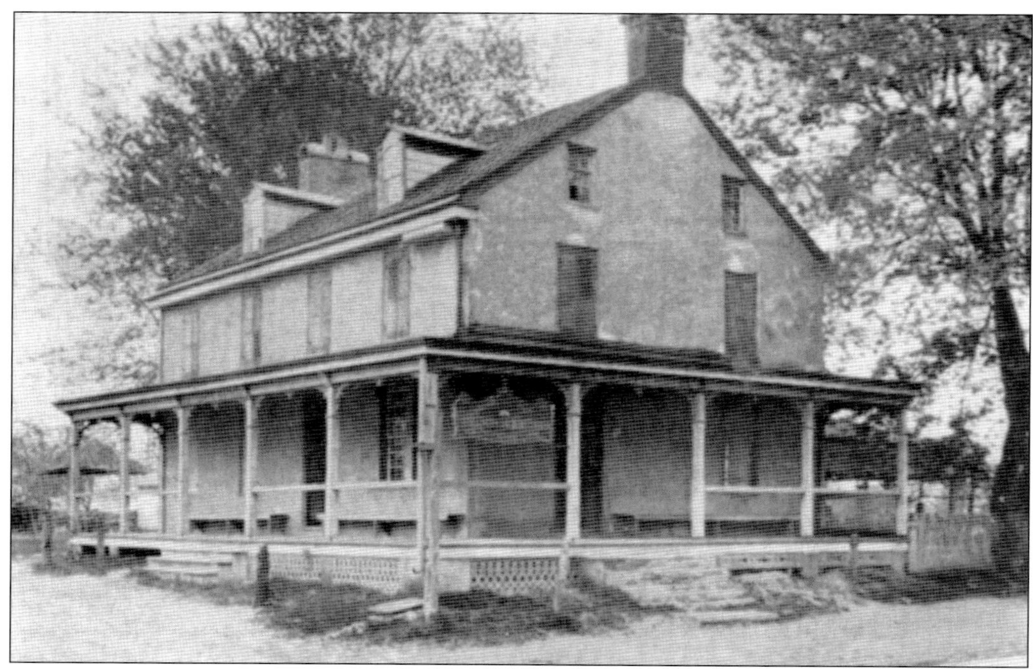

La Trappe Hotel, Bensalem. A mile east of Trevose on Street Road at Old Lincoln Highway was the site of a village and hotel called La Trappe or Trappe. Named by a Frenchman who supposedly trapped animals in the area, the Trappe Hotel dates to the 1700s. The construction of the Pennsylvania Turnpike caused the demolition of the old hotel in the late 1950s. (Arnold Brothers postcard.)

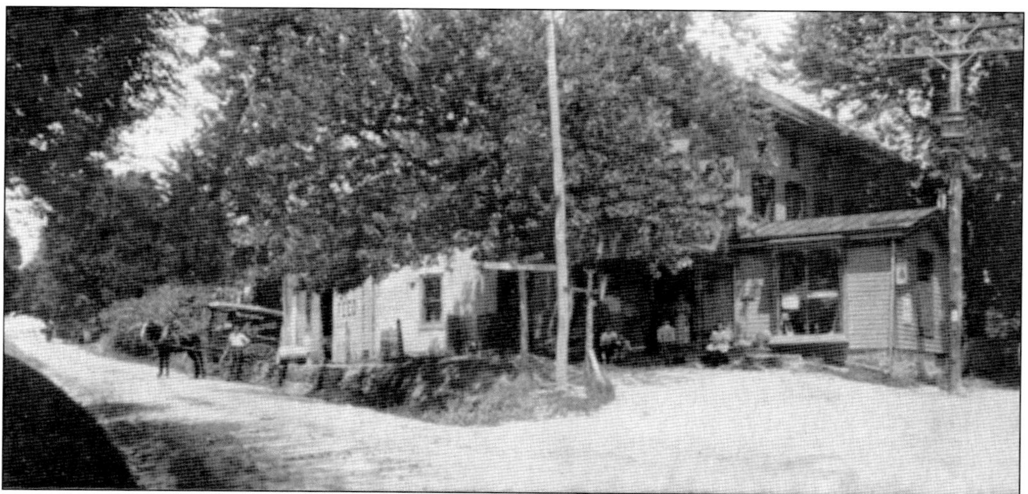

Trevose Store and Post Office. Looking west on Street Road from Brownsville Road, this Arnold Brothers postcard shows the Trevose Store. Built in the 1800s, many generations of Moyers operated the store. It was torn down in the 1960s. As Street Road was widened, this stretch of the road remained untouched as the new road bypassed Trevose Village. Today, this section of Old Street Road is lined with a few old Colonial structures and large trees. It remains a small glimpse of old Trevose bypassed by modern progress.

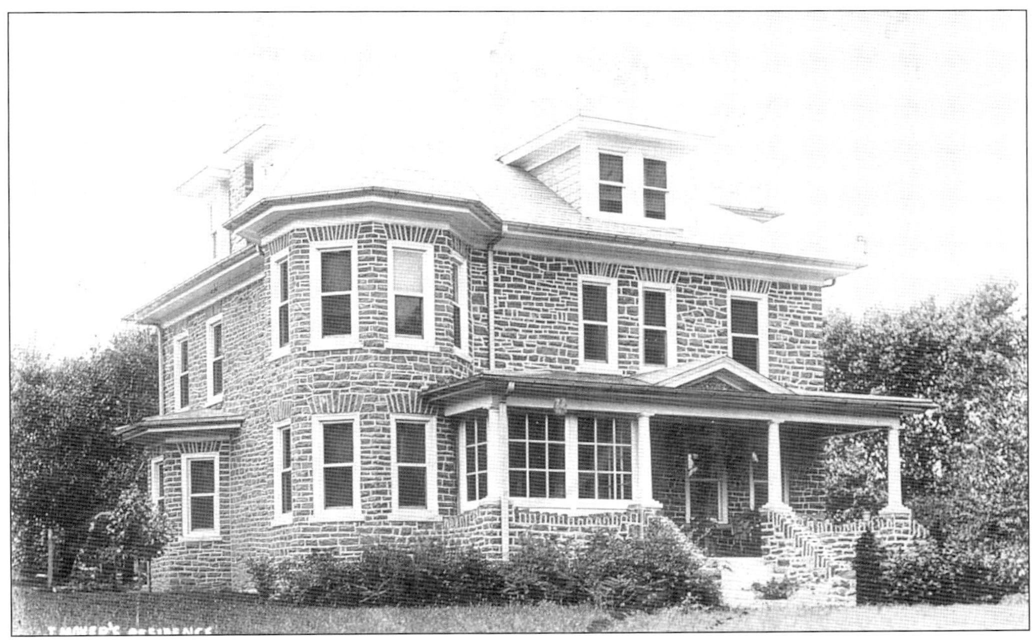

J. Moyer's Residence, Trevose. The Moyer residence is an attractive stone house that was built on Brownsville Road next to the Trevose Store. The Moyer family operated the store for many years. Although the store has been demolished, this residence is still standing and looks almost identical to this 1910 view. (Sliker postcard.)

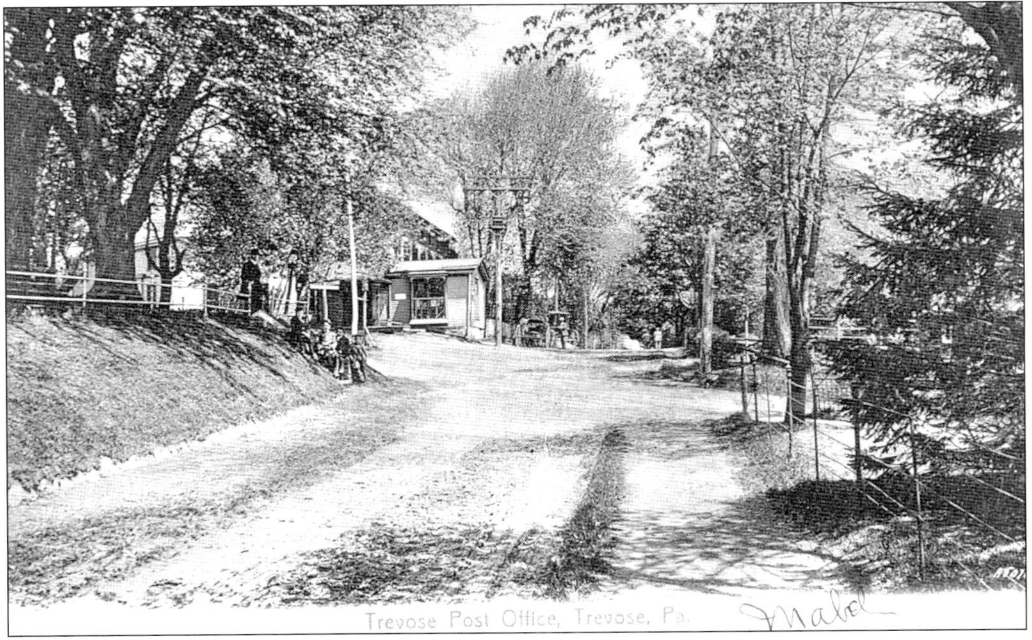

Trevose. This is the intersection of Brownsville and Street Roads, looking north. Moyer's Trevose Store and Post Office is seen on the left, facing Brownsville Road. (J.K. Streeper postcard.)

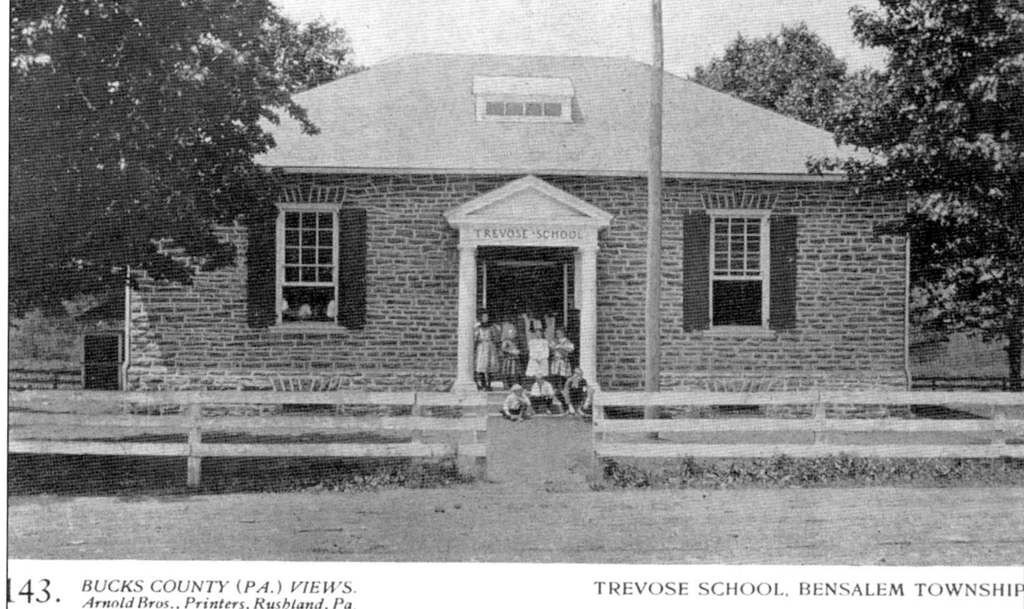

TREVOSE SCHOOL. Built as the Penn Valley School on Old Lincoln Highway above Street Road, this building still stands as part of an industrial complex. The first school on this site was built in the early 1800s. The present building, with two classrooms, was built in the early 1900s. The school closed in 1966. (Arnold Brothers postcard.)

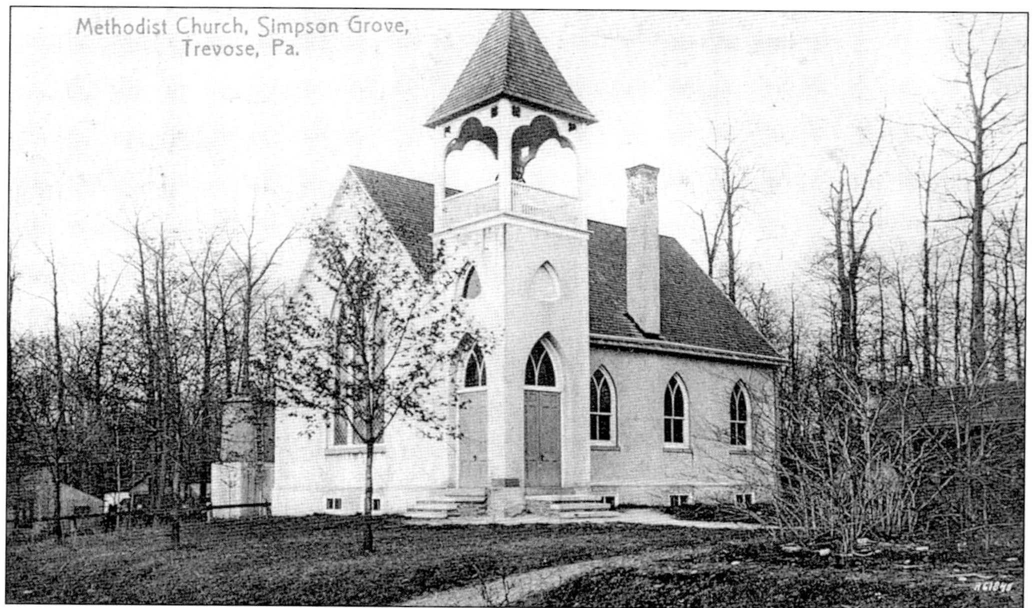

TREVOSE M.E. CHURCH. Churches in Bucks County all seem to have distinctively unique architecture. The Trevose Methodist Church is a fine example of late Gothic Revival architecture with its arched windows and a beautiful bell tower. Built in 1895 at Brownsville Road and Church Avenue, the building has changed very little in its 105 years of existence. (J.K. Streeper postcard.)

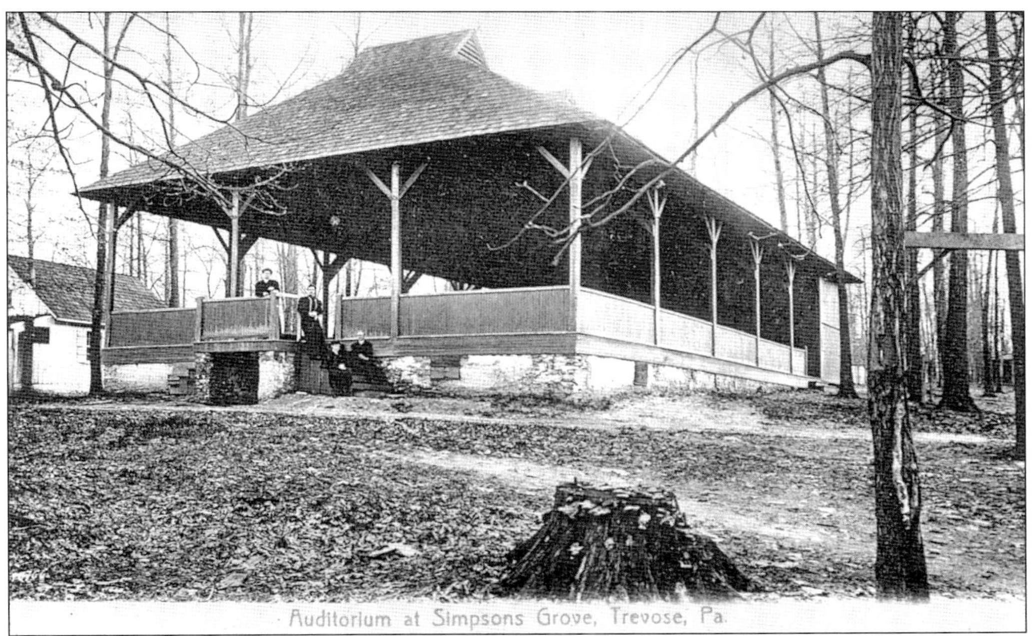

Auditorium, Simpson Grove, Trevose. In Bensalem Township, between Brownsville Road and Trevose Station, once stood Simpson Grove. Simpson Grove was a Methodist camp meeting ground that contained many outdoor facilities. Shown here in a wooded setting is the auditorium. (J.K. Streeper postcard.)

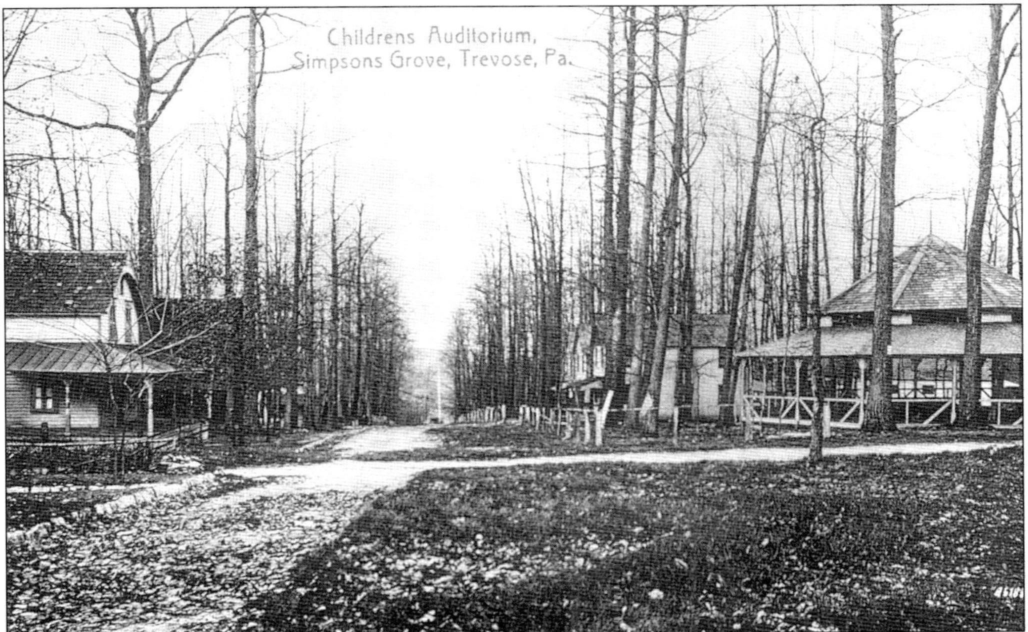

Children's Auditorium, Simpson Grove. This 1908 view of the attractive children's auditorium at Simpson Grove. Its wooded location gave the area a rather rustic look. (J.K. Streeper postcard.)

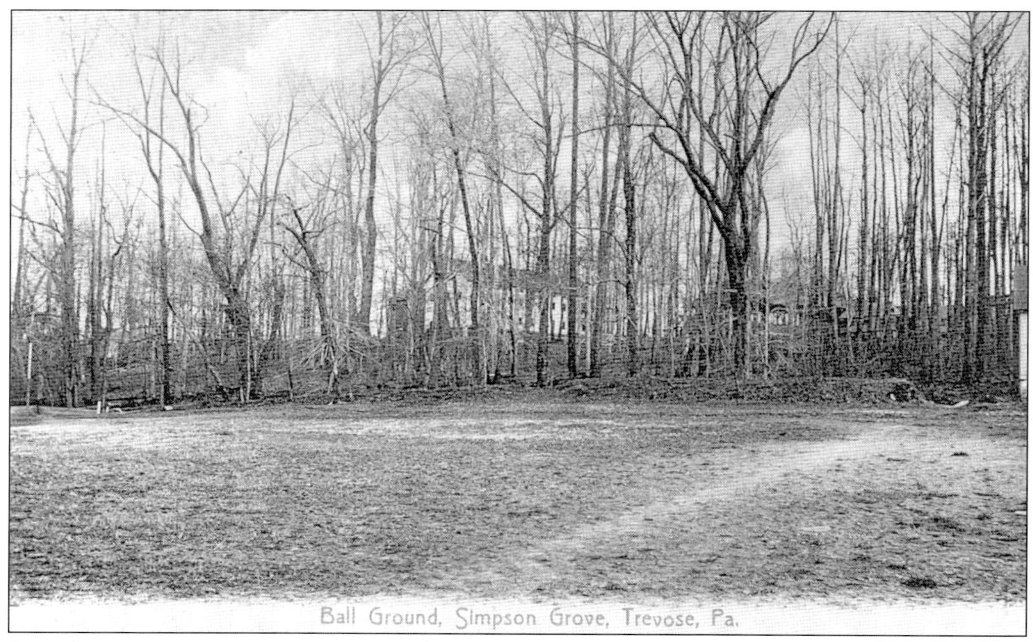

BALL GROUNDS, SIMPSON GROVE. Aside from religious purposes, Simpson Grove also contained recreational facilities such as this ball field. The Methodist Meeting at Simpson Grove was responsible for the creation of the Trevose Methodist Church on Brownsville Road. (J.K. Streeper postcard.)

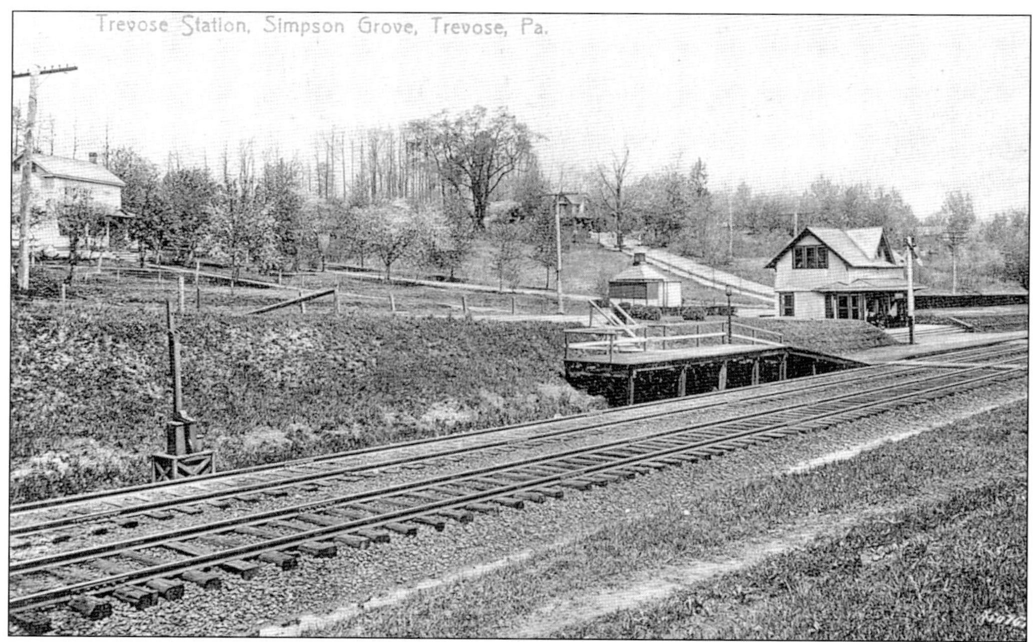

TREVOSE STATION. Trevose Station was built in 1893 on the Philadelphia to West Trenton Line. As indicated on this J.K. Streeper postcard from 1911, it was also the stop for Simpson Grove. Although trains still stop at Trevose, the old wood station was replaced 30 years ago.

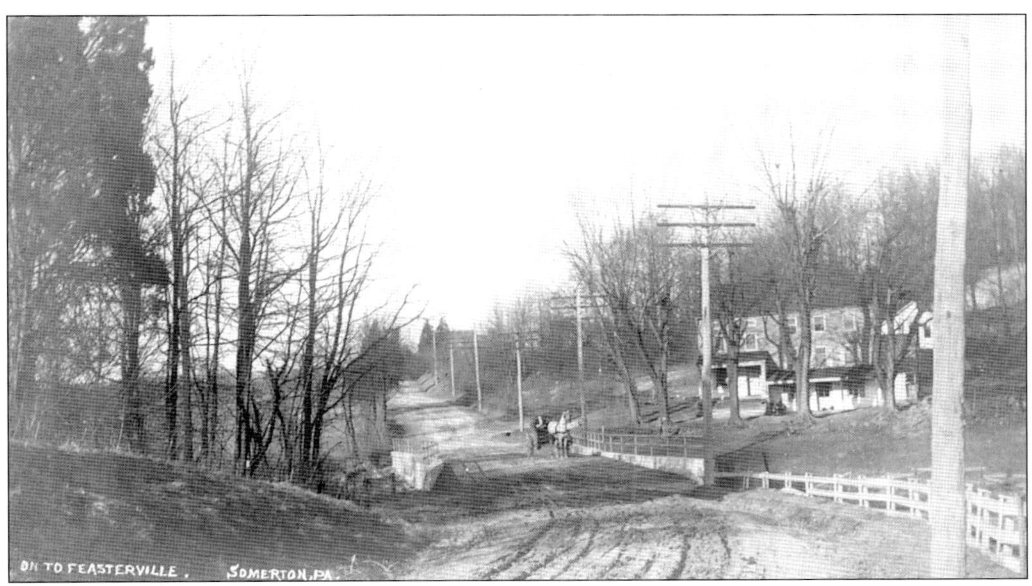

ON TO FEASTERVILLE. This *c.* 1908 view looks from Somerton in Northeast Philadelphia over the Poquessing Creek into Bucks County. The dirt road is today's Bustleton Pike with Feasterville in the far distance. The old farmhouse is still standing amid a golf course, swim club, and other commercial buildings. (Sliker postcard.)

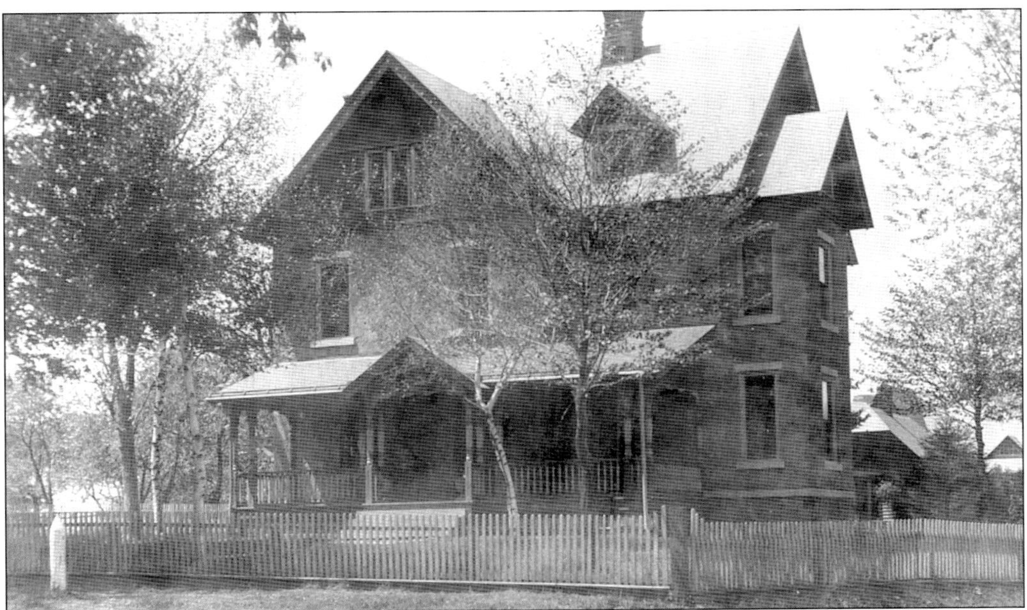

RESIDENCE OF A. JOHNSON, FEASTERVILLE. The village of Feasterville was named after the John Feaster family, who settled the area in the 1730s. The village was centered around the crossroads of Bustleton Pike and Street Road. The Johnson family at one time occupied many different farms in the area. This house, built in the latter half of the 1800s, stood near the village crossroads and is a fine example of a middle-class residence. (Sliker postcard.)

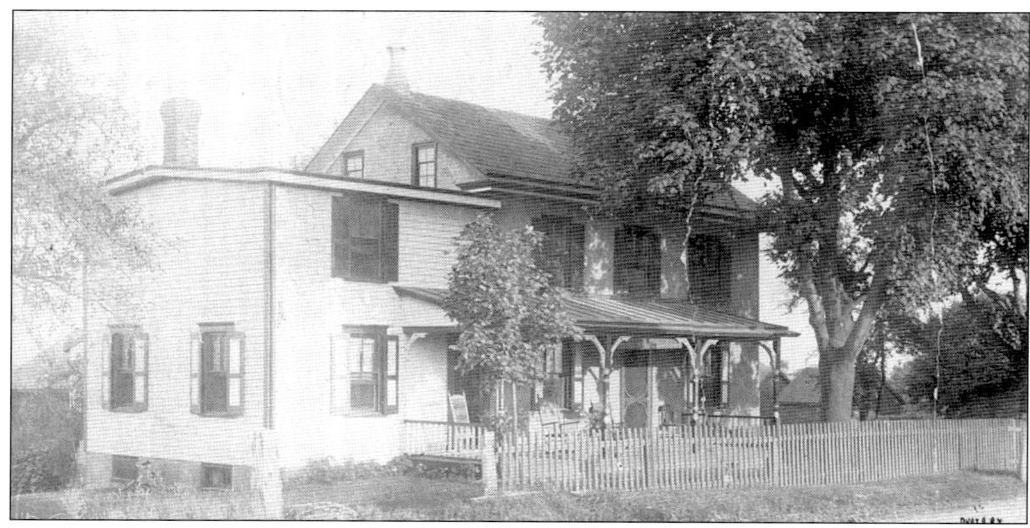

Snyder Residence, Feasterville. Since the 1960s, Feasterville has experienced tremendous residential and commercial growth. Very little of the old village and its old farms survive, although there are several curious old stone and brick houses on Bustleton Pike. The Snyder residence, found on an old atlas of the area, was once located on Bustleton Pike south of Street Road where stores and shopping centers now stand. It was a typical old dwelling in Feasterville dating back to the 1800s. (Sliker postcard.)

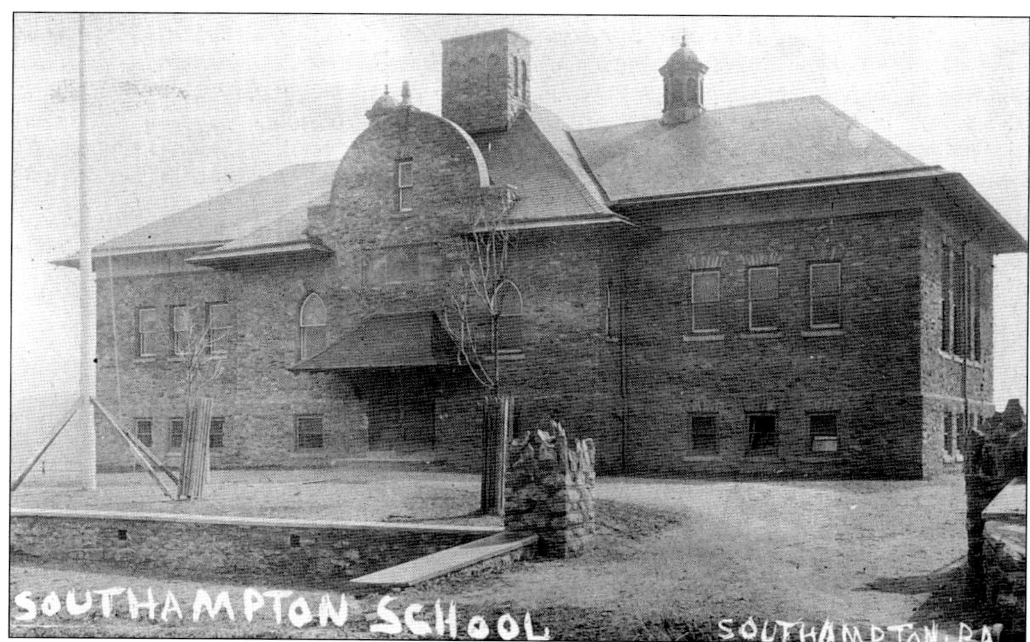

The Feasterville School. The date stone above the door of this school reads, "Southampton Township School, Built 1904." This Hay Photo postcard must have been produced before 1909, as the school was destroyed by a fire that year, with all students escaping without injury. The school was located on Bustleton Pike north of Street Road and was rebuilt only to be torn down in the 1960s.

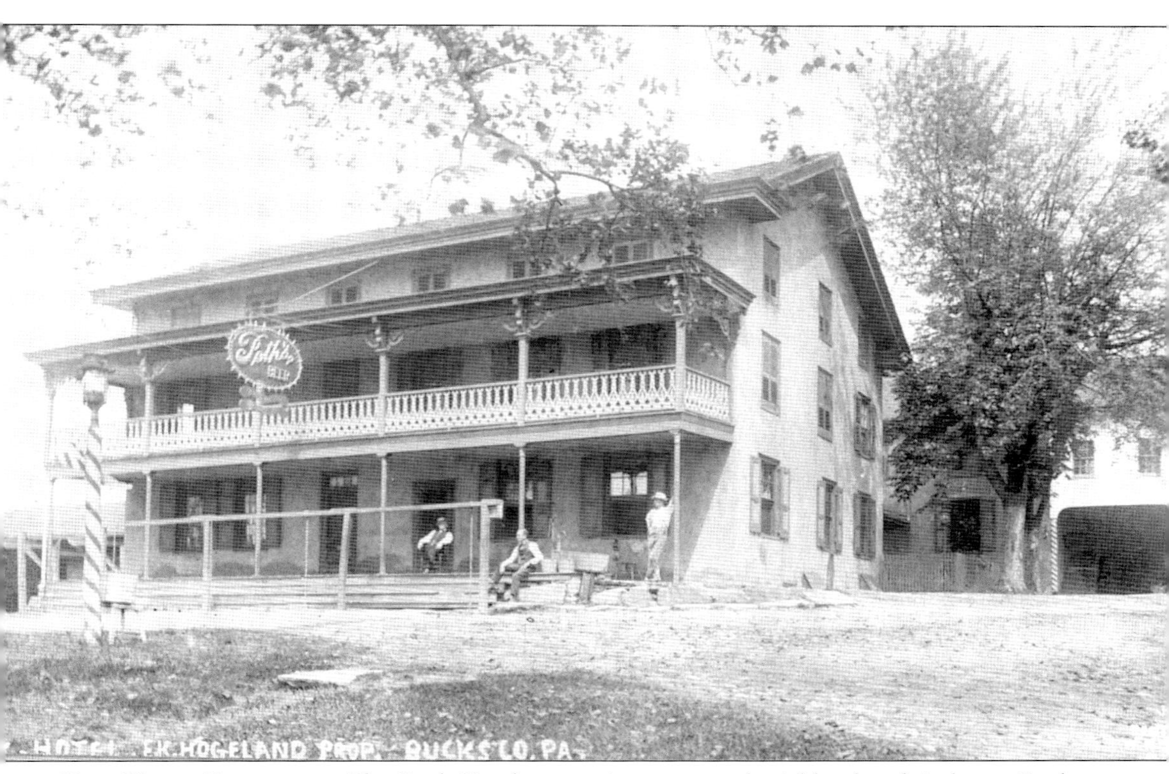

Buck Hotel, Feasterville. The Buck Hotel was an important colonial landmark in lower Bucks County. Situated on Bridgetown Pike at Bustleton Pike and Buck Road, it was an early stagecoach tavern built in 1735. Unlike the Red Lion Hotel, the Buck Hotel had been altered many times. This Sliker postcard is quite rare and shows the hotel in 1909, when E.K. Hogeland was the owner. Even in this view, "the Buck" had been altered and enlarged. The old landmark was torn down in the late 1990s.

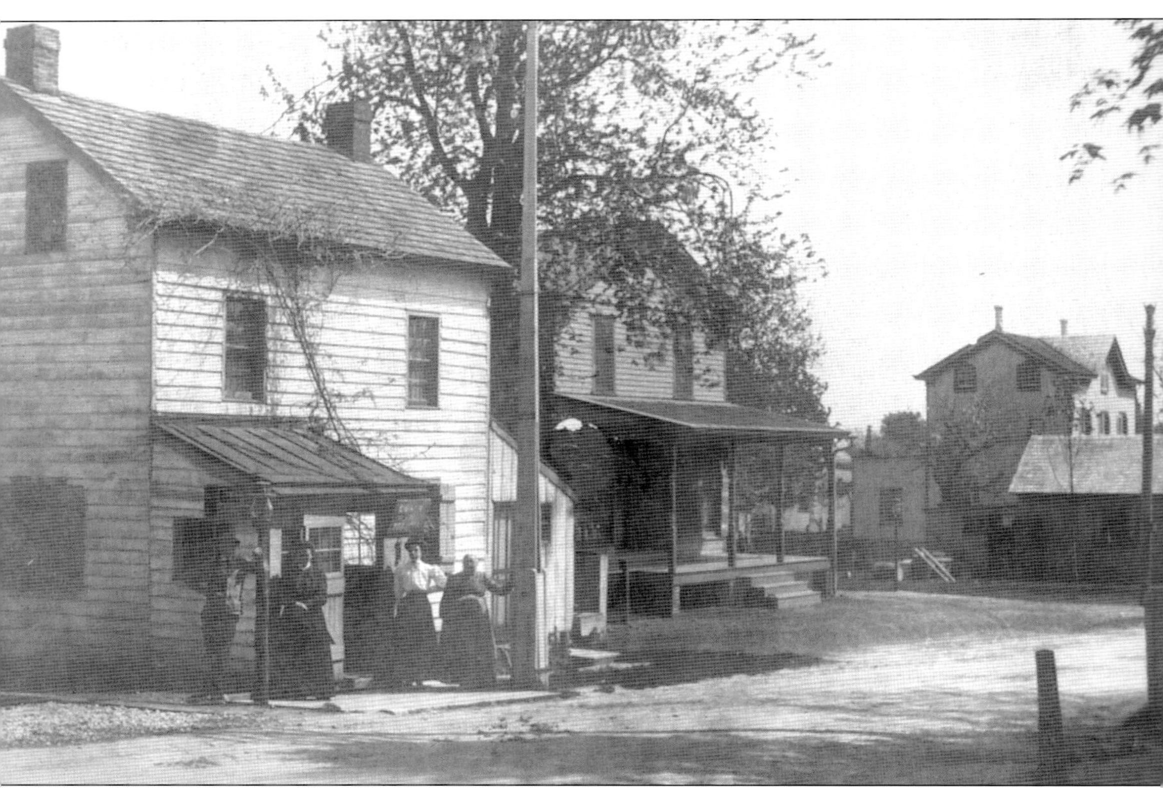

THE OLD TOLLGATE, SOUTHAMPTON. The village of Southampton was centered around the intersection of Second Street Pike and Street Road. This old tollgate stood on the southeast corner of that intersection. It was part of the turnpike that ran from Fox Chase through Huntingdon Valley to Wrightstown. The tollgate was moved to a nearby site on Plum Street in 1919 and is used as a residence. (Sliker postcard.)

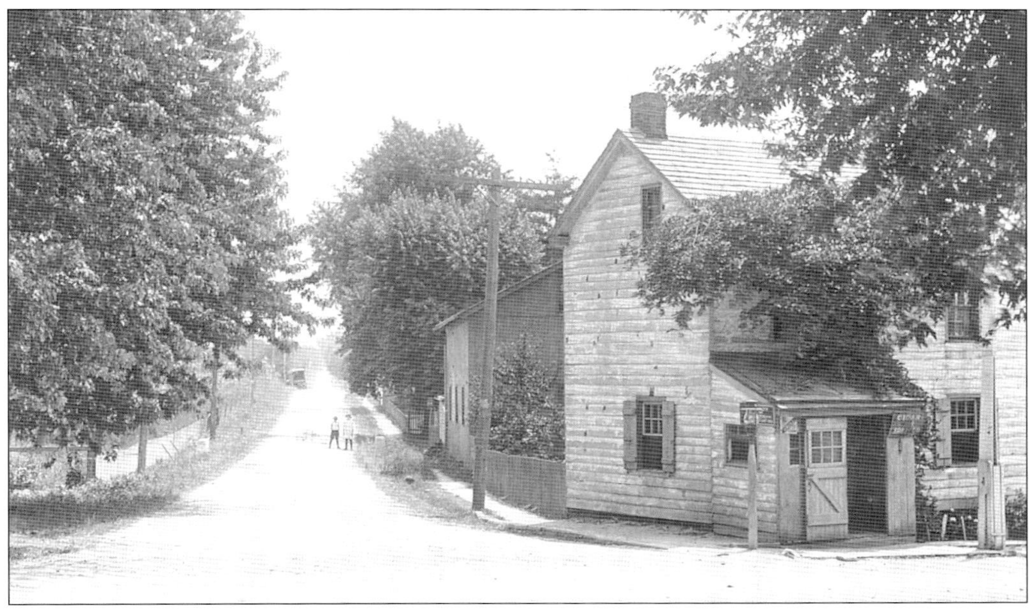

Street Road, Southampton. The narrow country dirt lane pictured here in 1910 is today's five-lane, macadam Street Road. Looking east from the tollgate at Second Street Pike, this quiet country scene is quite a contrast to today's busy Southampton. (Sliker postcard.)

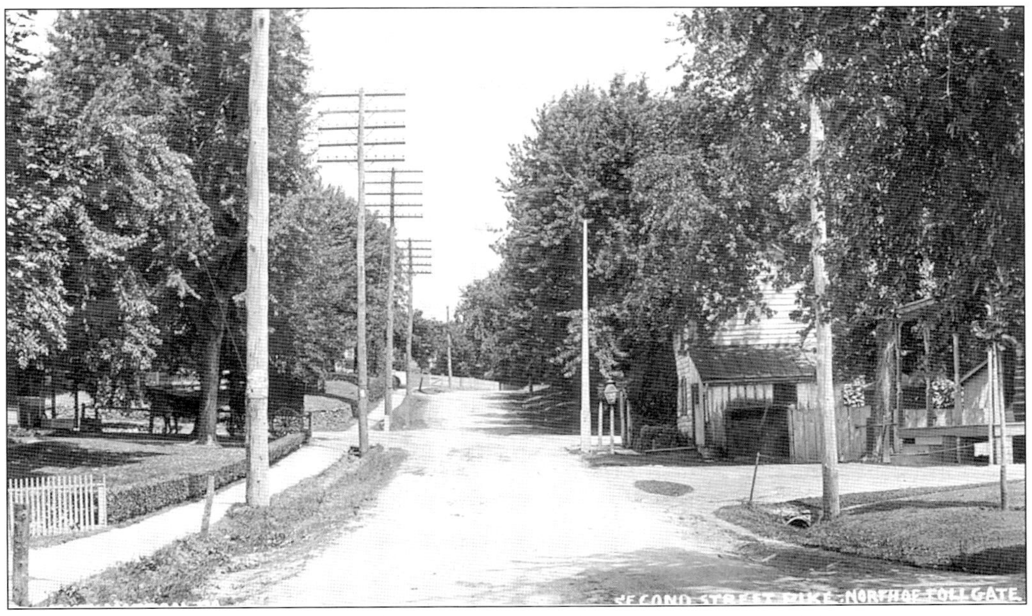

Southampton. This rare view, looking north toward the intersection of Street Road, shows Second Street Pike. The building on the right is the old tollgate. This area has undergone many changes since this 1911 postcard was made. (Sliker postcard.)

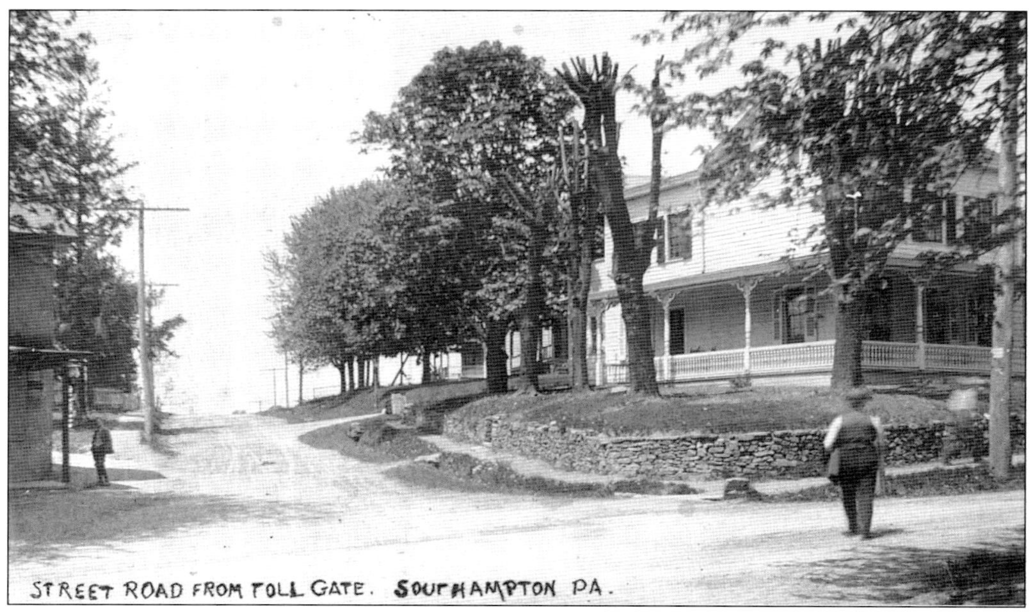

STREET ROAD, SOUTHAMPTON. A man casually walks into the intersection of Street Road and Second Street Pike in Southampton. This 1908 view looks west on a very empty Street Road. (Sliker postcard.)

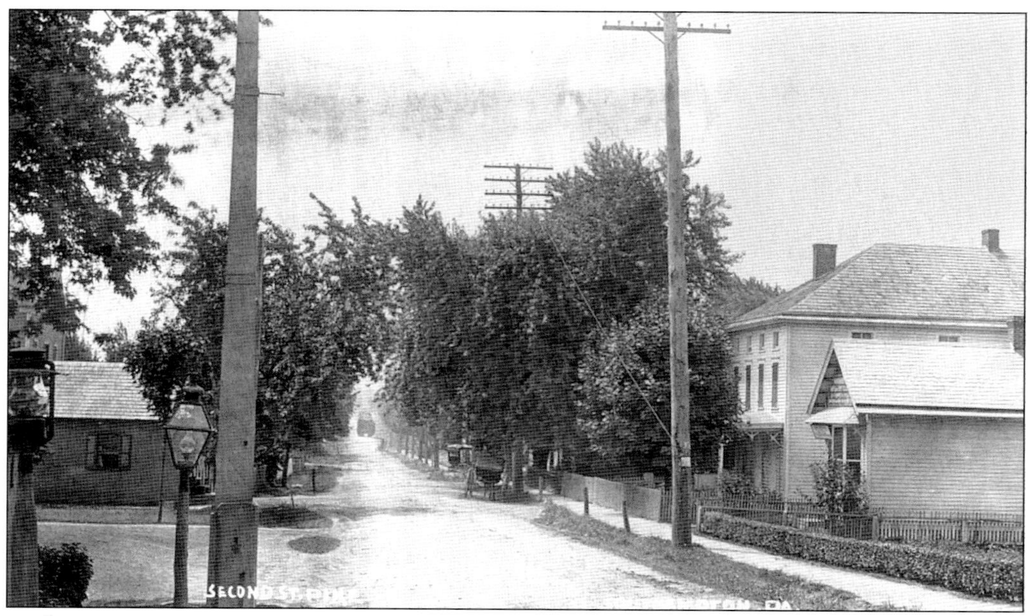

SECOND STREET PIKE, SOUTHAMPTON. Looking south from Street Road, this 1912 Sliker postcard shows Second Street Pike. The old tollhouse would be to the left, while on the right is the old harness shop. Both buildings shown on the right have recently been replaced by a new drugstore. With much fanfare, the harness shop was saved and moved to another site.

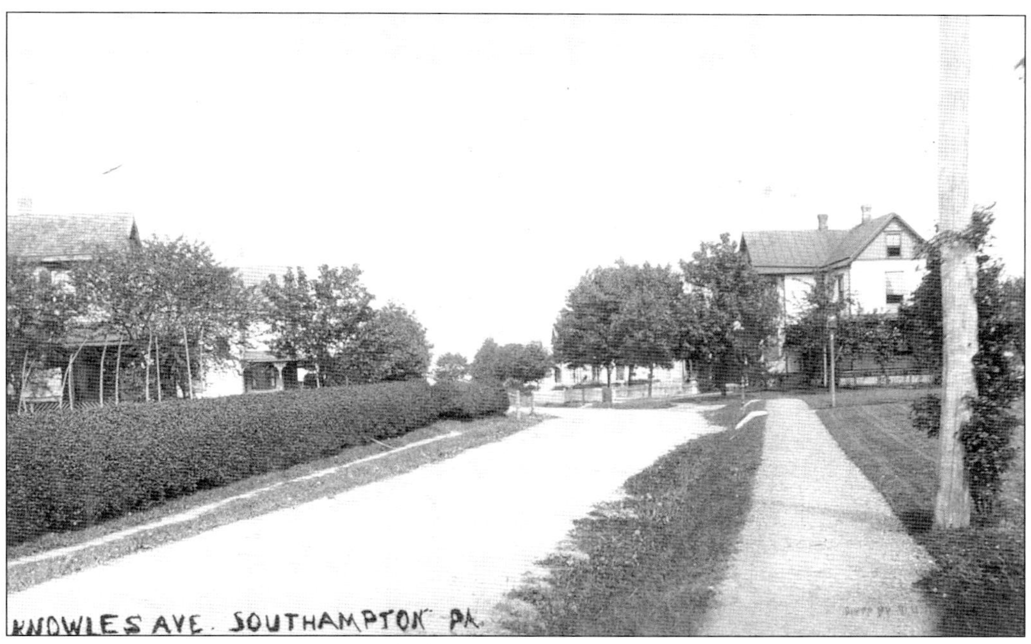

KNOWLES AVENUE, SOUTHAMPTON. Aside from Street Road and Second Street Pike, Southampton was large enough to have several small side streets with old houses. Knowles Avenue is one of these streets, and most homes shown here are still standing. This 1910 view looks north from above the Second Street Pike toward Street Road. (Sliker postcard.)

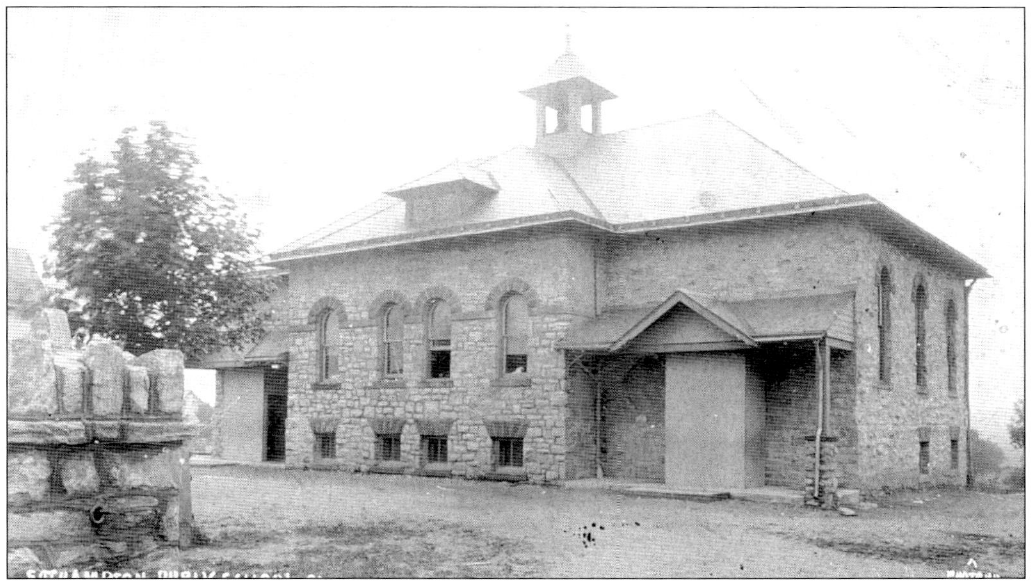

SOUTHAMPTON PUBLIC SCHOOL. The erection of this school in 1898 on Street Road in Southampton more or less replaced all one-room school facilities in Southampton Township. The school was used for many years and eventually gave way to bigger, more modern schools built in the area. Today, its stone facade can still be seen on Street Road. The building is now occupied by a credit union. (Sliker postcard.)

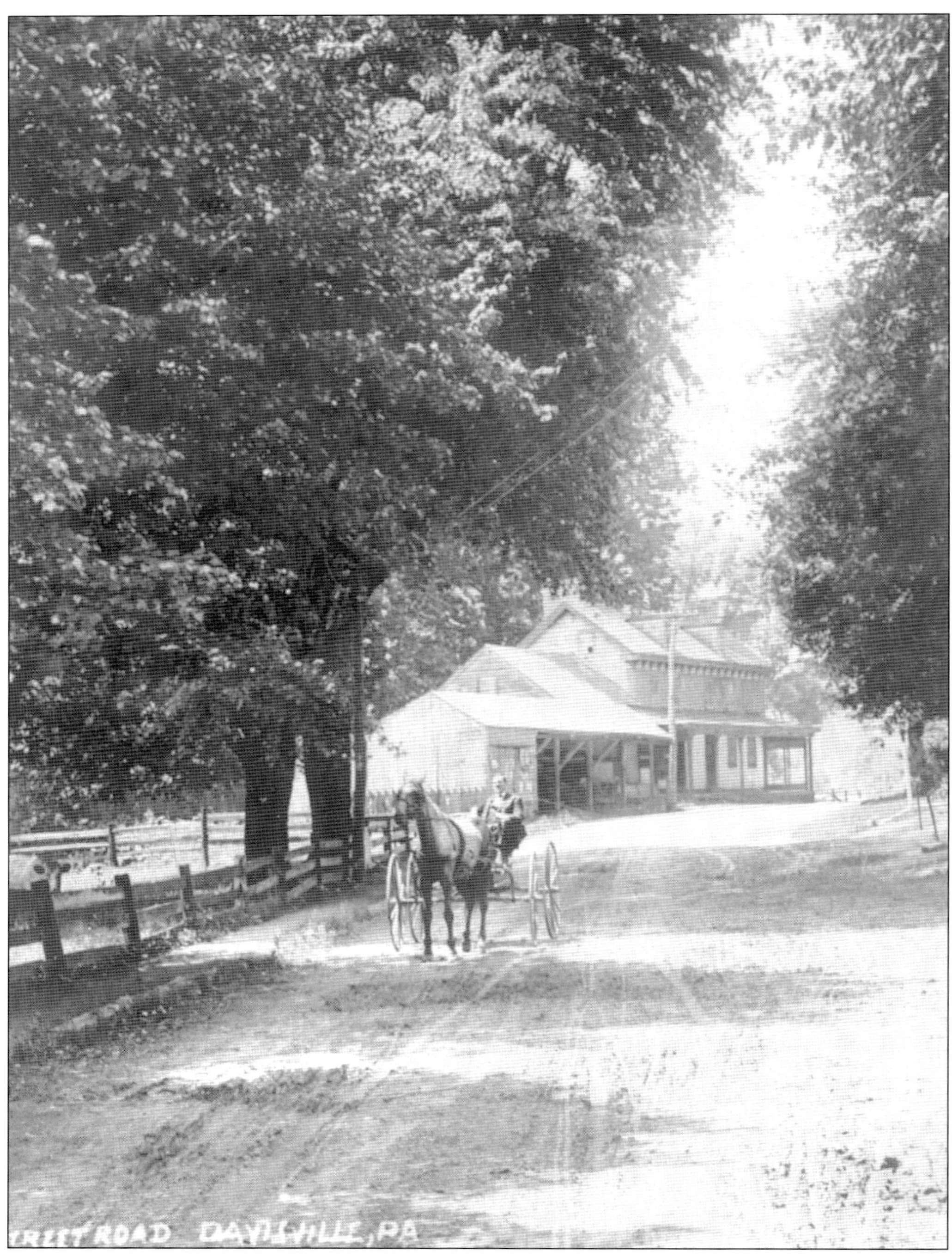

STREET ROAD, DAVISVILLE. The upper end of Street Road looked very rural in 1914, as seen here in Davisville. Looking west, this view shows the old Davis Mansion on Street Road at Davisville Road. The old mansion, built in 1827, was the home of Gen. John Davis, who became the village's first postmaster. The town was named after him. The old mansion was torn down when Street Road was widened. (Sliker postcard.)

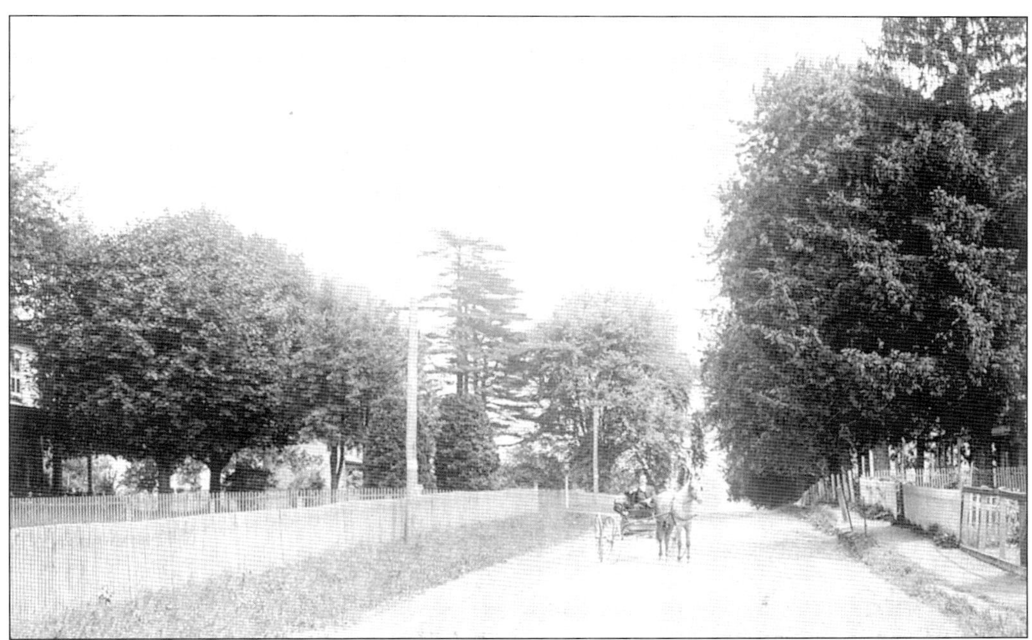

Street Road. In this *c.* 1910 view, a horse and carriage is all that is traveling on Street Road in Davisville. The once picturesque road was lined with old fences, large trees, and quaint buildings. Today, this has all been replaced by commercial development. (Sliker postcard.)

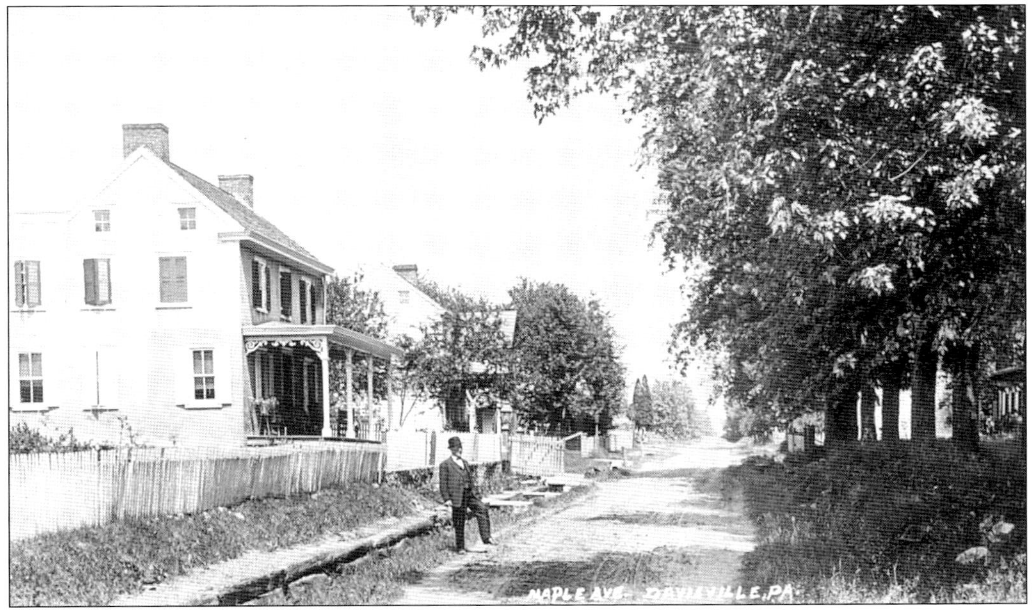

Maple Avenue, Davisville. Most of old Davisville along Street Road was demolished when the road was widened in the 1960s. However, Maple Avenue, a small side street off of Street Road, still contains all the old dwellings shown in this 1910 Sliker postcard. This is a nice glimpse of old Davisville.

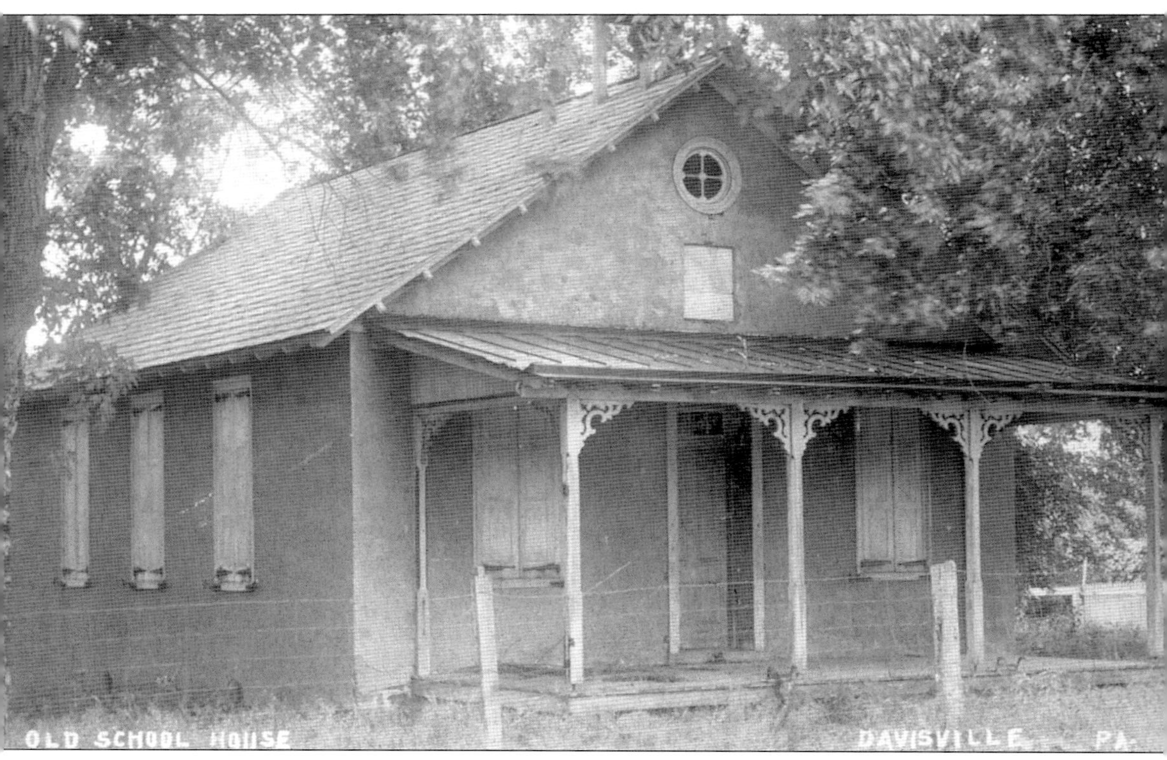

The Old School, Davisville. Constructed in 1843 as the Davisville Seminary for the education of children, regardless of religious background, this building eventually became a public school. The building is still standing on Street Road without its front porch and is a rare survivor of old Davisville. (Sliker postcard.)

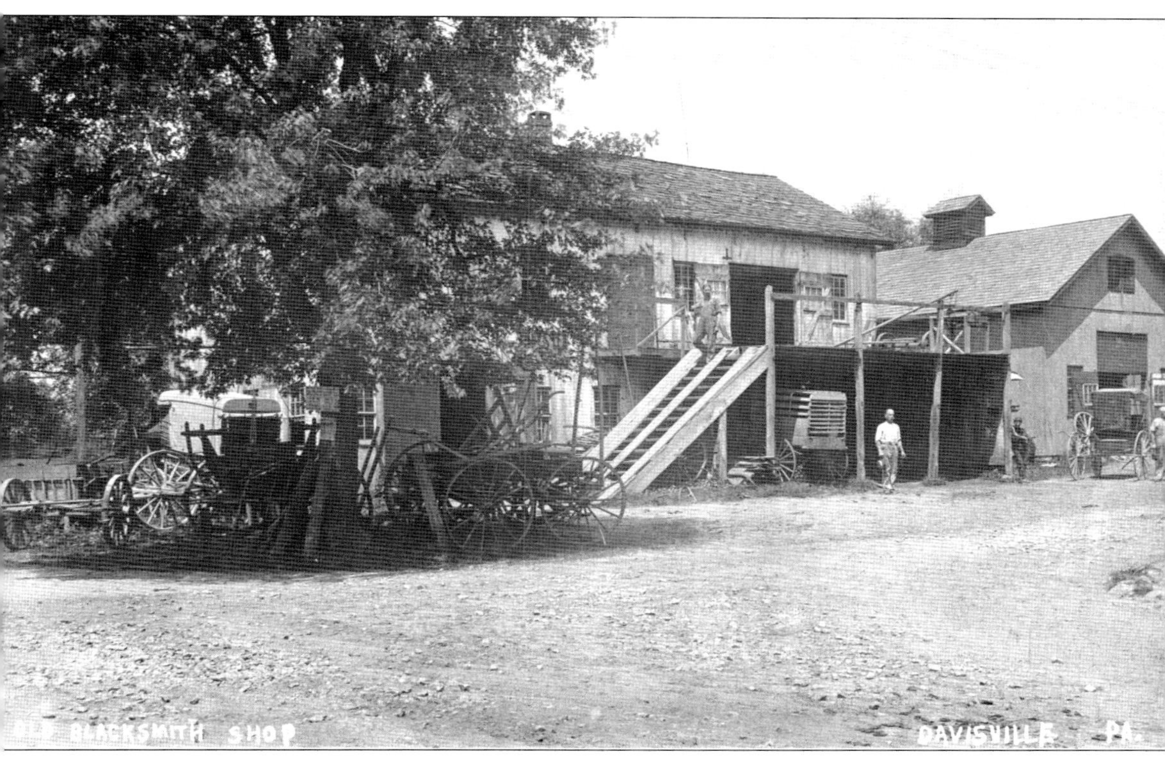

BLACKSMITH SHOP, DAVISVILLE. An important aspect of rural life in Bucks County was the village blacksmith. Blacksmiths provided a vital function to the people traveling by horse before the advent of the automobile. They would fit horseshoes and often repair carriages. This Sliker postcard shows some of the busy activity at the Davisville shop once located at the northwest corner of Street and Davisville Roads. The building is no longer standing.

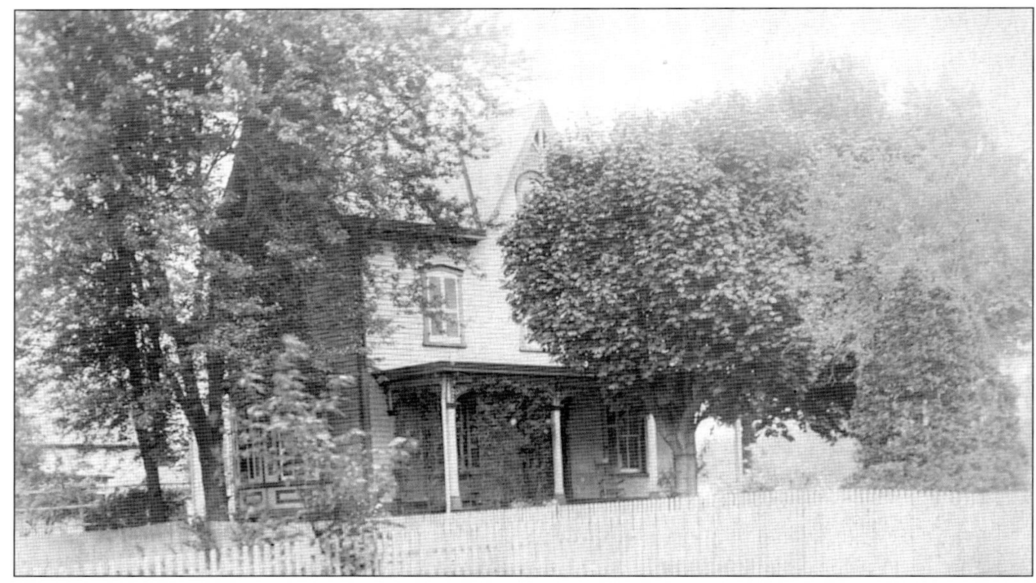

The Residence of A.M. Delany. The old Delany house was an attractive Victorian home complete with a wooden porch and curved windows. This house is typical of a village dwelling found throughout lower Bucks County. The home once stood on Street Road and is no longer standing. (Sliker postcard.)

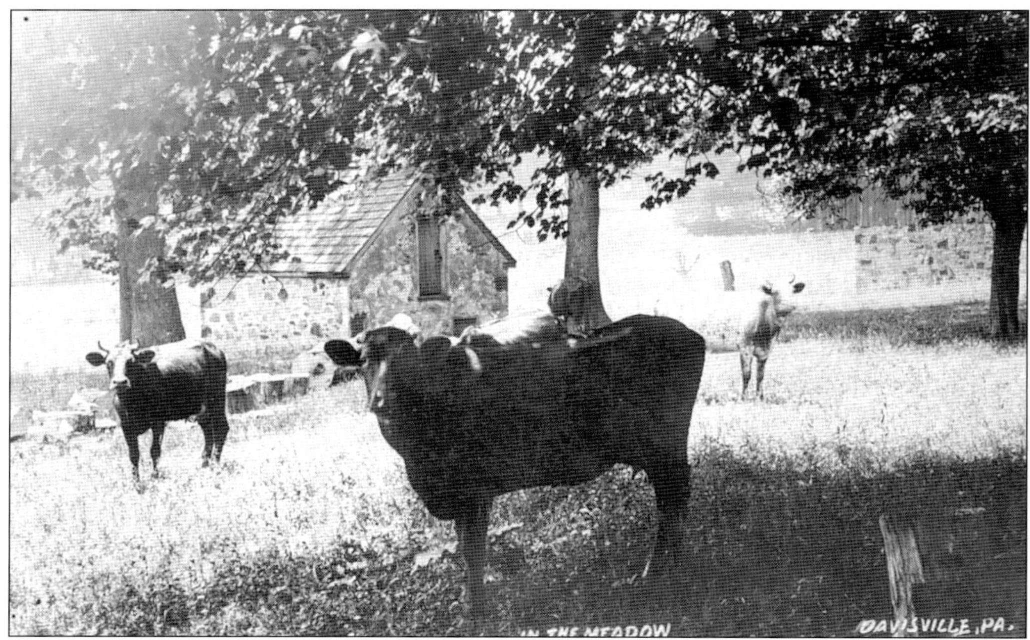

In the Meadow, Davisville. Beautiful country scenes dominated the lower Bucks County landscape in the early 1900s, as seen in this 1910 Sliker postcard of a farm on Street Road in Davisville.

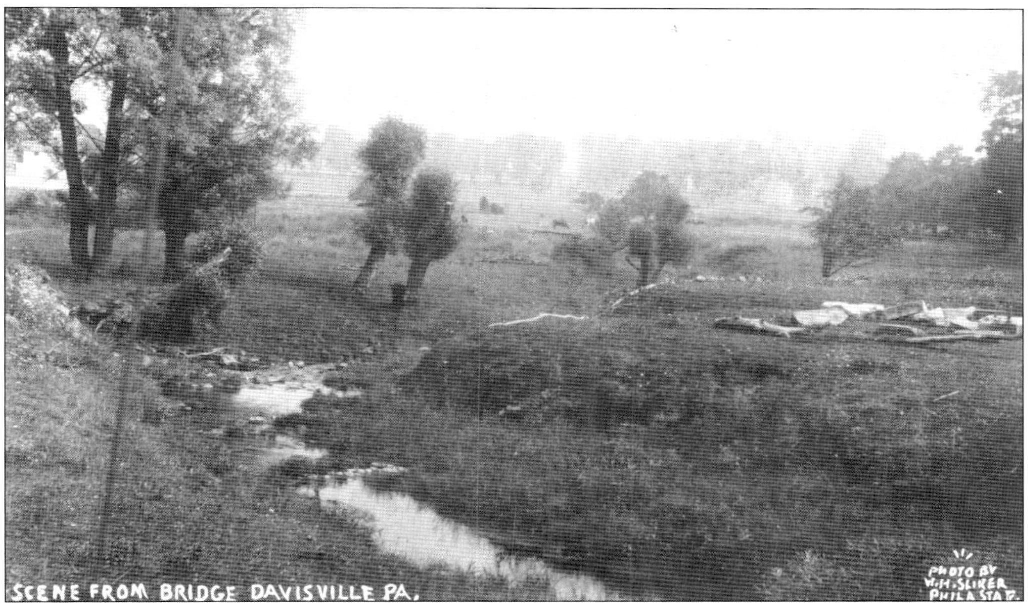

SCENE FROM A BRIDGE, DAVISVILLE. This *c.* 1910 view shows a beautiful, pastoral landscape with a small creek in Davisville. Today, this area is heavily developed with houses and shopping centers. (Sliker postcard.)

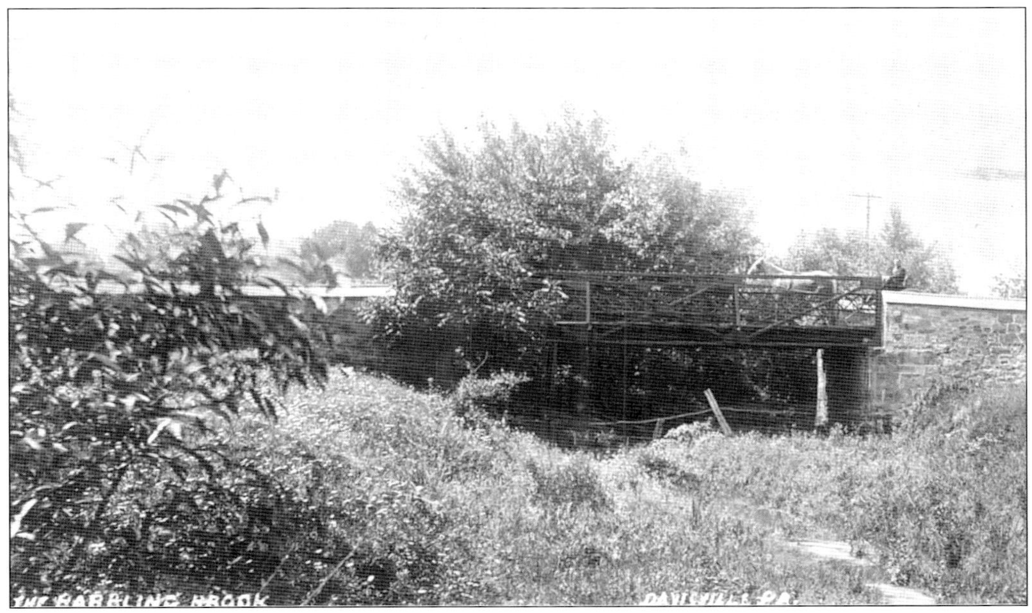

THE BABBLING BROOK, DAVISVILLE. Bucks County's natural features have attracted the attention of many people throughout the years. So it is no wonder that many old postcard images feature fields, trees, and creeks. This beautiful spot was near Davisville. Note the horse-drawn carriage on the bridge. (Sliker postcard.)

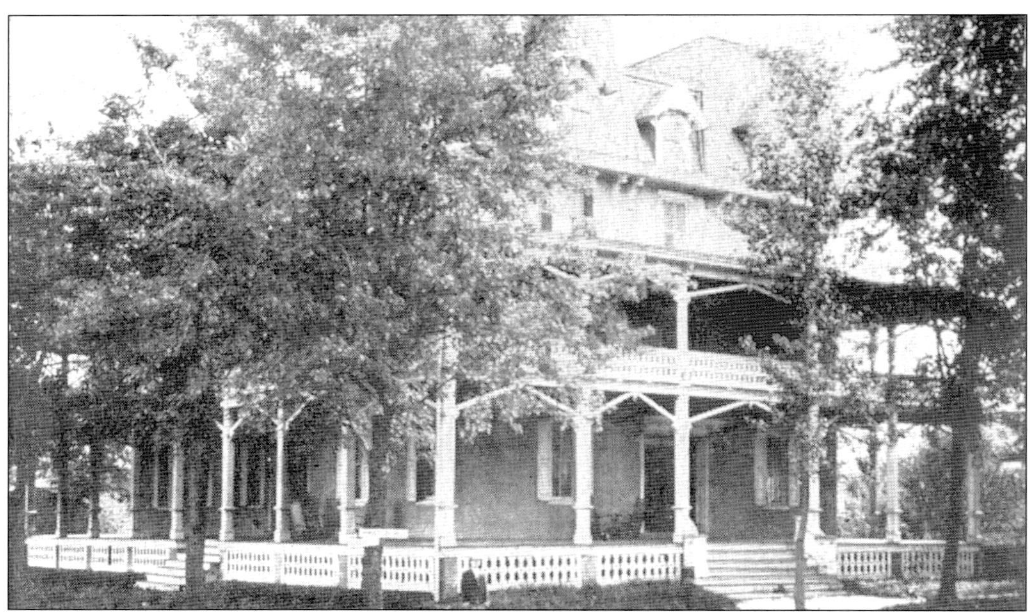

The Temperance Hotel, Ivyland. Ivyland Borough was incorporated in 1873. Its founder, Edwin Lacey, built this hotel in 1875. Lacey sold the hotel in 1879, and by 1895 John Davenport became the owner. At the time this Arnold Brothers postcard was made, it was the Davenport residence. Davenport owned the building until 1948. Today, the building on Gough Avenue still stands among many beautiful late Victorian homes.

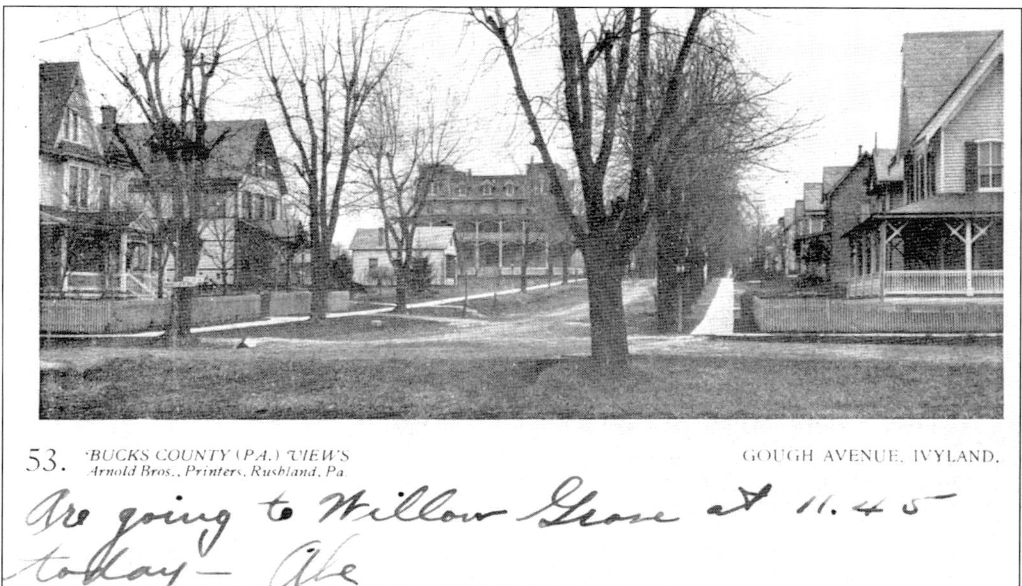

Gough Avenue, Ivyland. Lacey named the streets in Ivyland after local political figures. Gough Avenue was named after John B. Gough, a temperance speaker. Other streets include Lincoln, Wilson, and Chase. This 1907 view of Gough Avenue looking east from Greeley Avenue, shows the Temperance Hotel. Ivyland is the second smallest borough in the state of Pennsylvania. (Arnold Brothers postcard.)

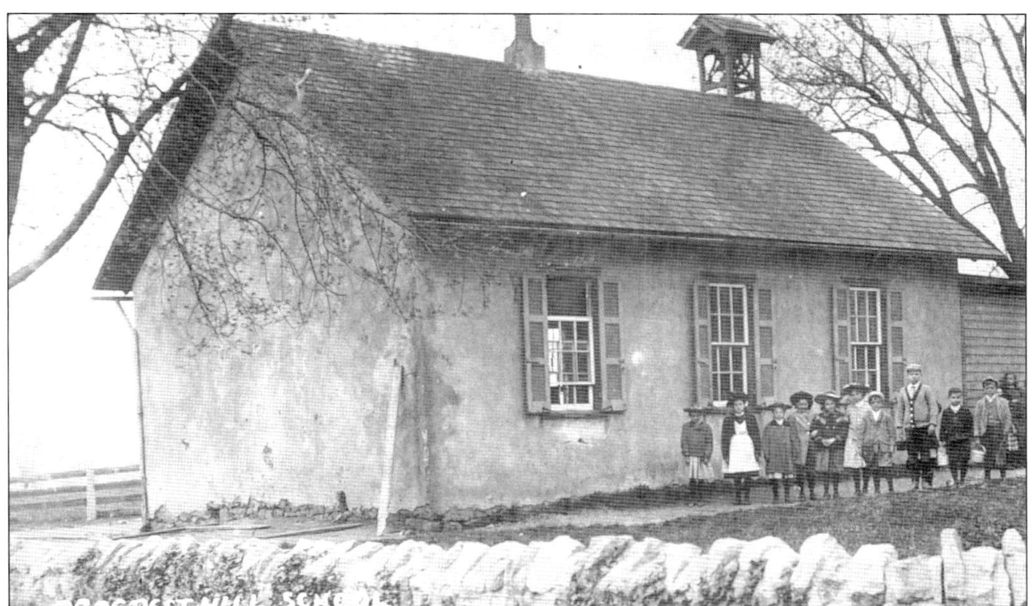

PROSPECT HILL SCHOOL, JOHNSVILLE. Another attractive one-room school was the Prospect Hill School, built in 1840 on Street Road at Centennial Road. This image shows the side and rear of the school with the students dressed with fancy hats and neat suits. The school is no longer standing. (Sliker postcard.)

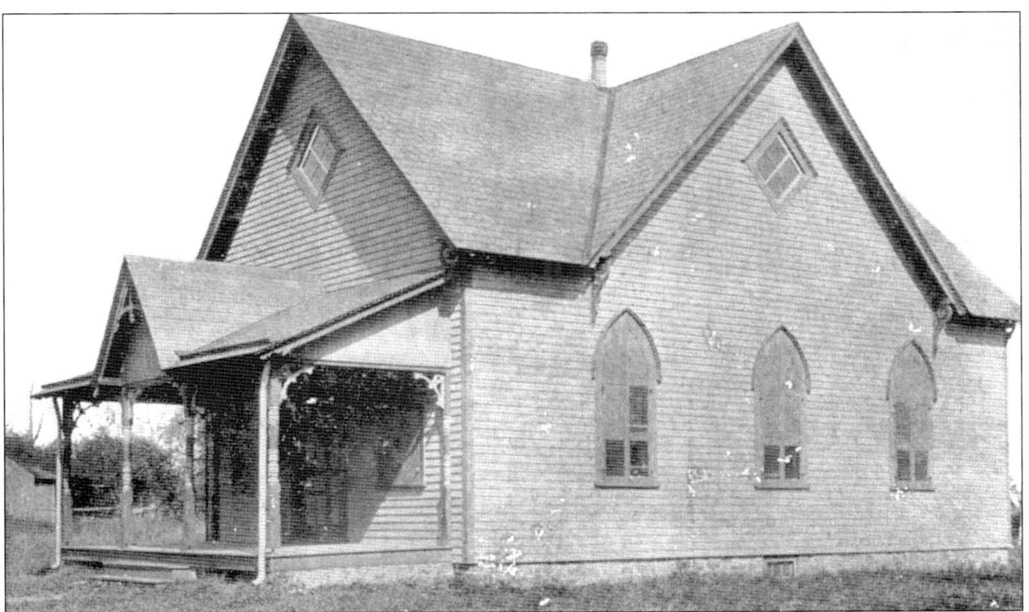

THE UNION CHAPEL, JOHNSVILLE. A rare survivor of the modern Street Road commercial area is the Union Chapel in the bygone village of Johnsville. The village was named after John Craven, whose family settled the area in the 1700s. Although no longer a chapel, the old country Gothic structure still stands at Newtown and Street Roads and currently houses a business. (Arnold Brothers postcard.)

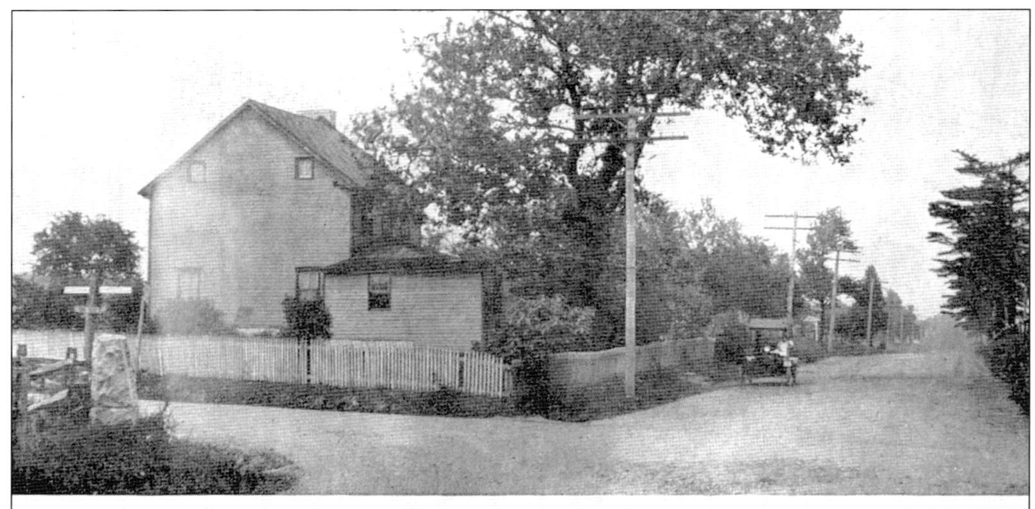

194. *BUCKS COUNTY (PA.) VIEWS.* *Chas. R. Arnold, Pub., Ivyland, Pa* CORNER YORK AND STREET ROADS, WARMINSTE Memorial to John Fitch, inventor of the steamboat, at the le

STREET AND YORK ROADS, WARMINSTER. Warminster Township was settled in the late 1600s and incorporated in 1711. At the intersection of Street and York Roads was the village of Warminster. It is not clear which direction this Arnold Brothers postcard is showing. On a late-1800s atlas, the only house shown at this crossroads was at the northwest corner, which would make this view looking north on York Road. If that is true, then the John Fitch monument would have been moved from the southwest corner (shown on the lower left) to its present location at the northeast corner.

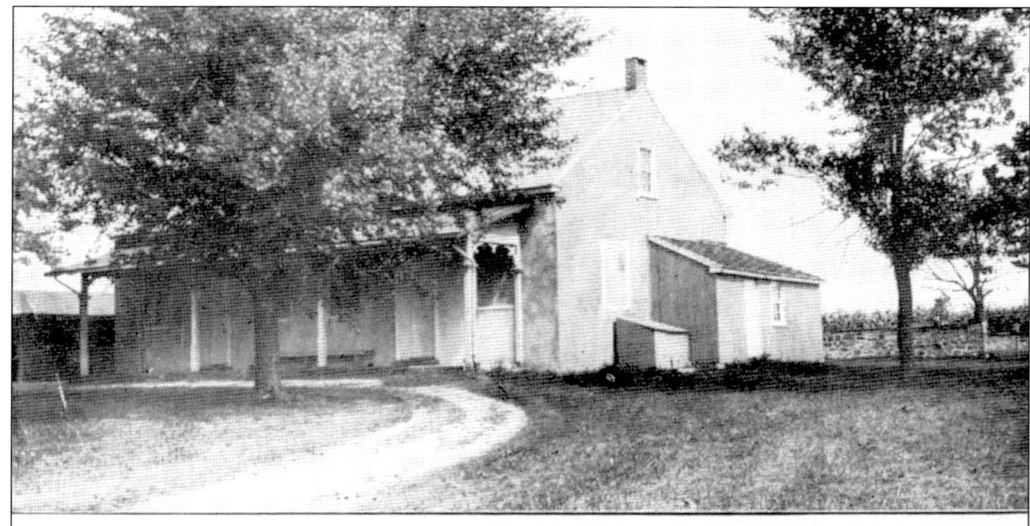

28 BUCKS COUNTY (PA.) VIEWS. Chas. R. Arnold, Pub., Ivyland, Pa WARMINSTER FRIENDS MEETING HOUS Erected 1842.

WARMINSTER FRIENDS MEETINGHOUSE. This Quaker meetinghouse was built in 1842 and was an outgrowth of the nearby Horsham Meeting. As the Warminster area became more suburban and the Quaker population decreased, this meeting closed. Today, the building on Street Road serves as another church. (Arnold Brothers postcard.)

Five

LANGHORNE AND MIDDLETOWN

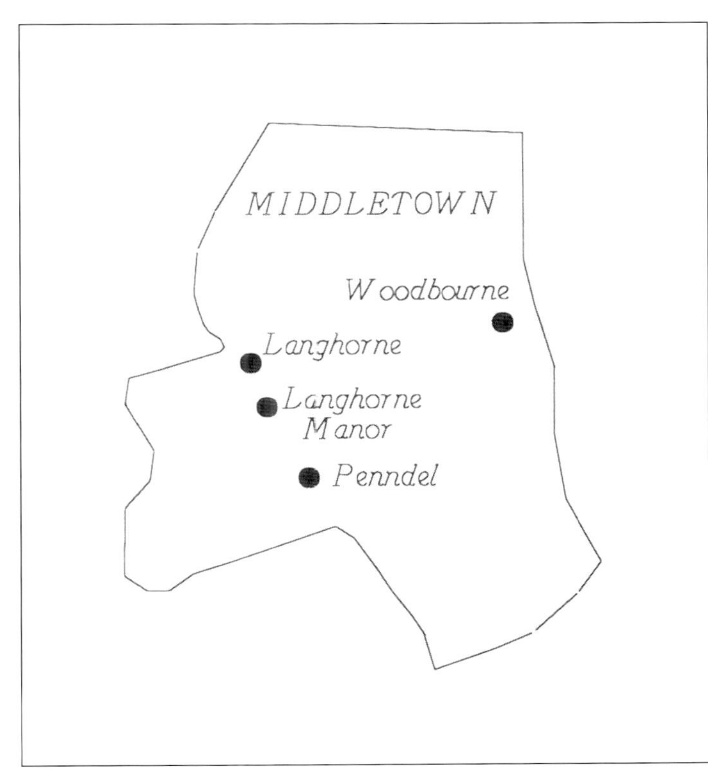

LANGHORNE AND MIDDLETOWN. In lower Bucks County, Middletown Township was the middle town, halfway between Bristol and Newtown. This area, along with Langhorne and Woodbourne, is represented in this chapter.

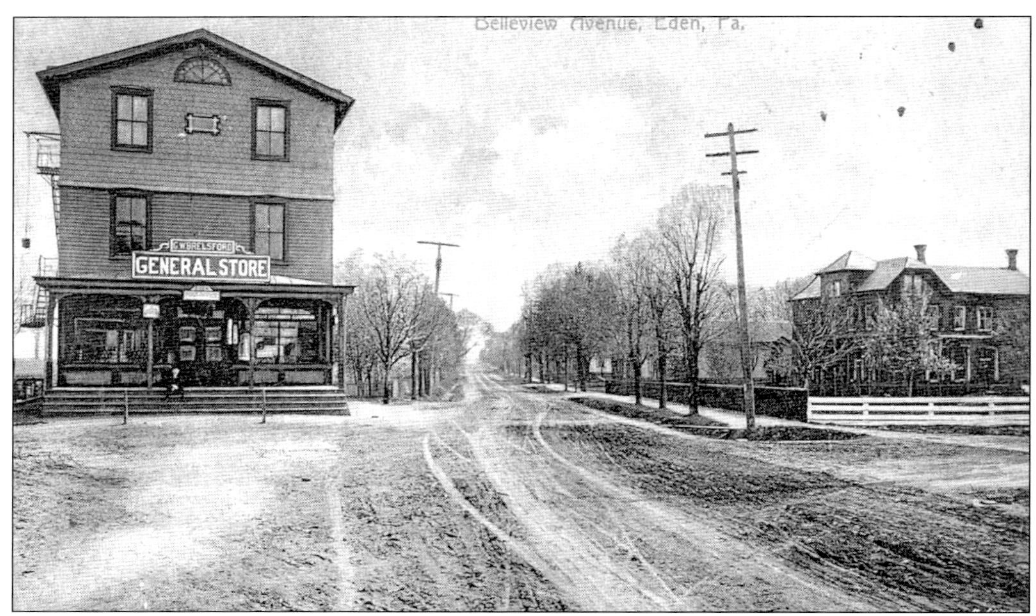

Bellevue Avenue, Eden. Eden may not be a familiar place to Bucks County residents since its name was replaced by Penndel in 1948. Prior to that, the name Eden was in conflict with another place bearing the same name in Lancaster County. Looking south with Bellevue Avenue in the center, this 1911 view shows the general store. Durham Road bears to the left of the store. The building now houses a bar.

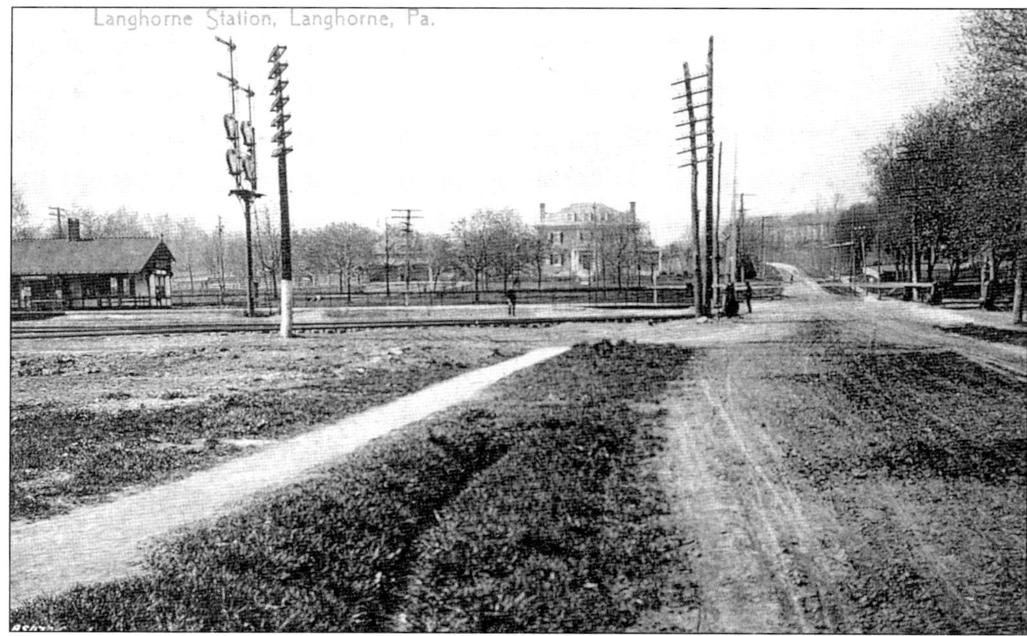

Langhorne Station. Bellevue Avenue is a lonely dirt road in this 1909 view looking north. Langhorne Station is still used today, although its appearance has changed and a smaller building now occupies this site. (J.K. Streeper postcard.)

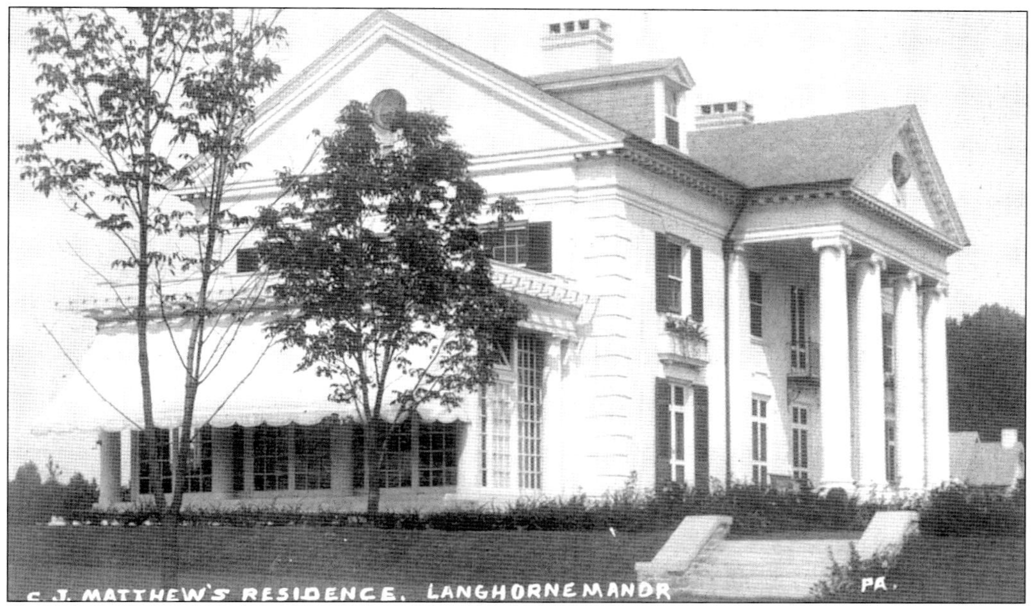

C.J. MATTHEWS RESIDENCE, LANGHORNE MANOR. Langhorne Manor is a quiet borough of homes incorporated in 1890. Most of the homes are quite large and are late Victorian, or in the case of the Matthews residence, Classical Revival in architectural style. (Sliker postcard.)

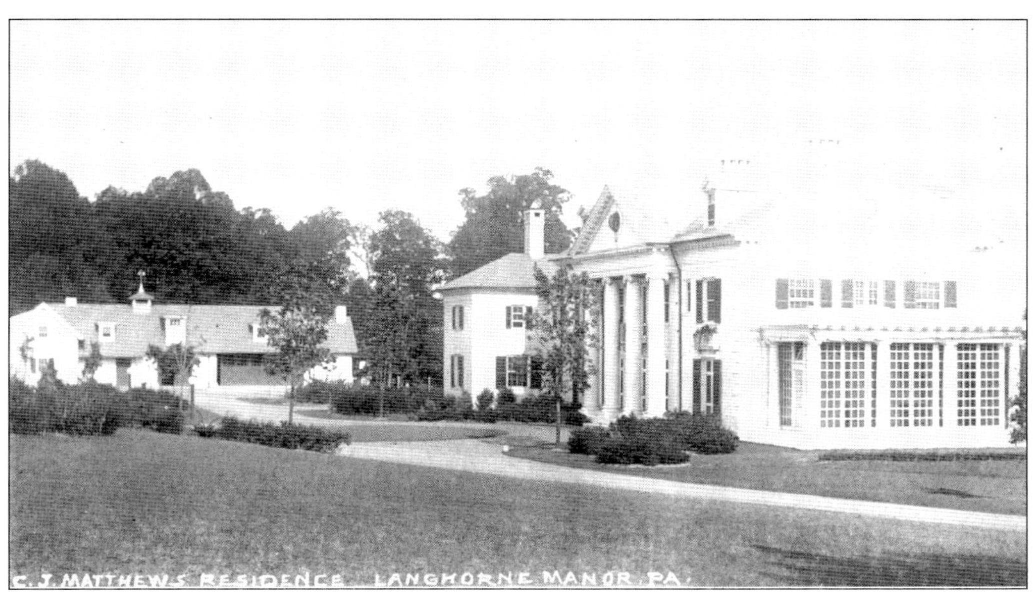

C.J. MATTHEWS RESIDENCE. This residence on Prospect Avenue has been beautifully maintained. The stable building shown to the left of the house has been converted to a private residence. (Sliker postcard.)

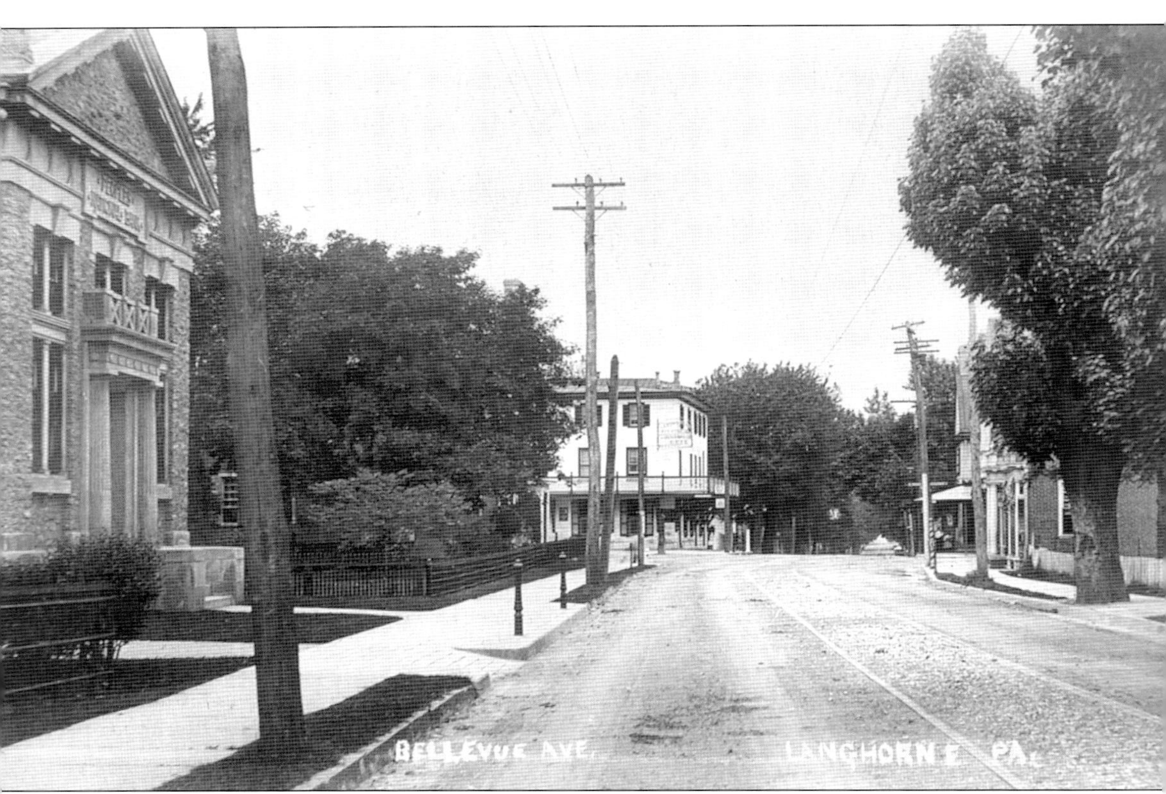

Bellevue Avenue, Langhorne. Langhorne was incorporated as a borough in 1874, although many of its buildings date from the 1700s, when it was known as Four Lanes End. Bellevue Avenue was the main north-south street in town. This 1910 view looks north toward Maple Avenue with the Peoples National Bank on the left and the Langhorne Hotel in the distance. (Hay Photo Postcard Company.)

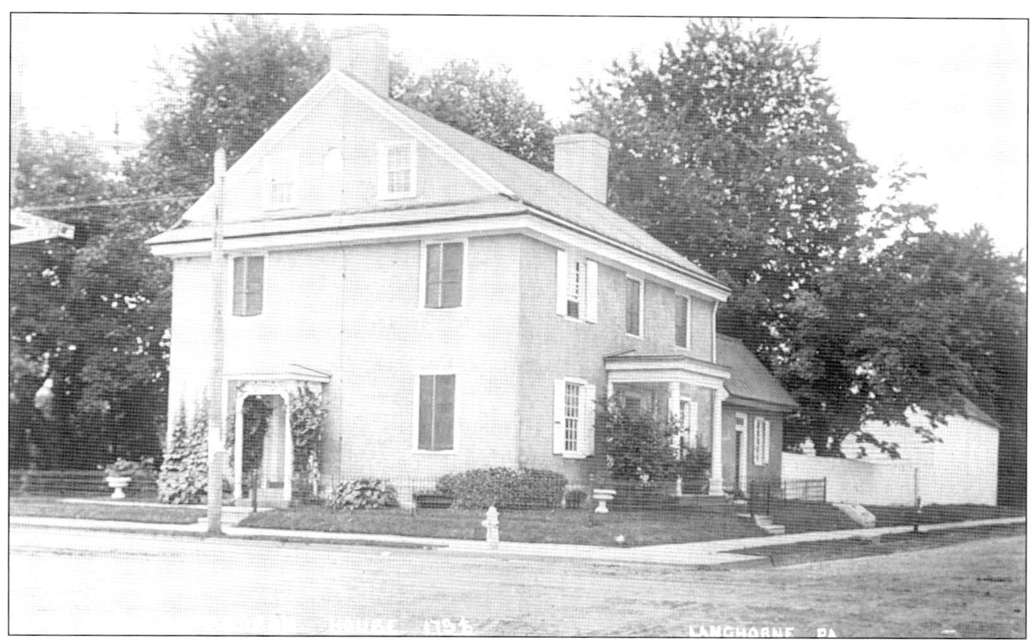

RICHARDSON HOUSE, LANGHORNE. At the corner of Maple and Bellevue Avenues stands the Richardson House, built in 1738. The Richardsons, an old Langhorne family, occupied this house until 1919. Since then, it has been owned by the Langhorne Community Association. (Hay Photo Postcard Company.)

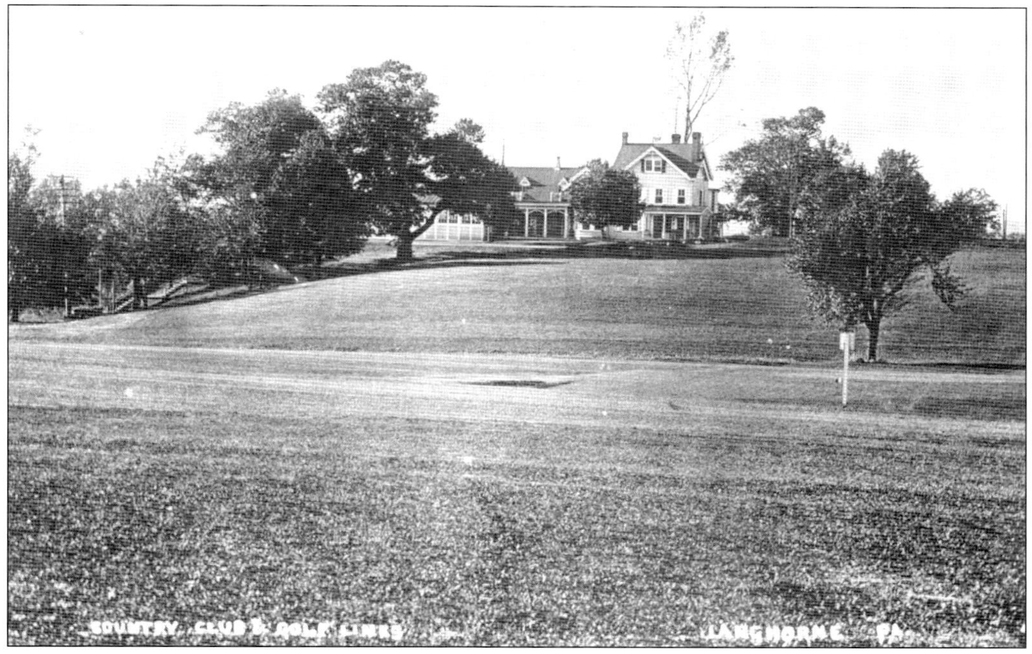

COUNTRY CLUB AND GOLF LINKS, LANGHORNE. The golf and country club in Langhorne was founded in 1901, making it the oldest institution of its kind in lower Bucks County. This 1910 view shows the beautiful golf course, which is still in use. (Hay Photo Postcard Company.)

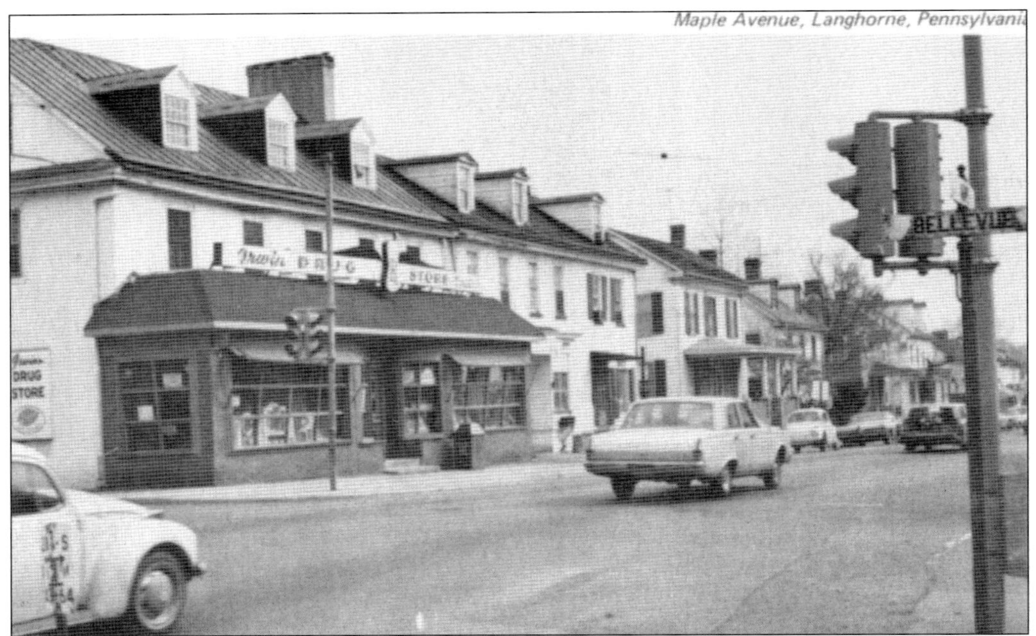

MAPLE AVENUE, LANGHORNE. This early-1970s view shows Maple Avenue, the main east-west thoroughfare through Langhorne. All buildings shown here are still standing, although the businesses have changed. (Merrimack Postcard.)

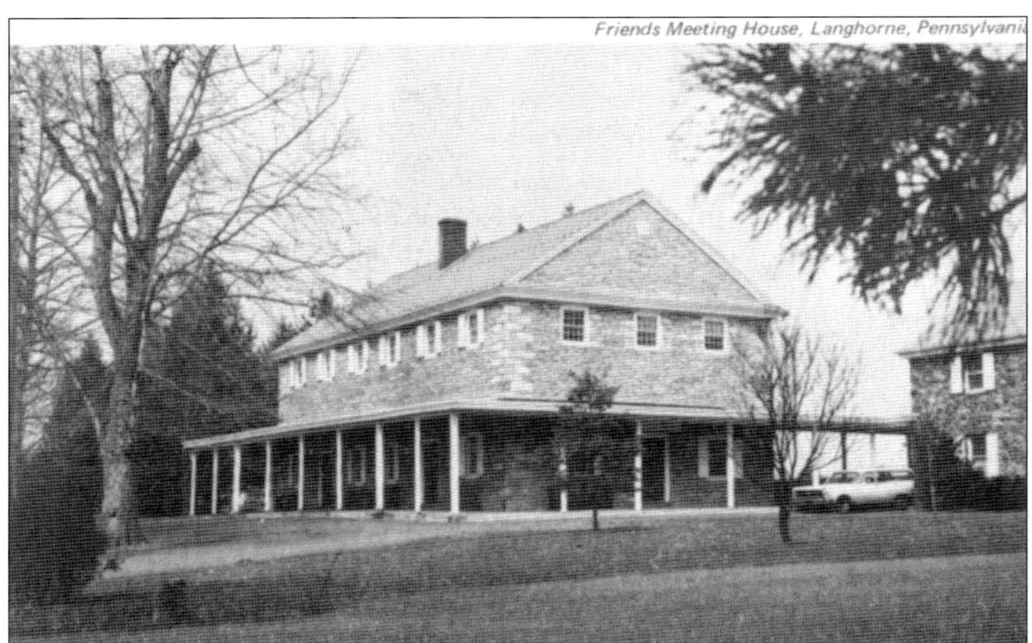

FRIENDS MEETINGHOUSE, LANGHORNE. The official name of this building is the Middletown Friends Meetinghouse. It is one of the oldest Quaker meetings in Bucks County, tracing its roots to 1683, although the present structure on West Maple Avenue dates to 1793. (Merrimack postcard.)

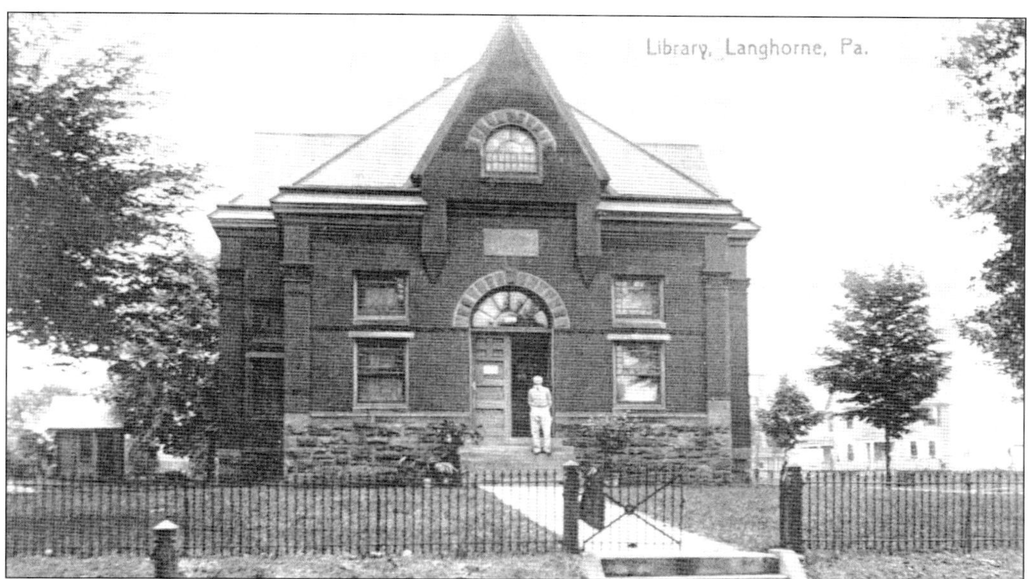

The Library. Built in 1888 at Maple and Hill Avenues, the Langhorne Library dates to 1802 when it was called the Attleborough Library Company. In the 1970s, the Pennwood Library was built to serve the community on Pine Street. Today, this building serves as a research facility for the Historic Langhorne Association. (J.K. Streeper postcard.)

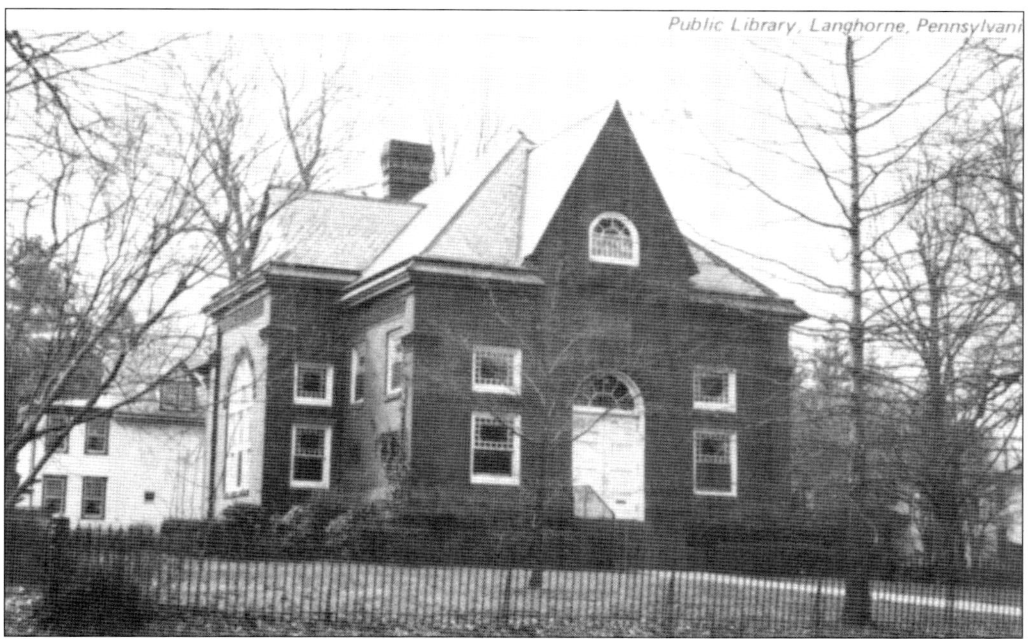

The Library, Langhorne. Not much has changed at the old library building as compared to this view taken almost 70 years after the image above. In fact, many Langhorne buildings have changed very little over the past century, making the borough one of the best-preserved historic districts in lower Bucks County. This view from the early 1970s was taken a few years prior to the removal of the library to its new branch. (Merrimack postcard.)

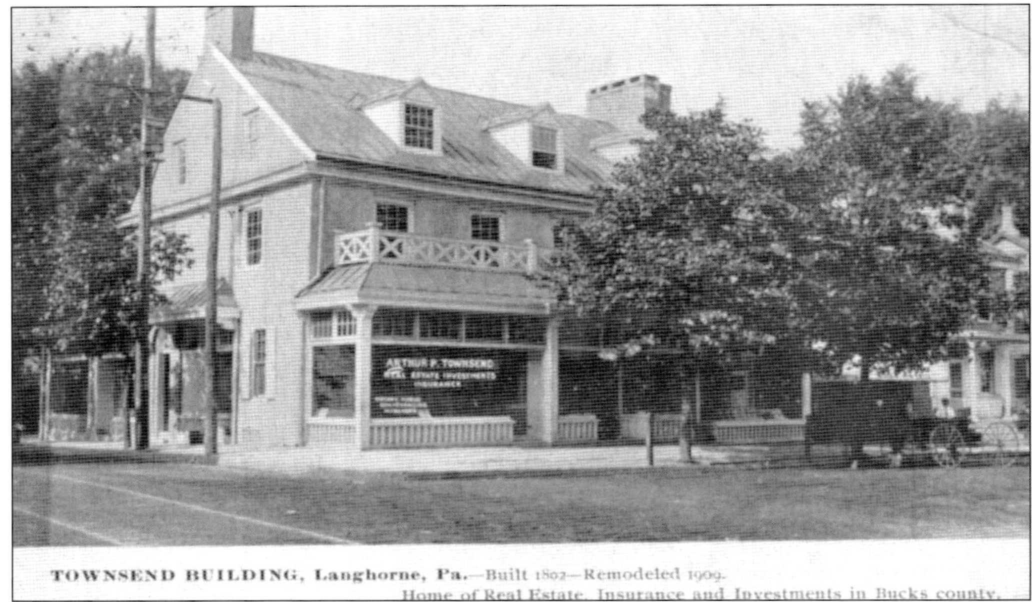

The Townsend Building, Langhorne. The Townsend building, located at the northeast corner of Bellevue and Maple Avenues, was built in 1802. This postcard shows the building a year after its 1909 remodeling. Arthur P. Townsend was a very prominent real estate broker and businessman in the early 1900s. The building was remodeled for his business. Today the structure is subdivided into smaller shops and offices.

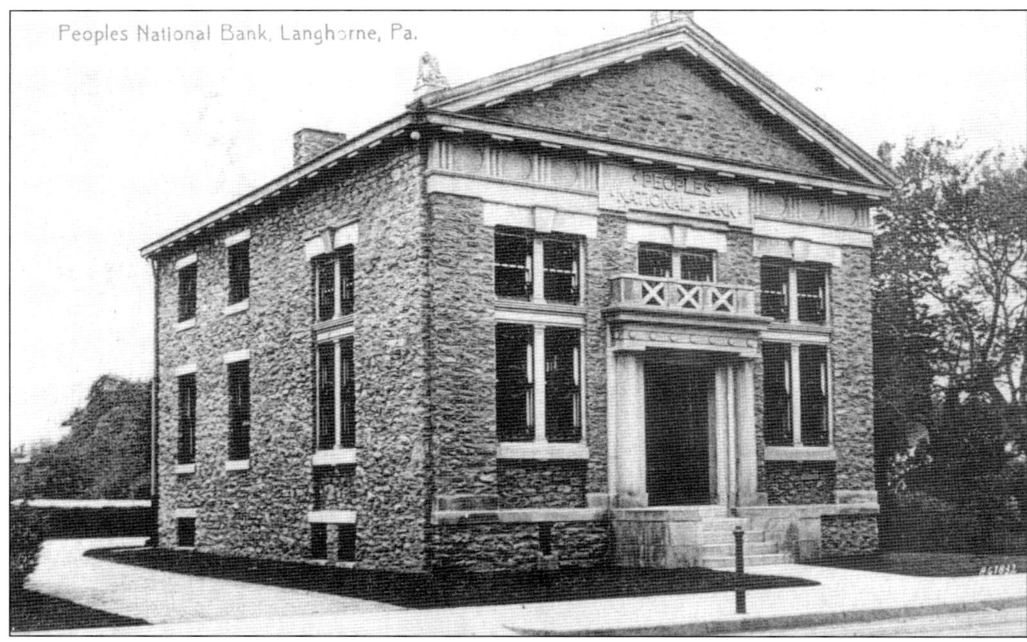

Peoples National Bank, Langhorne. This handsome bank building was built in 1901 on South Bellevue Avenue. The bank closed years ago, and the building was remodeled into another business. Unfortunately, the classic front facade has been completely obscured. (J.K. Streeper postcard.)

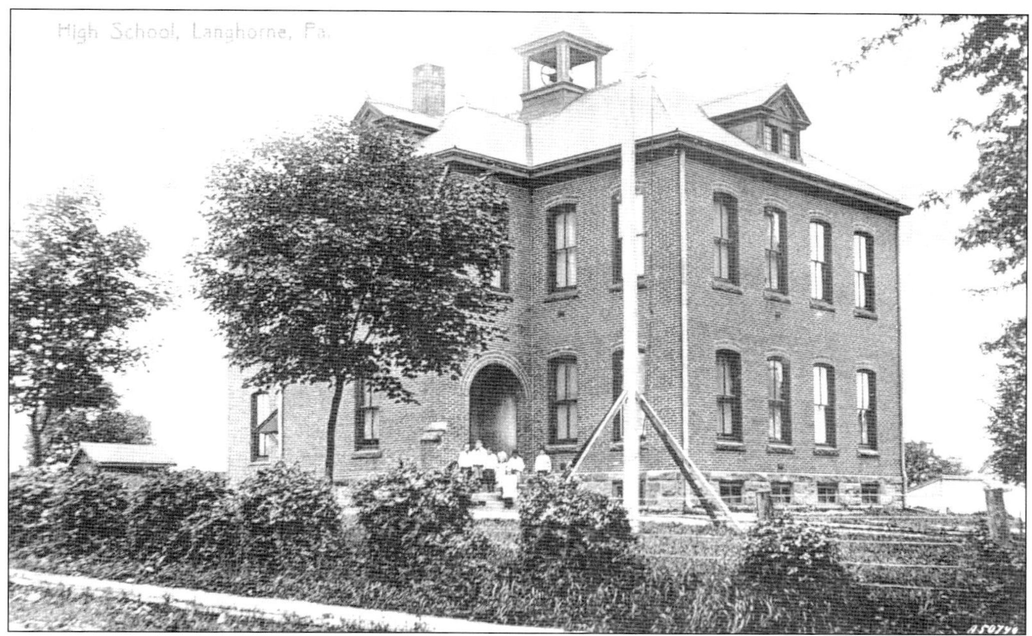

The High School, Langhorne. This was the public school in Langhorne from the late 1800s to 1965. Located at Pine Street and Maple Avenue, it is typical schoolhouse architecture from the late 1800s. (J.K. Streeper postcard.)

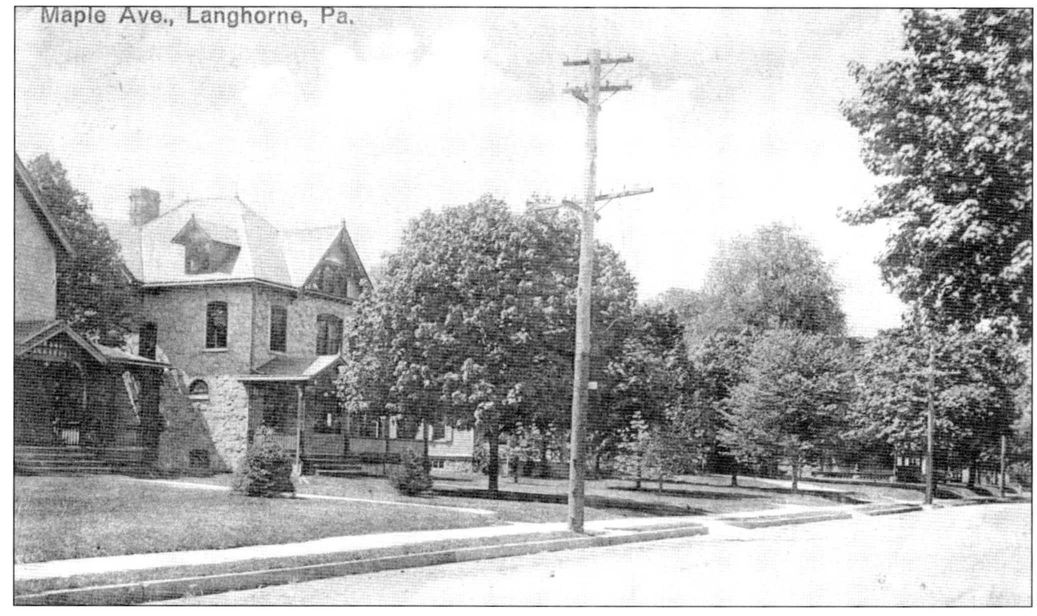

Maple Avenue, Langhorne. This 1914 view shows the beautiful residential area on Langhorne's Maple Avenue. Most old homes in Langhorne are well cared-for by the local citizens.

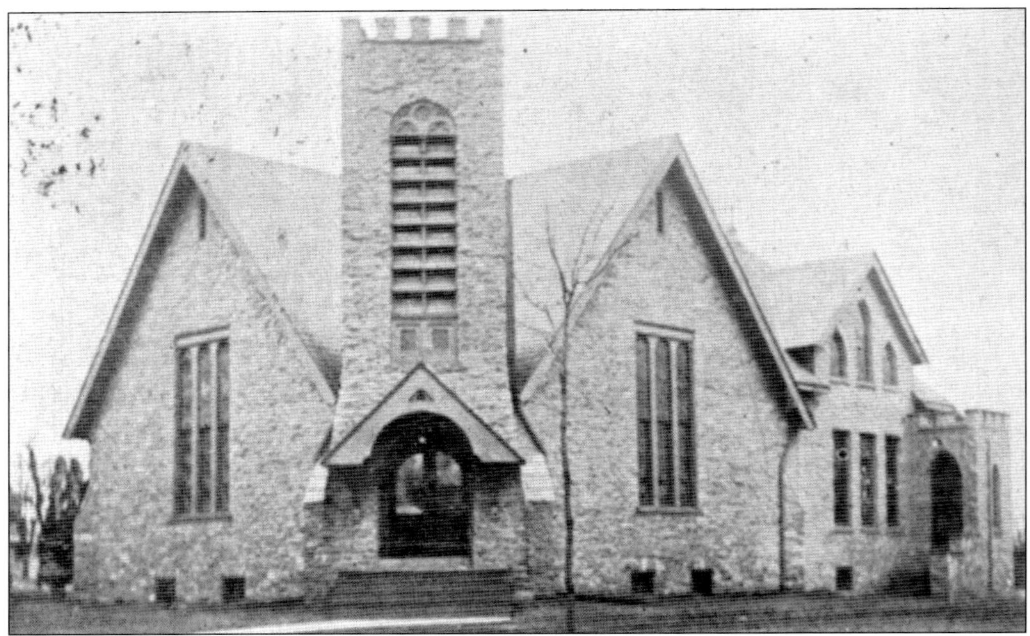

The Presbyterian Church, Langhorne. The Langhorne Presbyterian Church was originally built in 1892 at Bellevue and Gilliam Avenues. It is a good example of late-19th-century church architecture in Bucks County. Made of local stone, the building has many interesting windows and rooflines. This view shows the original building. Changes were made to the building in the early 1900s, and there have been recent additions and alterations.

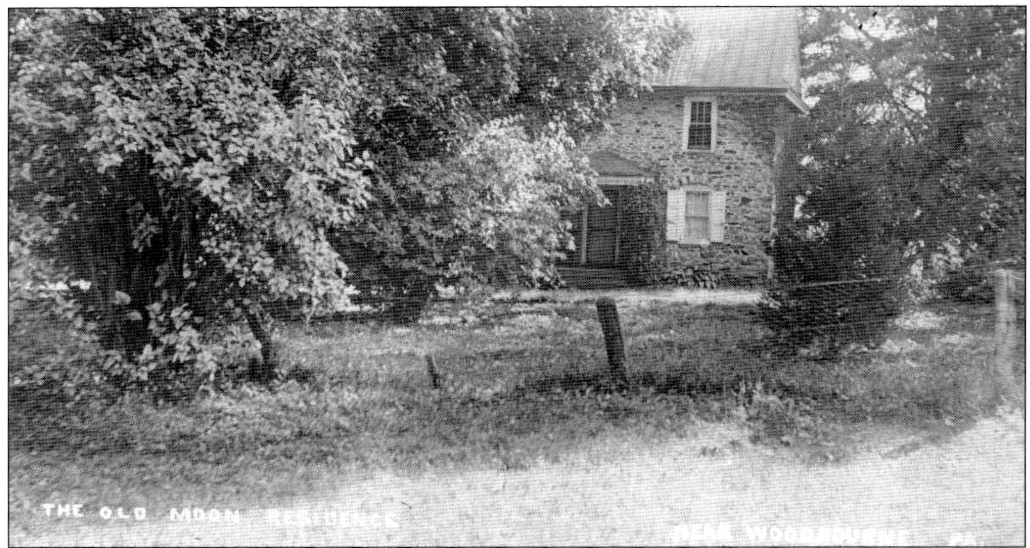

The Old Moon Residence, Woodbourne. The village of Woodbourne was along Woodbourne Road near the Woodbourne Station in Middletown Township. Unfortunately, U.S. Route 1 and Interstate 95 were built directly through Woodbourne, and almost all the dwellings, including the Moon residence, were demolished. The Moons were an old Quaker family from Middletown and Falls. This house was built in 1757 and demolished in 1967.

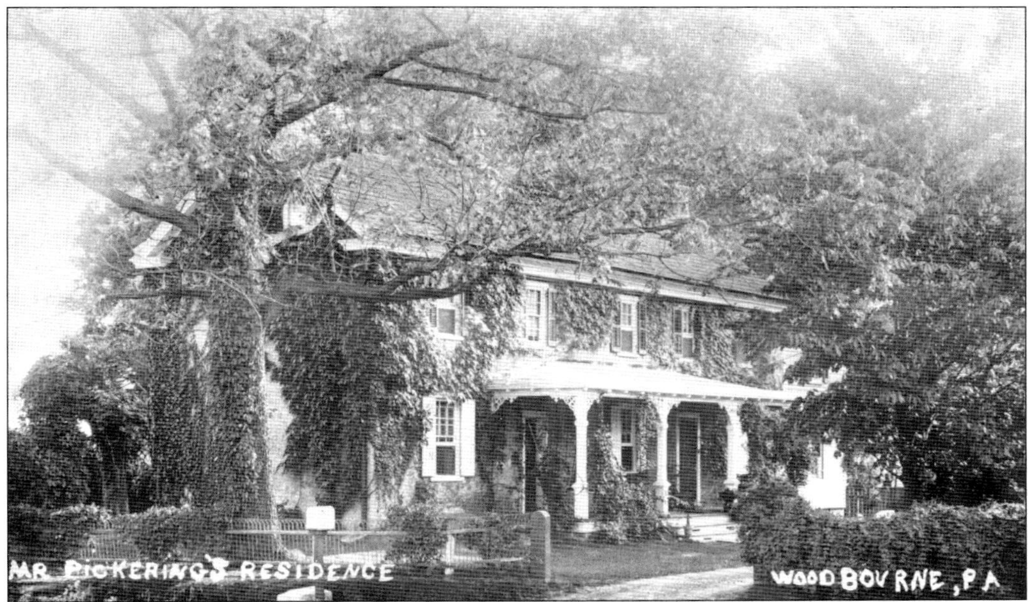

Mr. Pickering's Residence, Woodbourne. This picturesque old farmhouse, with its beautiful trees and lovely wrought-iron fence, stood along the west side of Woodbourne Road near Interstate 95. In the late 20th century, the house was boarded up and abandoned. It was later demolished to make way for a new housing development that includes "Pickering" for one of its street names.

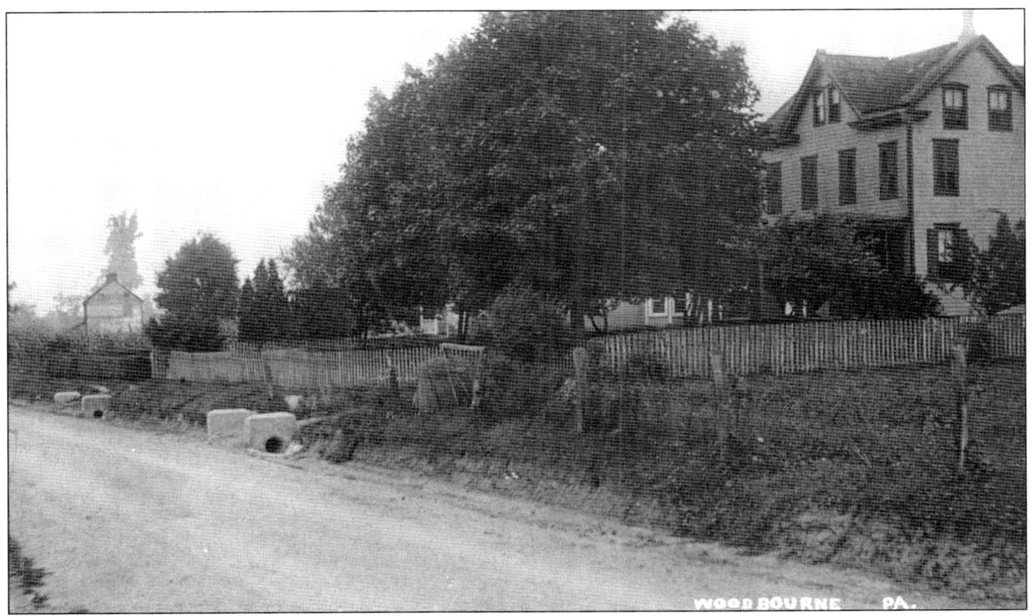

Woodbourne. This postcard was mailed from the Woodbourne Post Office in 1908 and shows a peaceful country scene along Woodbourne Road. Before the shopping malls and the expressways, this is what rural Middletown Township looked like.

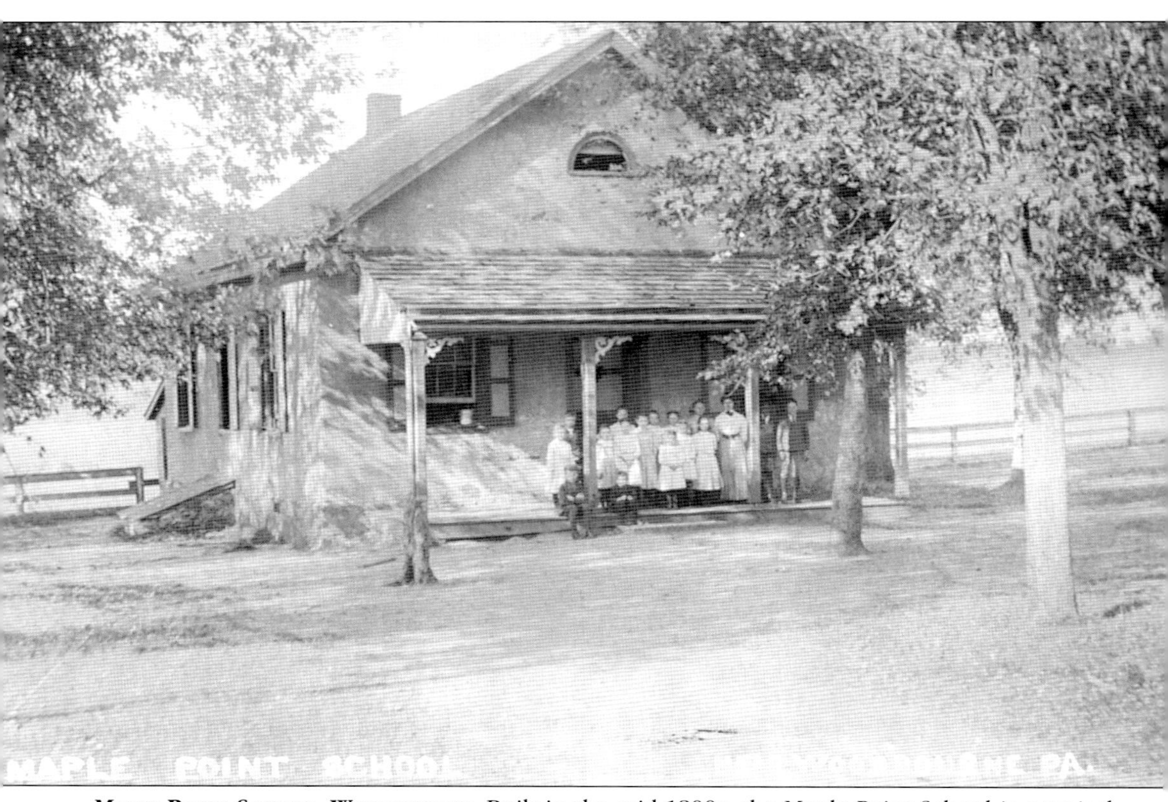

Maple Point School, Woodbourne. Built in the mid-1800s, the Maple Point School is a typical one-room country school built in Bucks County. As seen in most postcard views of schools, the children are neatly posed for the photograph. Today the old school is a private residence at the northwest corner of Woodbourne and Langhorne-Yardley Roads in Middletown Township. (Hay Photo Postcard Company.)

Six

Northampton, Newtown, and Yardley

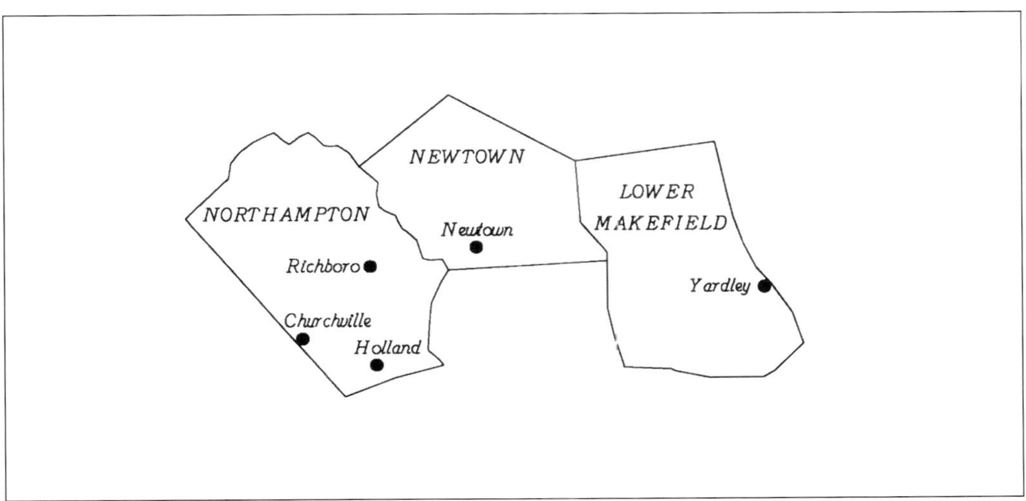

Northampton, Newtown, and Yardley. Detailed in this chapter are the northern sections of lower Bucks County. Places depicted include Newtown and Yardley Boroughs, Churchville, Holland, and Richboro.

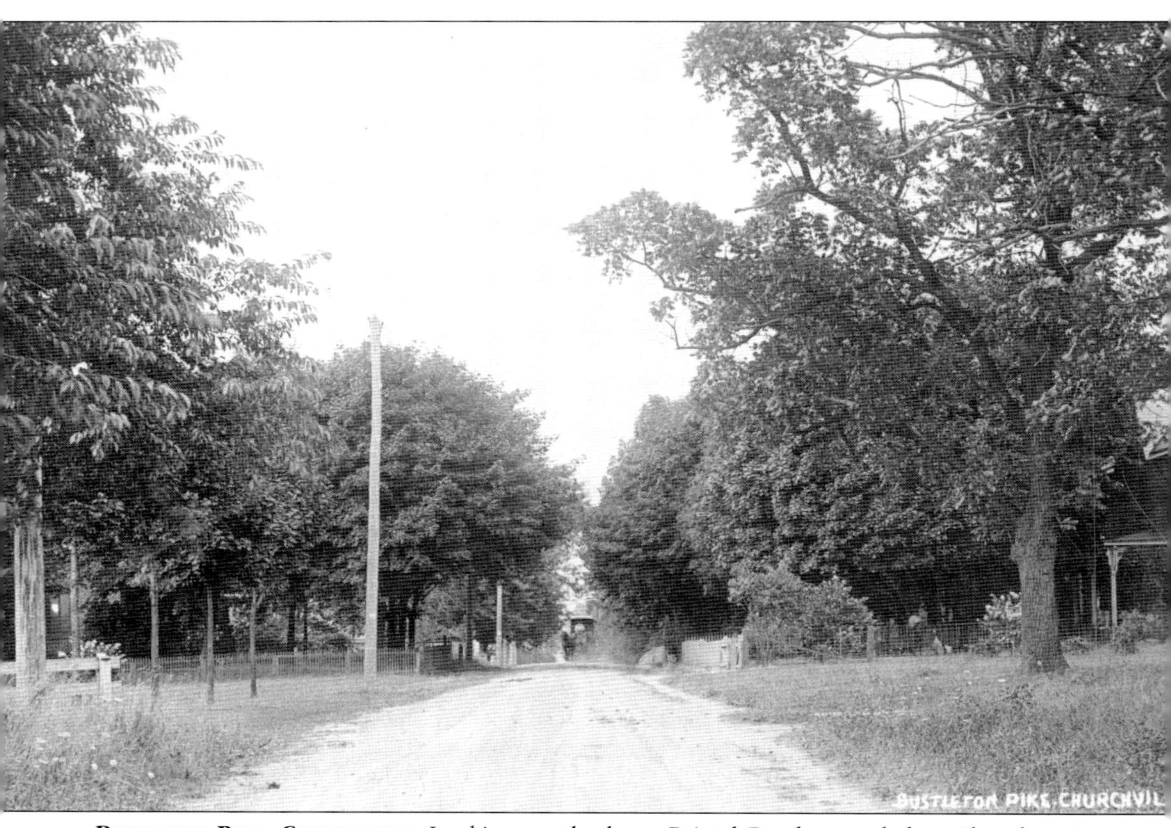

Bustleton Pike, Churchville. Looking north above Bristol Road toward the railroad station, this William Sliker postcard shows Bustleton Pike. It is difficult to imagine that our major thoroughfares of today were once tranquil dirt roads. Street views like this one provide excellent insight into how Bucks County has changed over the past 100 years.

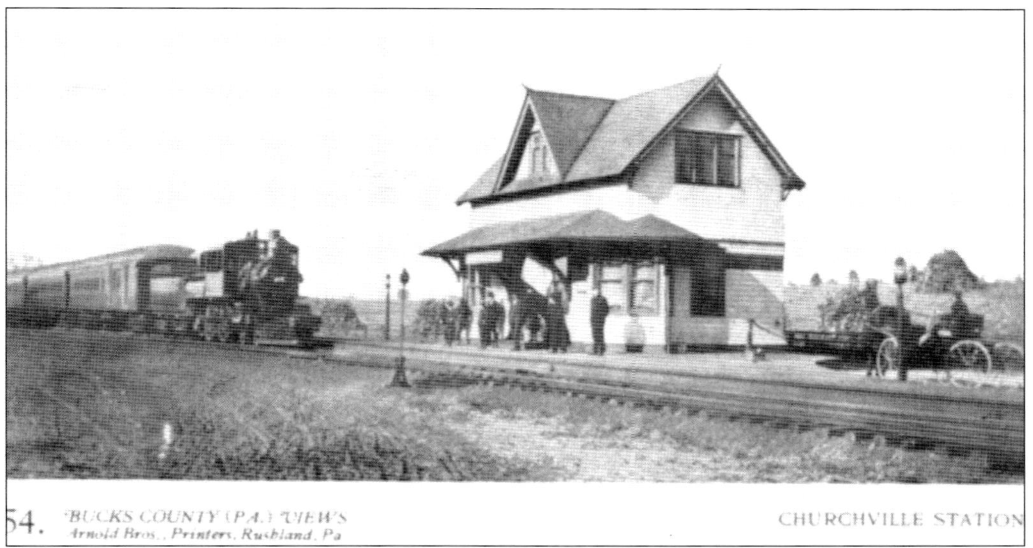

Churchville Station. Much of the old village of Churchville still remains. Various homes from the 1700s to 1900s, the old store, school, and this train station all are standing among a number of new buildings. Churchville Station was built in 1892. (Arnold Brothers postcard.)

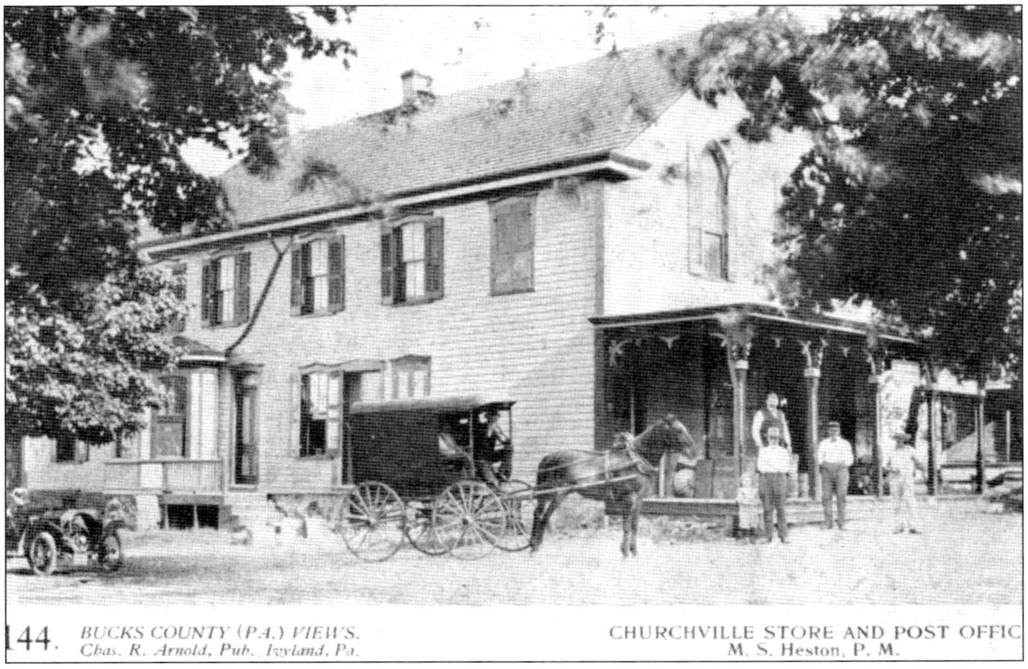

Churchville Store and Post Office. The Churchville General Store was built in 1883 on Bustleton Pike at the railroad crossing. Today, the building houses a grocery store. (Arnold Brothers postcard.)

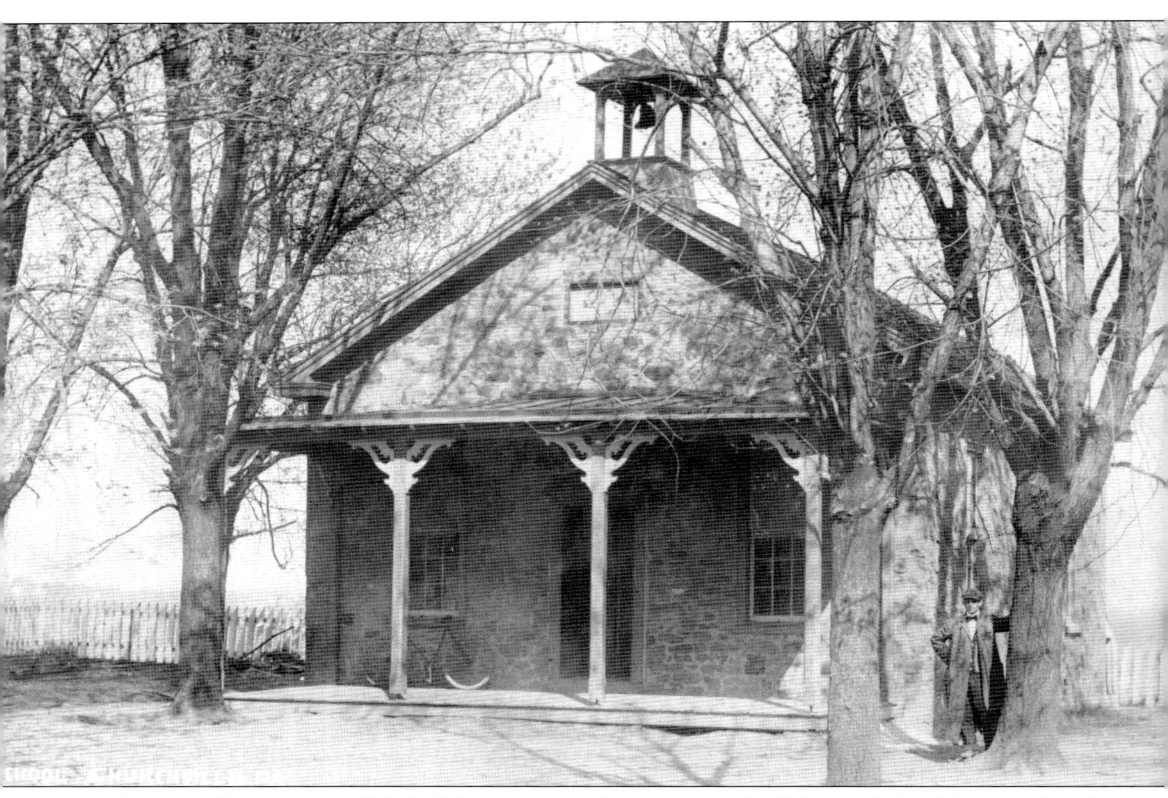

A School, Churchville. This building, commonly known as the Fairview School, is typical of the beautiful stone, one-room schoolhouses. Note the fancy wood trim on the porch and the old school bell and belfry. Built in 1868, it ceased functioning in 1928 and is now remodeled into a private residence on Bustleton Pike. (Sliker postcard.)

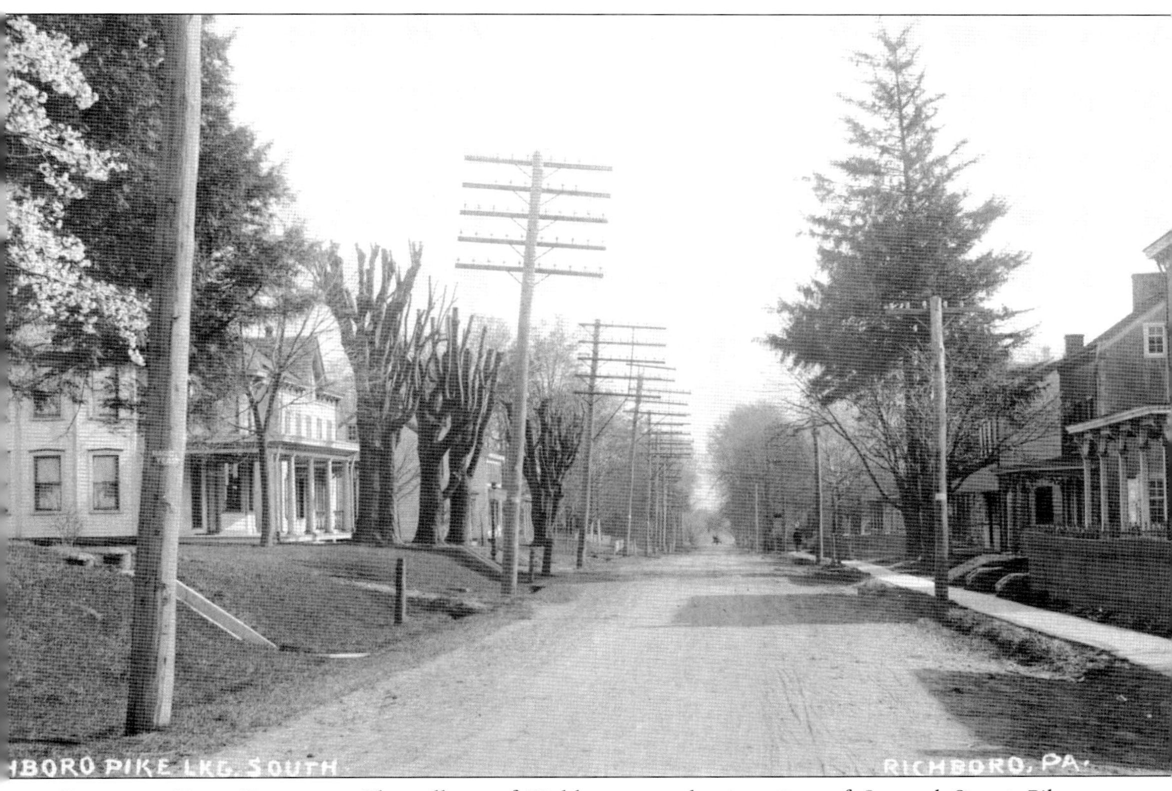

Richboro Pike, Richboro. The village of Richboro—at the junction of Second Street Pike, Bustleton Pike, Almshouse Road, and Newtown-Richboro Road—is an old settlement dating to the mid-1700s. This is a rare glimpse of Richboro from *c.* 1910. Of particular interest is the variety of old buildings shown here. Although many old buildings remain, the area has been heavily commercialized, and some of the old structures have been torn down. (Sliker postcard.)

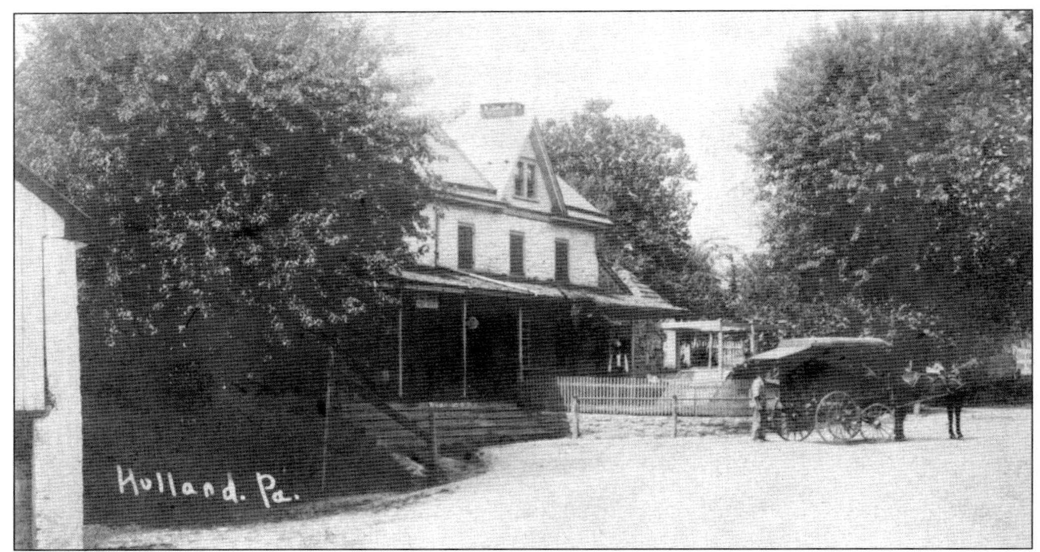

Holland. Where Buck Road crosses the Mill and Ironworks Creeks is the village of Holland in Northampton Township. Holland is an old settlement with several mills dating to the mid-1700s. This building dates to the early 1800s and was the Holland Store and Post Office. The building still stands on Buck Road opposite the Mill Race Inn. (Craven postcard.)

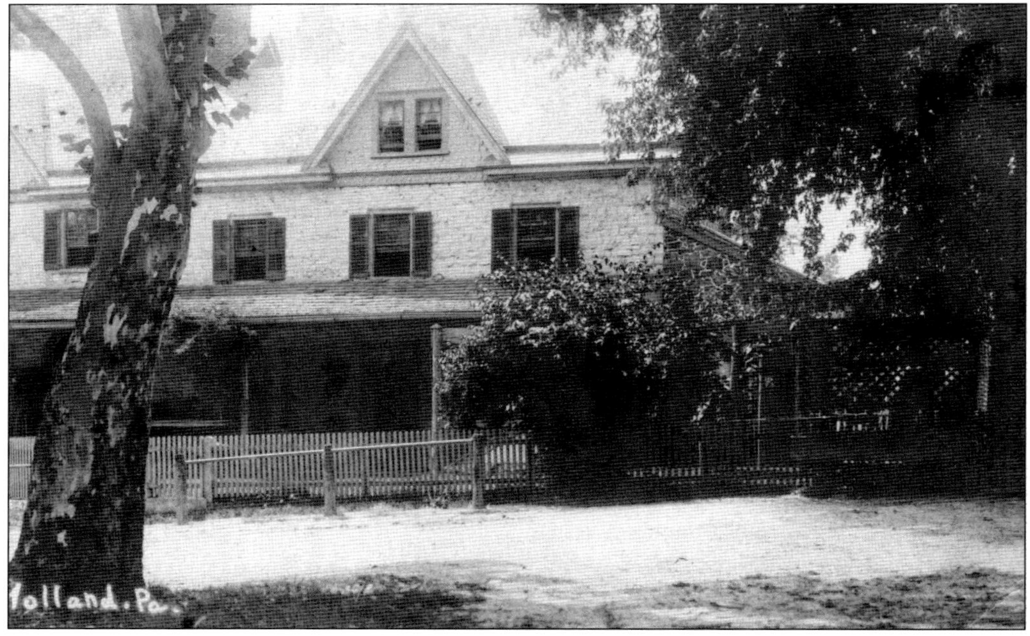

Holland Store and Post Office. This postcard shows a close-up view of the old Holland Store and Post Office. This building was originally the Rocksville Store. Prior to 1870, Holland was known as Rocksville. (Craven postcard.)

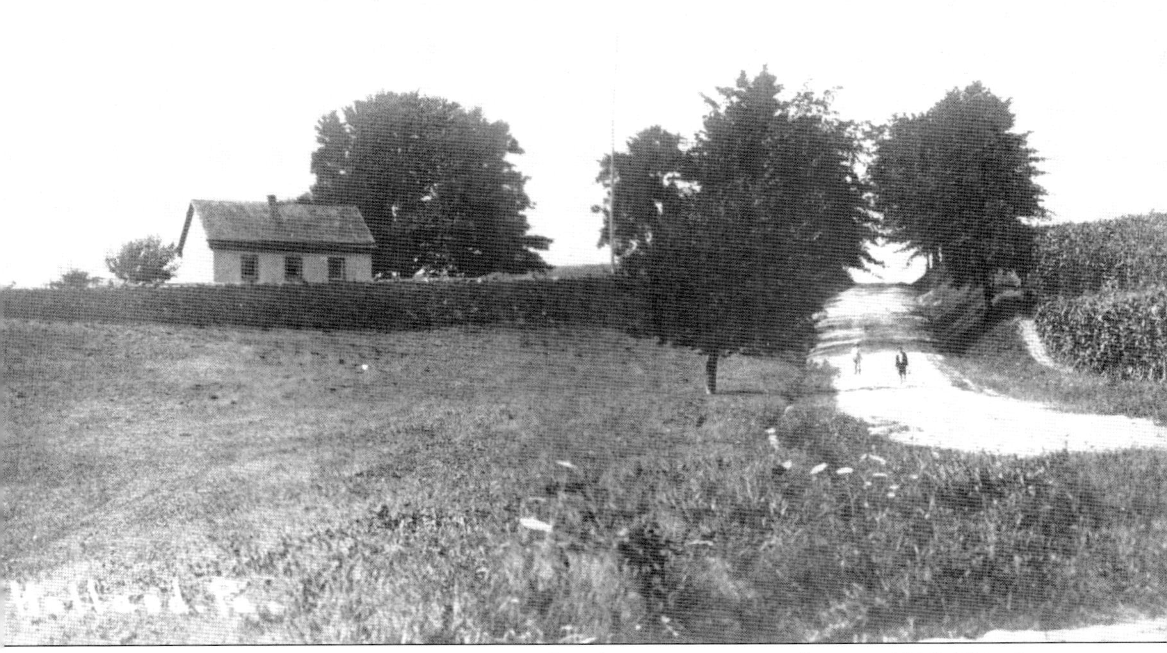

Buck Road, Holland. Holland was a tranquil and scenic country village in 1906. This Craven postcard shows the old Rocksville or Holland School with Buck Road to the right, looking north from Holland Road. The school dates from the 1850s and is still standing as a private home. Today, this area is quite busy with traffic and shopping centers.

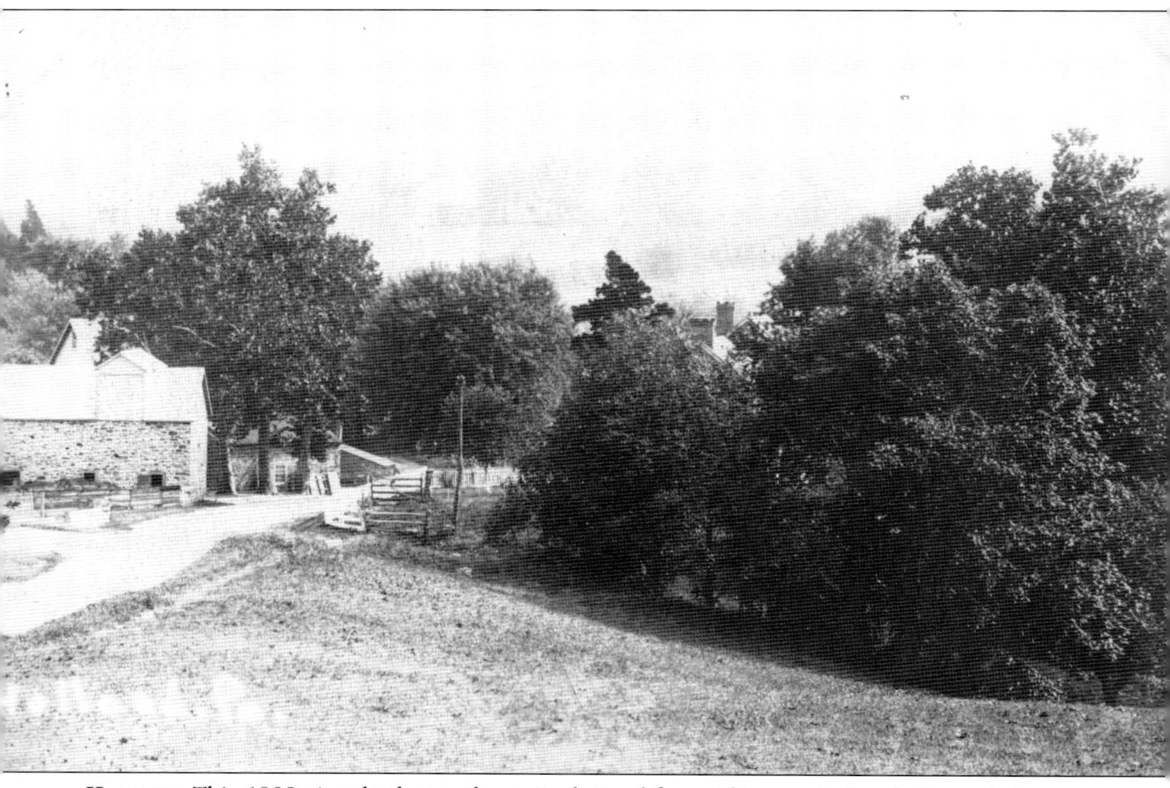

HOLLAND. This 1909 view looks south on Buck Road from Chinquapin Road. Beyond the stone barn is the old Holland Mill, currently the Mill Race Inn. Part of a covered bridge entrance over Mill Creek can be seen next to the mill. In the center is the roof and chimneys to the old store and post office.

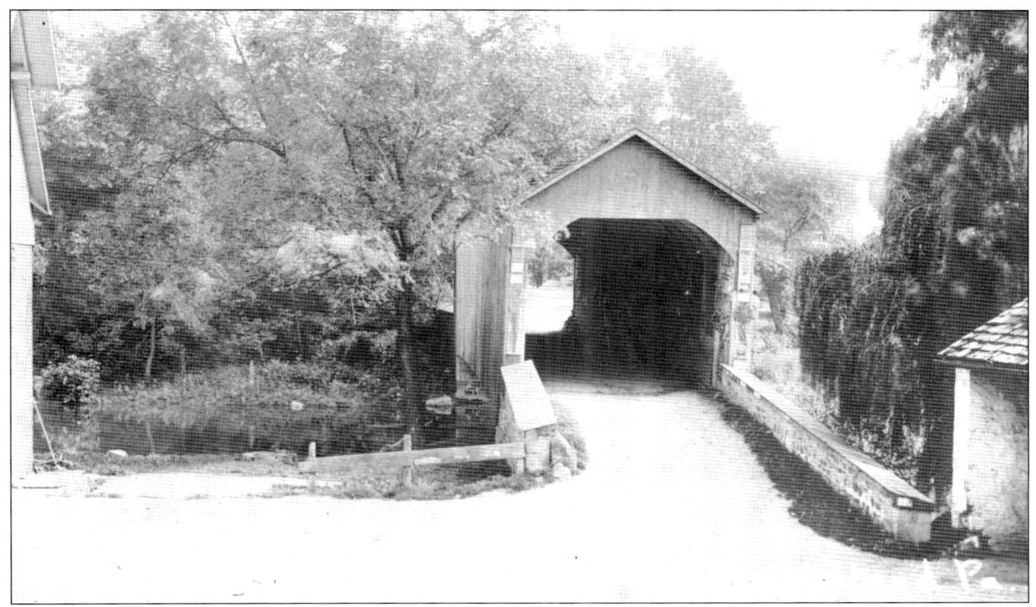

A Covered Bridge, Holland. The Rocksville Covered Bridge carried Buck Road over Mill Creek in Holland from 1830 to 1932. A concrete bridge now carries very busy traffic at this location. (Craven postcard.)

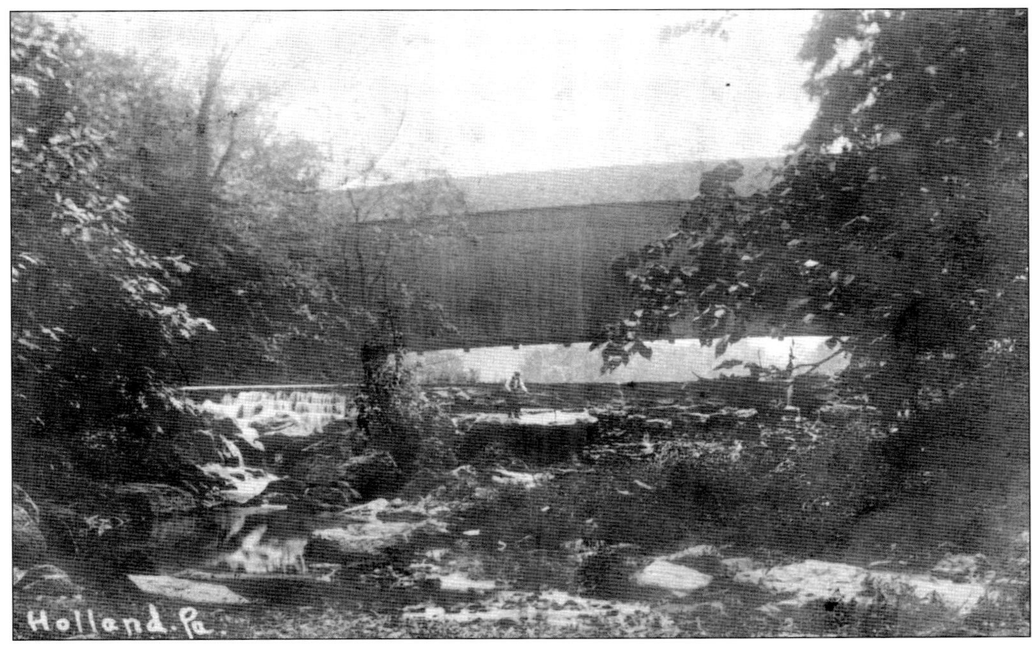

A Side View of the Rocksville Covered Bridge. The bridge, shown here in 1907, was quite long, measuring 139 feet across the Mill Creek. (Craven postcard.)

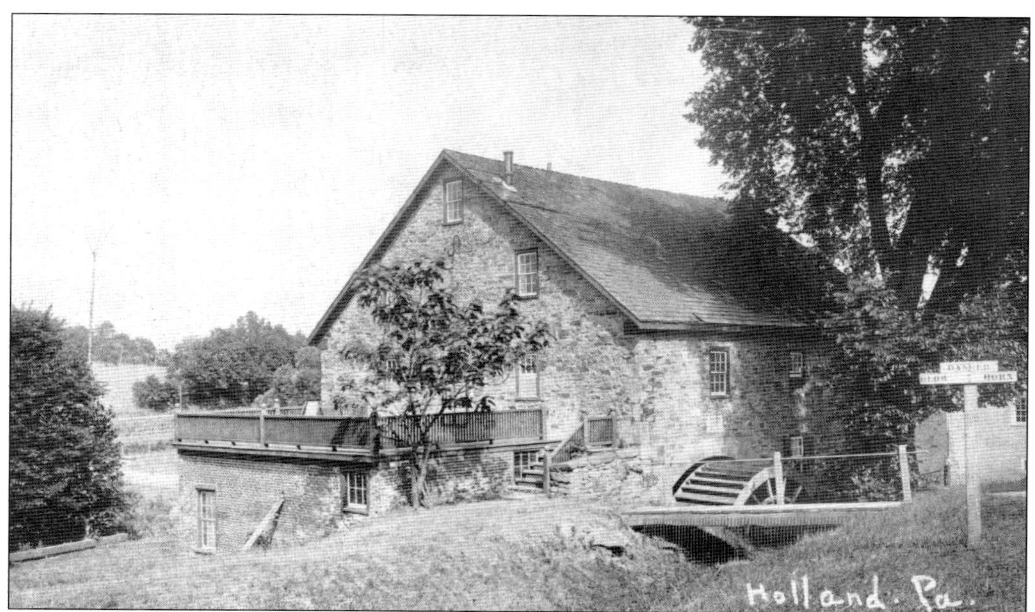

FAIRVIEW MILL, HOLLAND. The old Fairview Mill is now a private residence on Chinquapin Road. The mill, located along Ironworks Creek, was built in 1773. A date stone is visible above the waterwheel. (Craven postcard from 1907.)

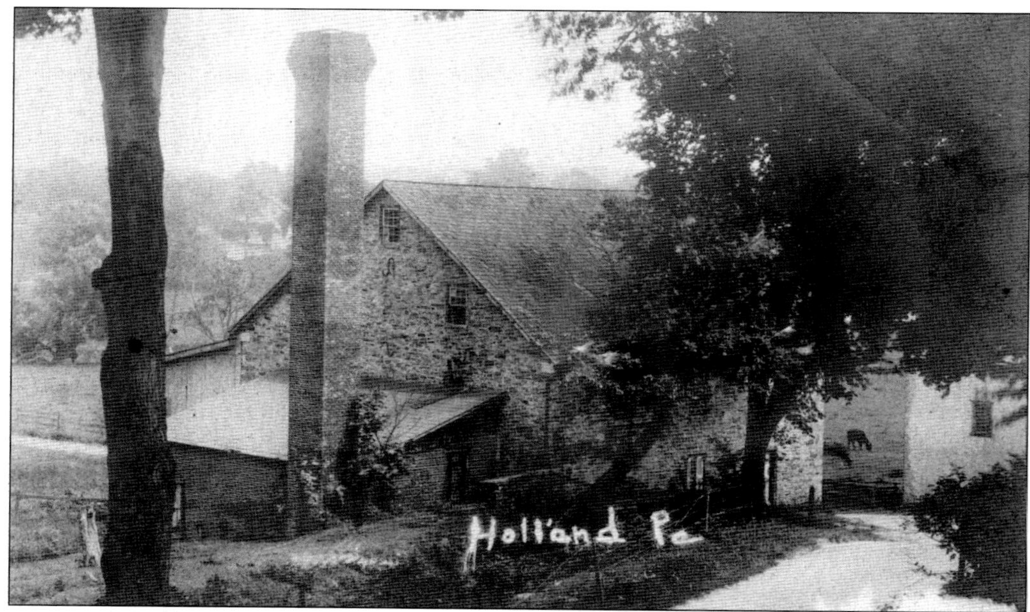

FAIRVIEW MILL. Changes to the mill are evident in this postcard view taken a few years later than the one above. The old water-driven wooden wheel is gone, and now present is a large brick smokestack, which may signify the conversion of this mill from water to steam. Chinquapin Road is to the right and makes a sharp turn in front of the mill and continues left toward Holland.

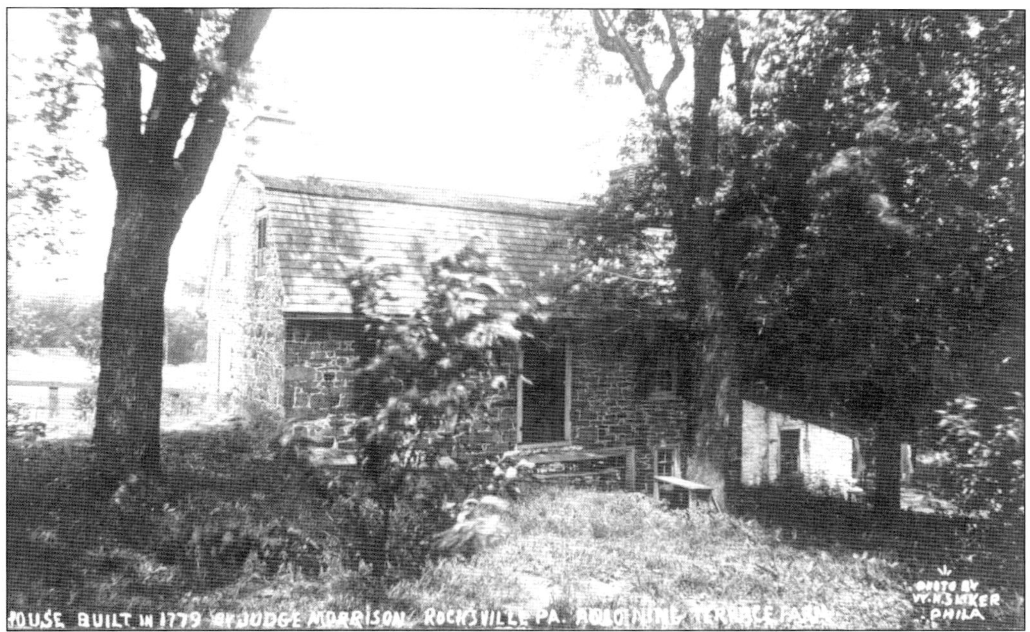

A 1779 HOME IN ROCKSVILLE. Across Chinquapin Road from the Fairview Mill stands this stone, gambrel-roof house, once the home of Judge Morrison. This home was said to be the miller's house and is still standing with some alteration and additions. Many times, the names Rocksville and Holland are interchanged. (Sliker postcard.)

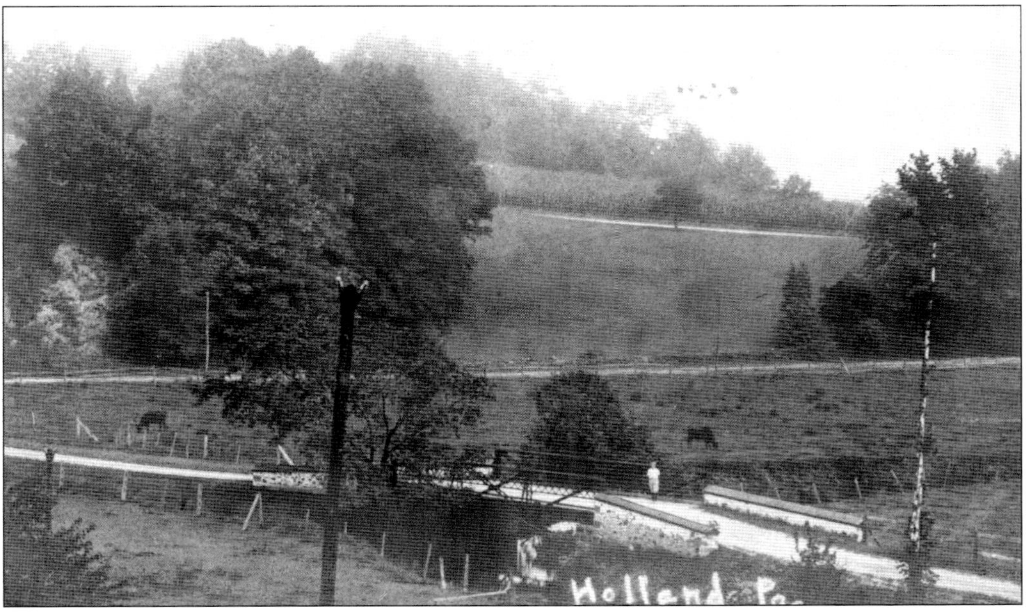

HOLLAND. Chinquapin Road zigzags near the Ironworks Creek in this 1910 view, looking east toward Buck Road. The area near the bridge remains an open field. (Craven postcard.)

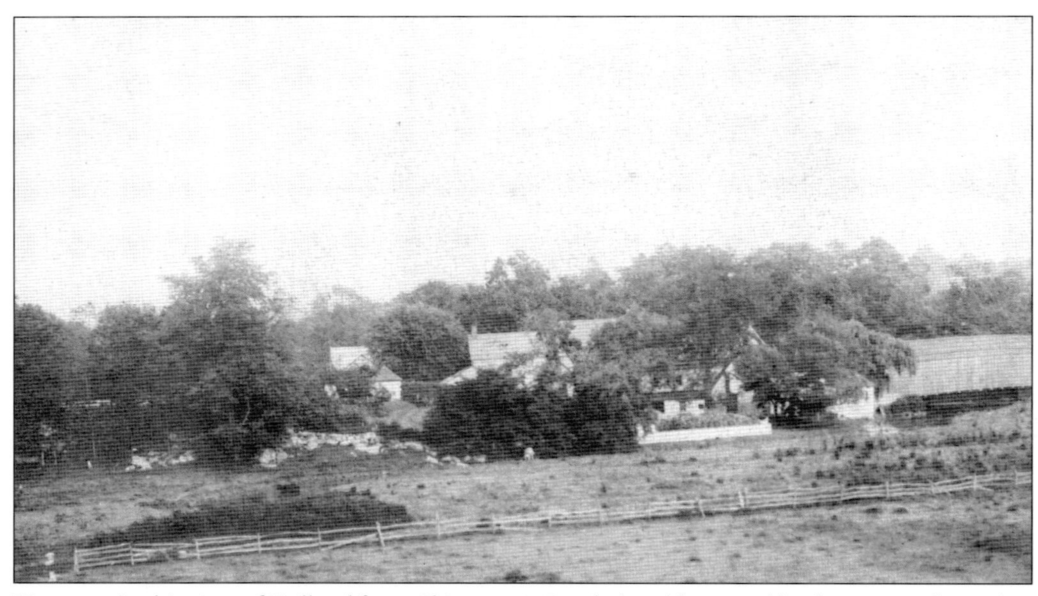

HOLLAND. In this view of Holland from Chinquapin Road, the old covered bridge over Mill Creek is on the right with the old store and post office barely visible behind the trees. (Craven postcard.)

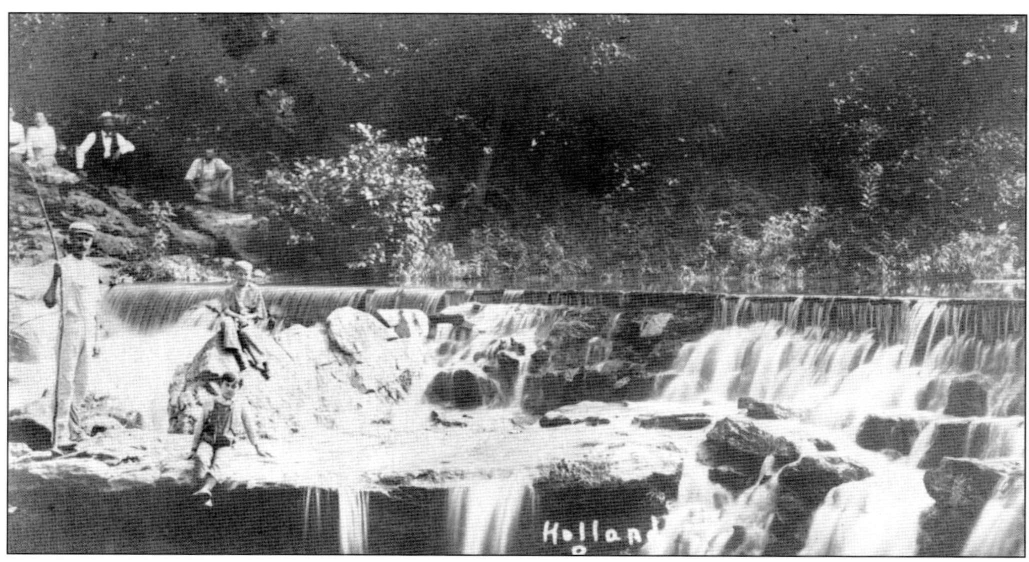

FISHING IN HOLLAND. A fisherman and a few children take time out to pose for this Linford Craven postcard from 1906. This location is the dam and falls on Mill Creek below the covered bridge, next to the present Mill Race Inn in Holland.

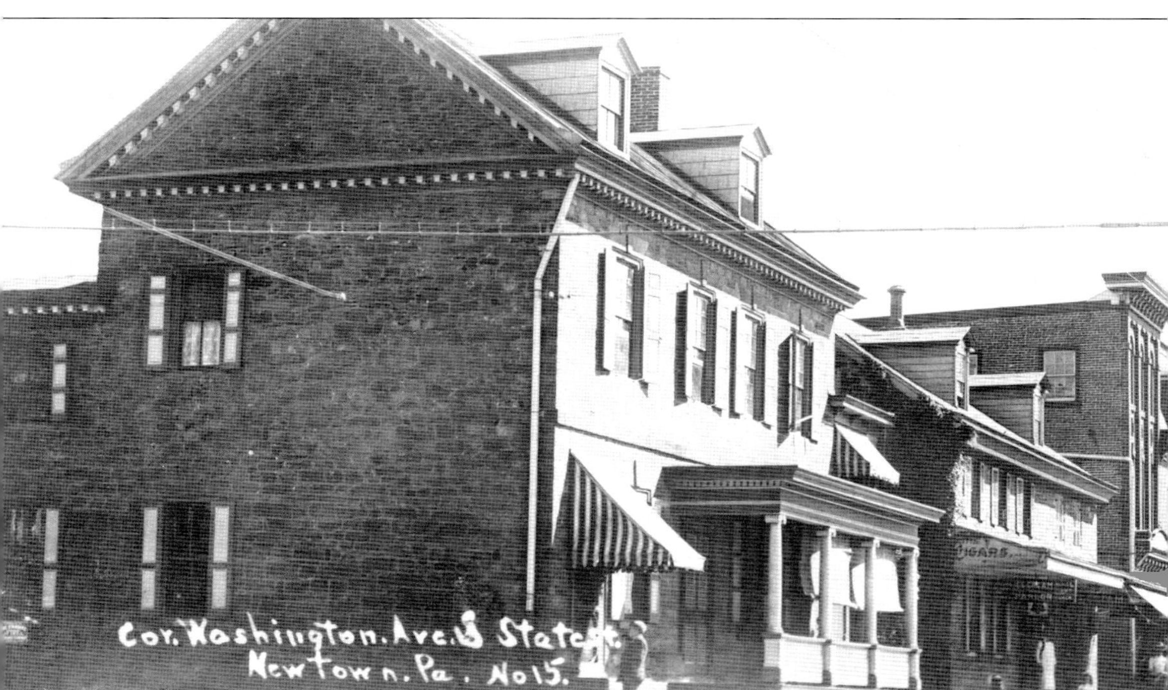

WASHINGTON AVENUE AND STATE STREET, NEWTOWN. This is Newtown's main intersection and the center of town. Newtown Township and what was later Newtown Borough was laid out by Thomas Holme, William Penn's surveyor, in 1684. This Craven postcard shows State Street looking south from Washington Avenue *c.* 1906. Most of the old stone buildings from colonial Newtown are still standing, including these structures. At the corner is the Smock House, followed by the Temperance House, built in 1774.

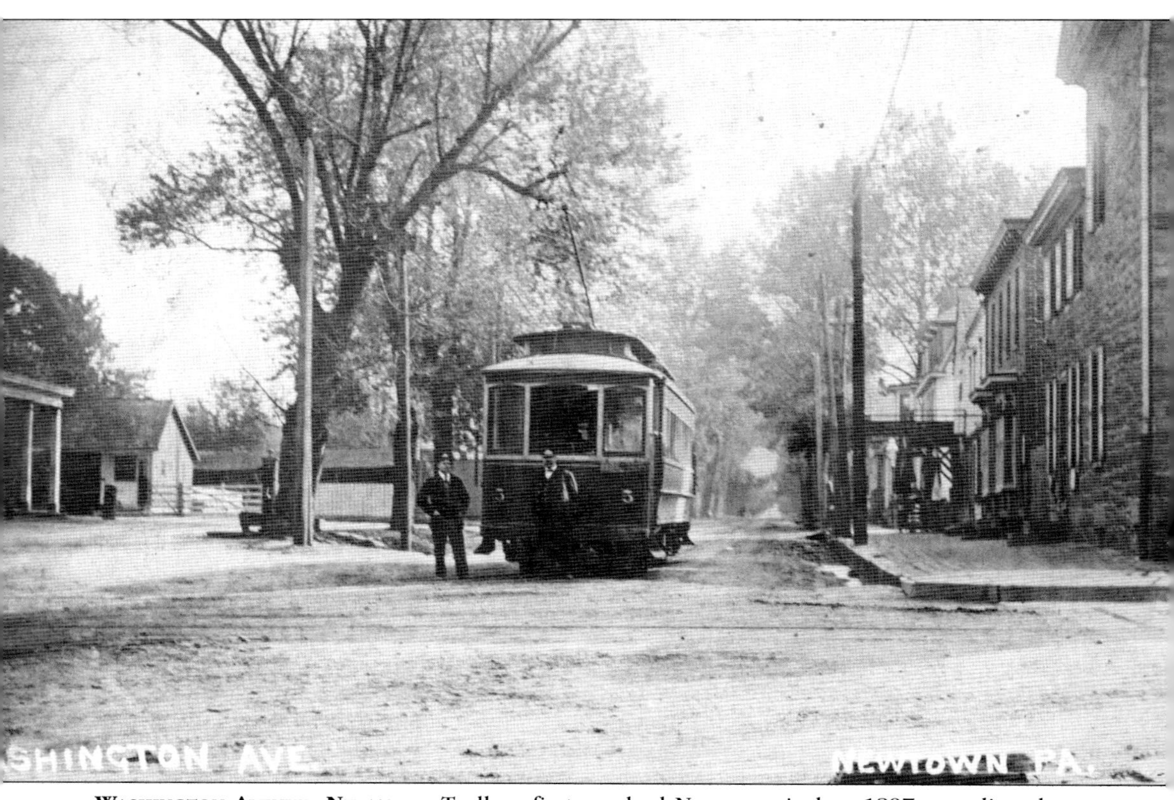

WASHINGTON AVENUE, NEWTOWN. Trolleys first reached Newtown in late 1897 on a line that ran from Bristol and Langhorne. In 1900, a line from Newtown to Doylestown was completed. Trolleys also ran from Newtown through Yardley to New Hope. Looking east from State Street, this 1908 postcard shows a trolley on Washington Avenue.

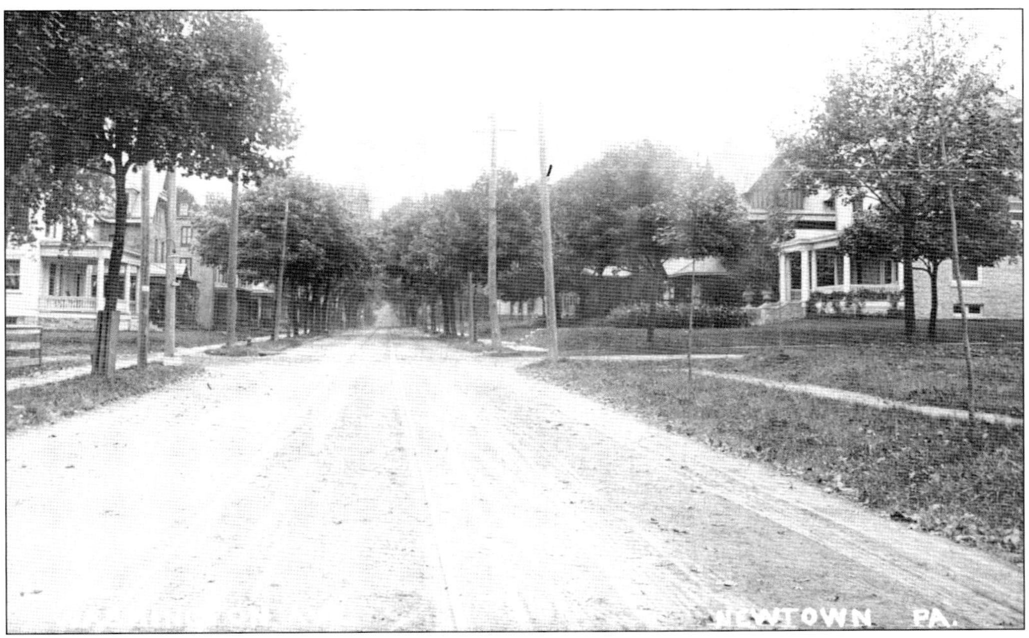

WASHINGTON AVENUE. Washington Avenue is the main east-west thoroughfare in Newtown Borough and contains many fine homes, as seen in this 1910 view. (Wharton postcard.)

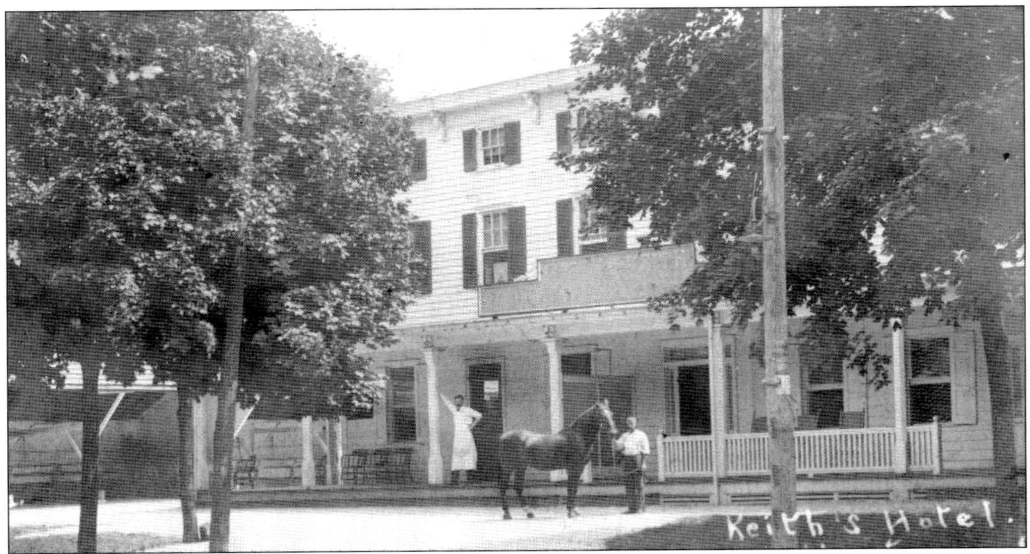

KEITH'S HOTEL, NEWTOWN. Newtown had a number of hotels and taverns, including this building, commonly known as the White Hall Hotel. Originally built in the early 1800s, it was owned by Sipron C. Keith at the time this Craven postcard was made in 1908. The hotel was destroyed by fire in 1979 and was rebuilt in the 1980s.

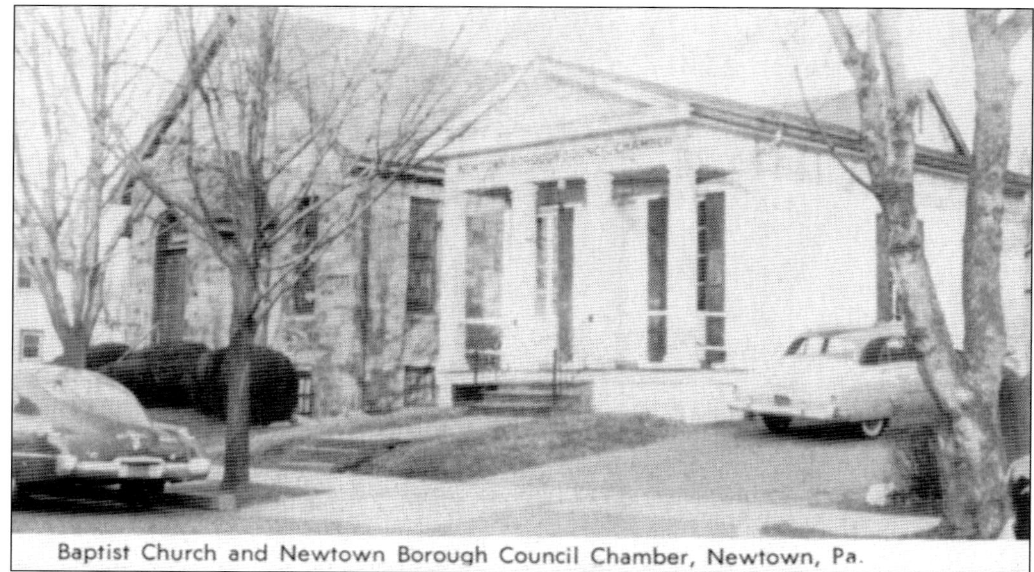
Baptist Church and Newtown Borough Council Chamber, Newtown, Pa.

The Baptist Church and Newtown Borough Council Chamber. The Newtown Baptist Church stands on State Street at Greene Street. The structure shown here was built in 1906, but since the time of this postcard, *c.* 1952, it has had numerous additions built onto it. The Newtown Borough Council Chamber was built in 1854 as a Greek Revival building with classic pillars. The chambers are still in use today. (Seeman postcard.)

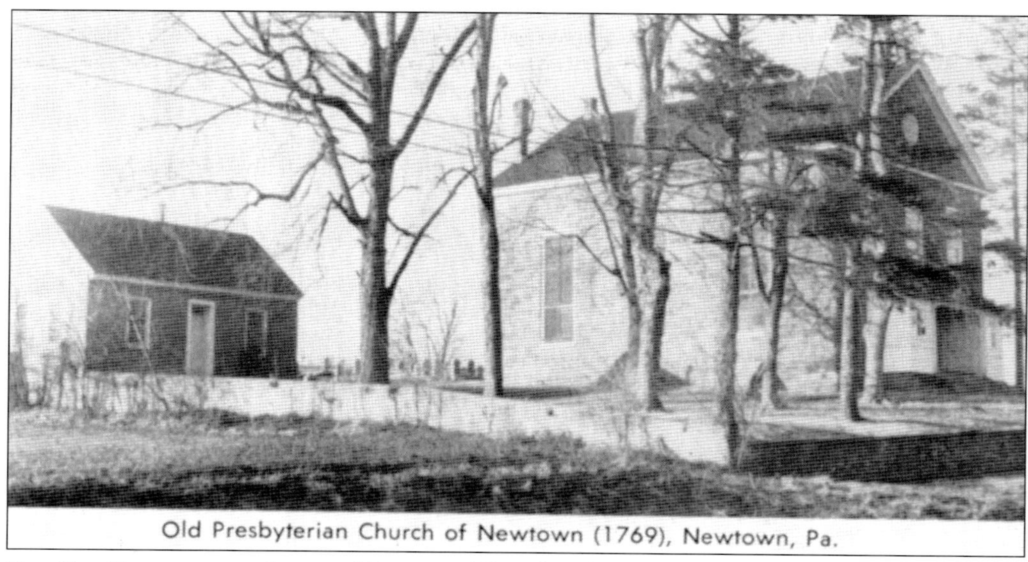
Old Presbyterian Church of Newtown (1769), Newtown, Pa.

The Old Presbyterian Church, Newtown. This church represents Newtown's oldest religious denomination, dating to 1734. The building shown here was built in 1769 and was the second church constructed. During the Revolutionary War, the church served as a barracks for the American Army as well as a prison for British soldiers. Some soldiers are buried in the church's graveyard. The structure has changed very little over the centuries, although the congregation has built newer churches at other locations in Newtown. This view from Sycamore Street is from the early 1950s. (Seeman postcard.)

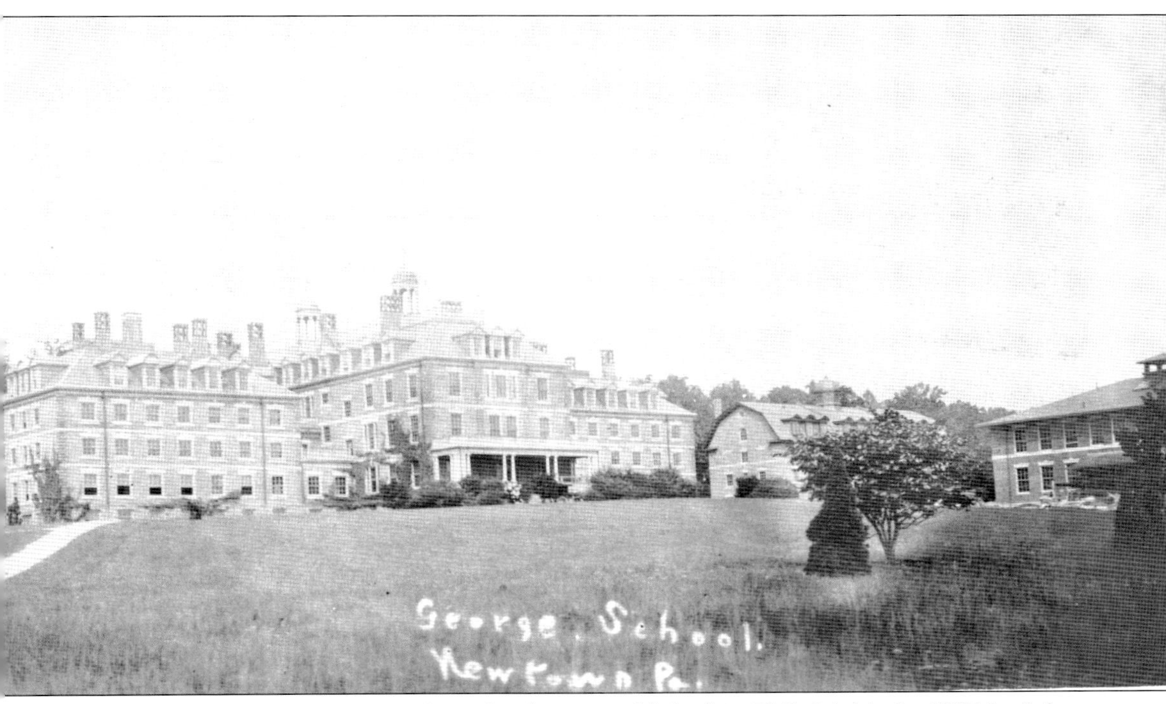

THE GEORGE SCHOOL, NEWTOWN. This school was established in Philadelphia in 1887 by John George to educate members of the Society of Friends, Quakers. More than 100 sites were considered for the new school. In 1891, a beautiful wooded property, bounded by the Neshaminy Creek, south of Newtown, was selected. The school opened its doors in 1893 and still functions as a private school. (Craven postcard.)

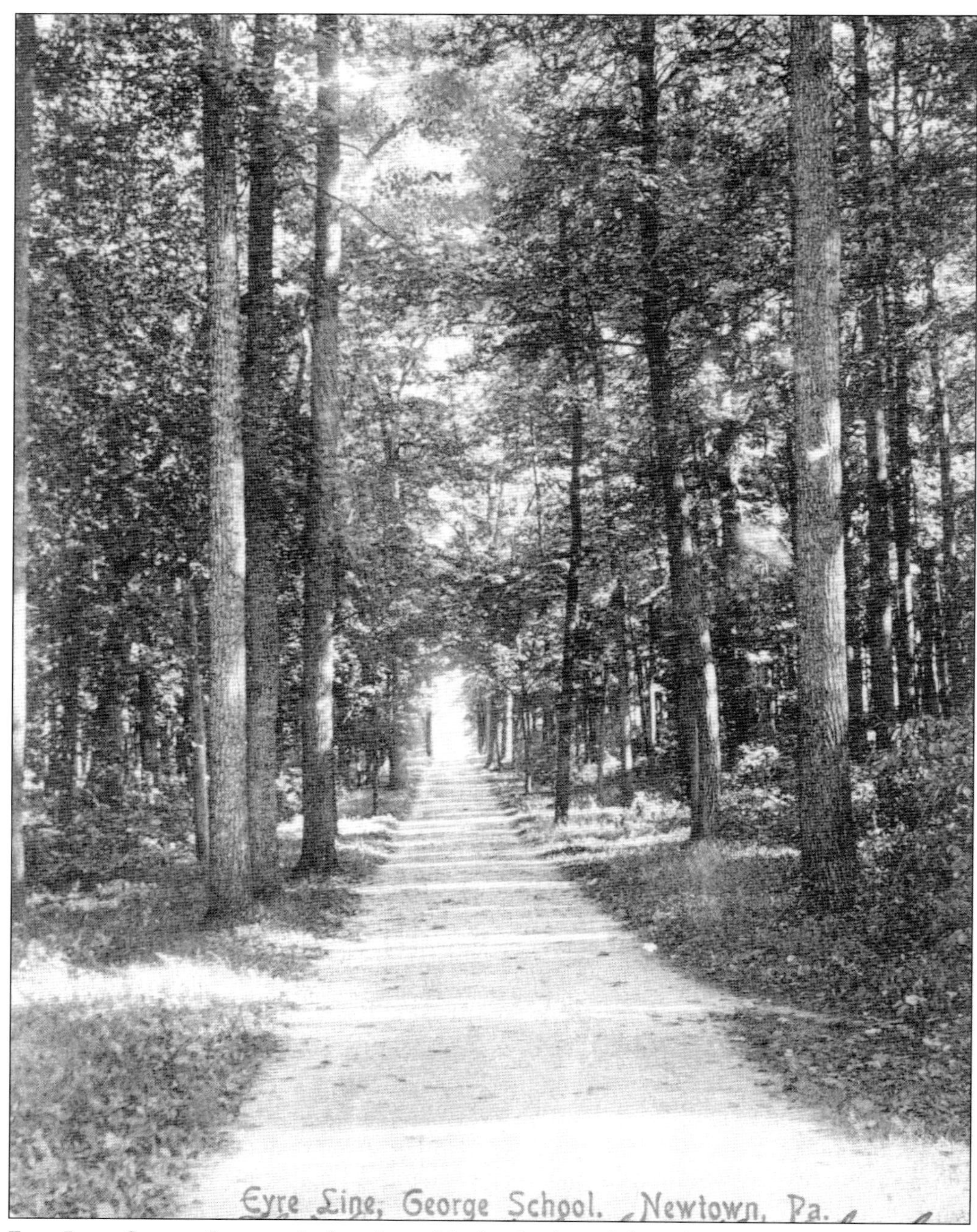

EYRE LINE, GEORGE SCHOOL. In keeping with the Quaker philosophy of respecting the natural landscape, the vast grounds of the George School contained a number of wooded areas and a large pond. Until the early 1970s, a magnificent oak tree, thought to have been more than 300 years old, stood where the Newtown bypass was built. The "George School Oak" fell victim to progress. Fortunately, much of the school grounds have been preserved. Issac Eyre from Newtown helped select the site for the school and aided in raising funds for the school. This path was named for him.

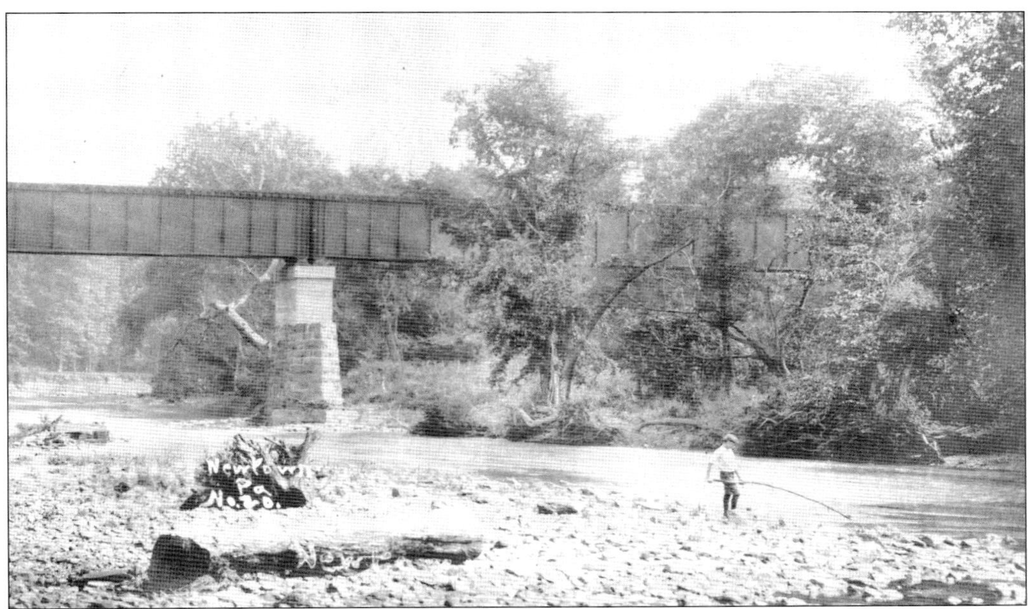

Railroad Bridge, Newtown. A young boy fishes in the Neshaminy Creek below the railroad bridge south of Newtown near the George School property in 1910. This steel bridge was built *c.* 1905 and replaced an old trestle bridge that burned in 1904. (Craven postcard.)

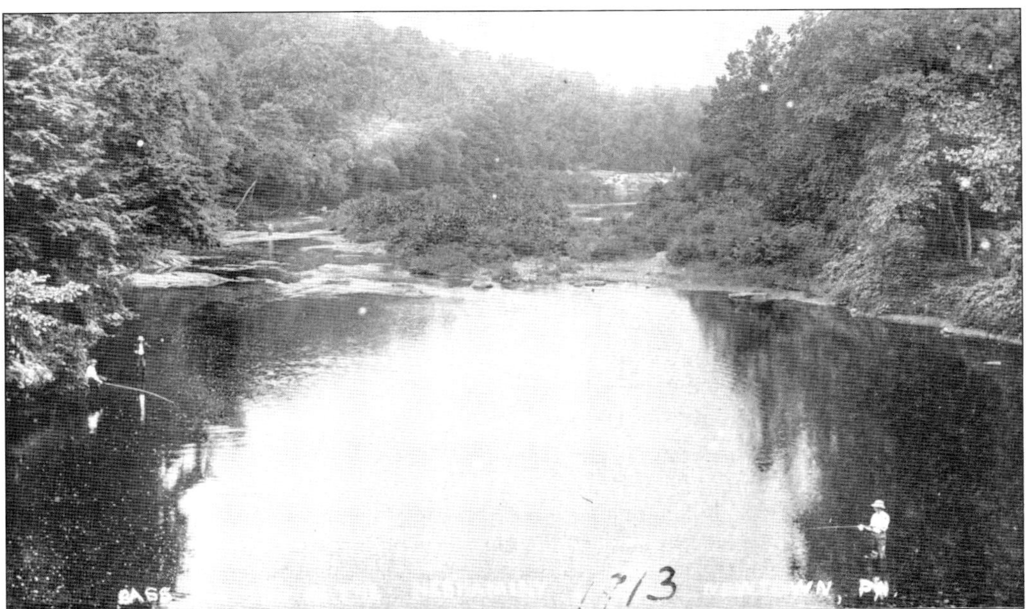

Bass Fishing along the Neshaminy, Newtown. The Neshaminy Creek has played an important role in life in lower Bucks County. The creek powered many early mills and, as shown in this view, provided some pleasant moments for bass fishing.

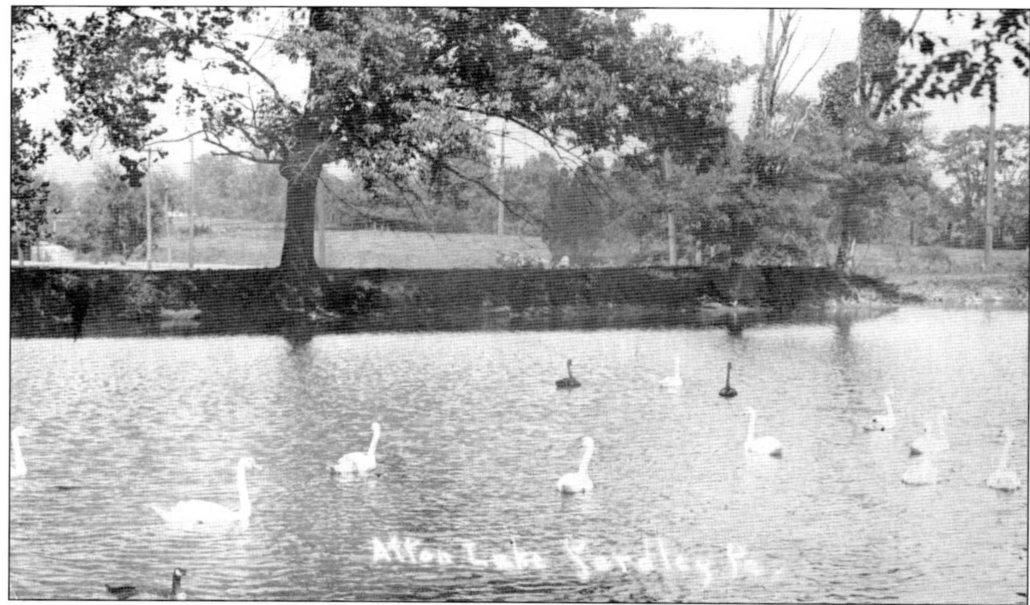

Lake Afton, Yardley. The centerpiece of historic Yardley is Lake Afton, situated in the middle of the borough. Originally Brock Creek was dammed before entering the Delaware River, creating a pond to supply water for the nearby mill. This Craven postcard from 1912 shows a variety of ducks and swans enjoying the lake.

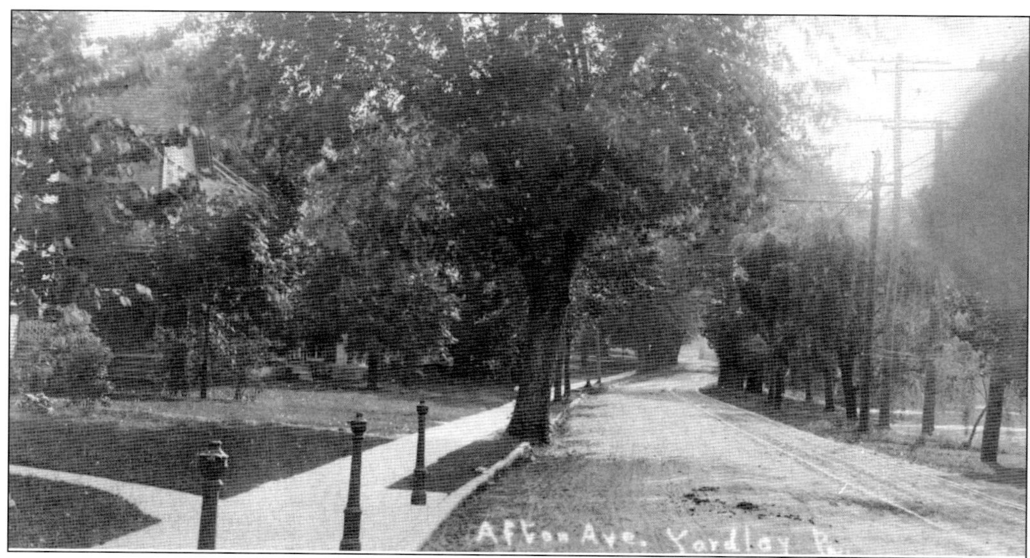

Afton Avenue, Yardley. Looking west from a vantage point near Main Street, this 1906 view shows Afton Avenue in Yardley. Lake Afton can be seen on the right. (Craven postcard.)

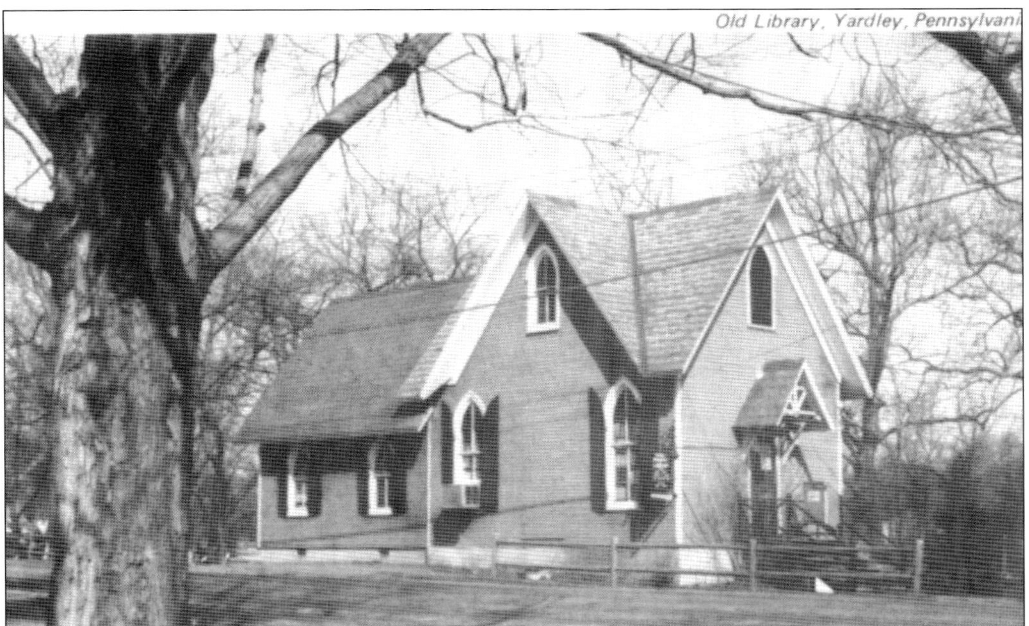

The Old Library, Yardley. The old Yardley Library was built next to Lake Afton in 1878. It remained the borough's library until the 1970s, when a new library was built in Lower Makefield. The building is presently the home of the local historical association. (Merrimack postcard.)

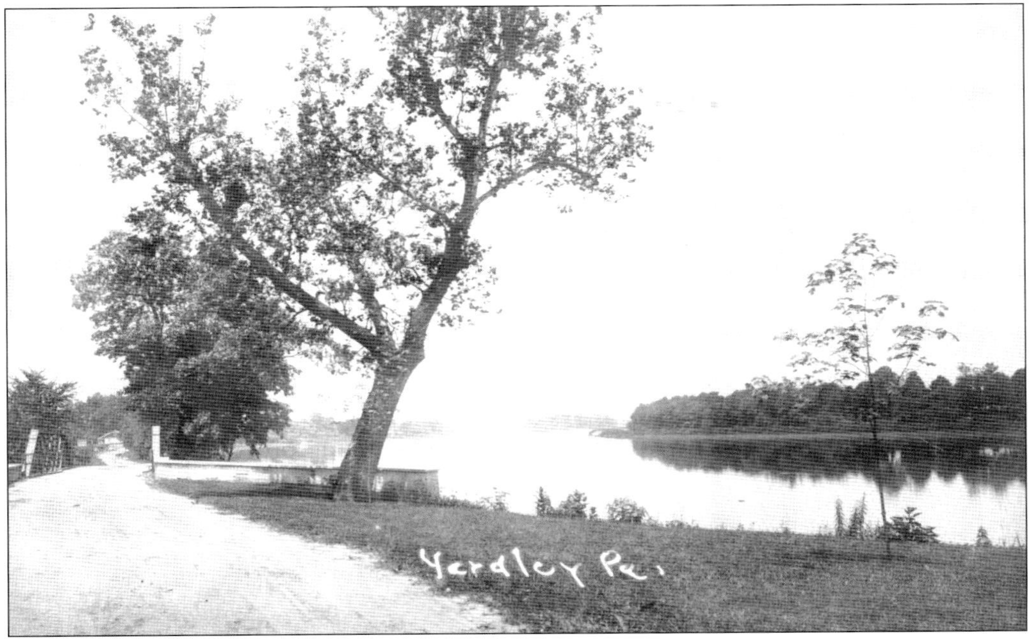

Yardley. Yardley Borough and River Road (Delaware Avenue) offer many beautiful views of the Delaware River, as seen in this 1913 view by Linford Craven of Doylestown.

Yardley. This view of the Delaware River shows the Reading Railroad Bridge, which was built in 1913. The span replaced a trestle bridge built in 1876. Linford Craven photographed both bridges for postcard views.

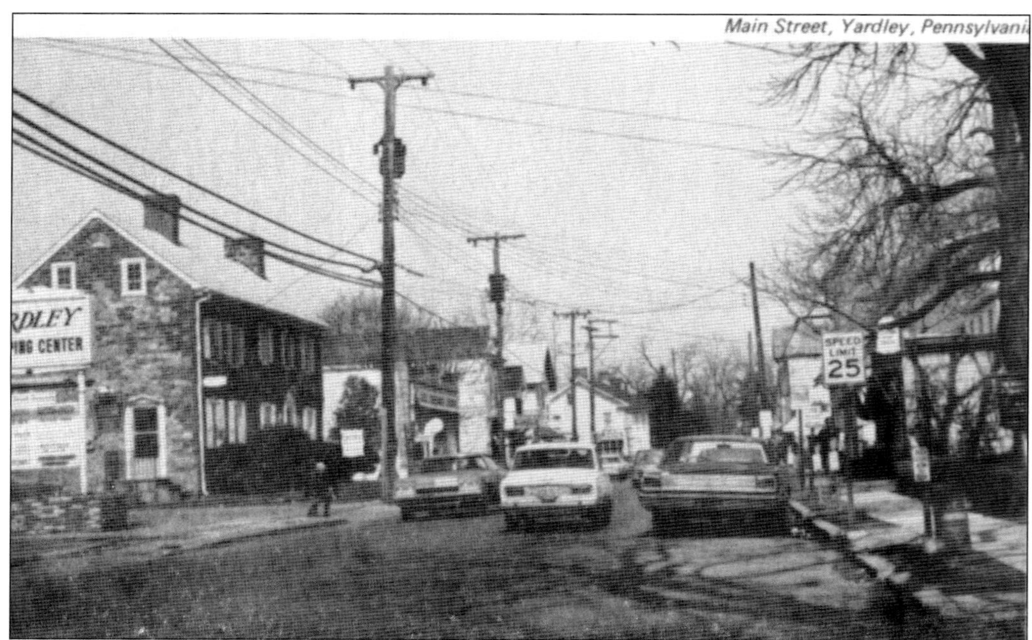

Main Street, Yardley. The Yardley name dates back to 1682 from an original land grant to William Yardley. The borough was incorporated in 1895. This 1970s view shows a thriving yet quaint Main Street area of Yardley that still exists today. Places like Yardley, Newtown, and Fallsington offer great visual reminders of Old Bucks County towns. (Merrimack postcard.)